TRANSPACIFIC DEVELOPMENTS

TRANSPACIFIC DEVELOPMENTS

The Politics of Multiple Chinas
in Central America

Monica DeHart

CORNELL UNIVERSITY PRESS   **ITHACA AND LONDON**

First published 2021 by Cornell University Press

Library of Congress Cataloging-in-Publication Data

Names: DeHart, Monica C. (Monica Christine), author.
Title: Transpacific developments : the politics of multiple Chinas in Central
    America / Monica DeHart.
Description: Ithaca [New York] : Cornell University Press, 2021. | Includes
    bibliographical references and index.
Identifiers: LCCN 2021014541 (print) | LCCN 2021014542 (ebook) |
    ISBN 9781501759420 (hardcover) | ISBN 9781501759451 (paperback) |
    ISBN 9781501759437 (pdf) | ISBN 9781501759444 (epub)
Subjects: LCSH: International economic relations—Political aspects—Central
    America. | Central America—Foreign economic relations—China. | China—
    Foreign economic relations—Central America. | Central America—Foreign
    economic relations—Taiwan. | Taiwan—Foreign economic relations—Central
    America. | Central America—Foreign relations—China. | China—Foreign
    relations—Central America. | Central America—Foreign relations—Taiwan. |
    Taiwan—Foreign relations—Central America.
Classification: LCC HF1483.Z4 D44 2021 (print) | LCC HF1483.Z4 (ebook) |
    DDC 338.91/510728—dc23
LC record available at https://lccn.loc.gov/2021014541
LC ebook record available at https://lccn.loc.gov/2021014542

All photographs are by the author.

For those who dream of more just future worlds

Contents

Acknowledgments

Just as transpacific developments span a broad range of sites, crossing space and time to reflect the work of many actors, so too does a project like this book. Indeed, this project stretched the bounds of my knowledge and proliferated the webs of collaboration like no other. Not only did it require me to reach beyond my area studies specialization in Latin America, but it also necessitated ethnographic research across multiple national territories over the course of eight years. It entailed learning a new language—Mandarin—and familiarizing myself with a new space—China. None of this would have been possible without the incredibly generous collaboration of colleagues, friends, and family spread across China, Latin America, and the United States. This brief acknowledgment will fall far short of expressing the depths of my gratitude but will hopefully acknowledge the collective labor that went into this book.

The material support for this project was provided by grants from the Trimble Foundation, the John Lantz Senior Fellowship for Advanced Study, a Martin Nelson Research Award, and the Dirk Phibbs Memorial Award for Faculty Research at the University of Puget Sound. These essential supports enabled multiple rounds of fieldwork in Central America, travel to China, and sabbatical leave during the period when this project was conceived, executed, and written up.

When I commenced this work, my first steps benefited from formidable Guatemalan scholar, lifelong activist, and good friend Julio Quan. His orientation and connections got me going in Costa Rica, while Aynn Settright helped ground me in Nicaragua. In Central America, I benefited from a wide array of especially generous and knowledgeable interlocutors who made this research both possible and meaningful. While I will not be able to individually name the majority of the people that made this true, my indebtedness to them is immense. Thaís Córdoba was an extremely generous hostess, colleague, and friend, serving as a sounding board and providing important feedback at many points along the way. I am similarly thankful to Carolina Arias Núñez, Sergio Cambronero, Rodrigo Alberto Carazo Zeledón, Mei Chi Cen, Ilien Kuo, Eduardo Lizano, Lily Man, Samuel San, and Elena Wachong for their ongoing counsel and collegiality. I offer special thanks to former president Oscar Arias Sánchez for his time and insights, as well as to Johnny Araya Monge and representatives from the office of National Concessions, PROCOMER, and COMEX. In Nicaragua, Fabio Lau Sandino graciously provided a wealth of his own amazing research knowledge and materials to guide my work, as did Mónica López Baltodano and Enrique Saénz. In Guatemala, Gloria and José Campang served as crucial guides to local Chinese diasporic history and community, while Diego Ubico and representatives from 4CG, the Guatemalan Chamber of Commerce, and the Ministry of Foreign Commerce provided important material for the analysis. I am also thankful to the Chinese embassy representatives (both PRC and Taiwan) in Costa Rica, Guatemala, and Nicaragua for their support of this project.

Of course, it was the myriad everyday Central Americans who shared their candid insights, opinions, and experiences that make up the heart of this book. Among these contributors, members of the Chinese Associations of Nicaragua, Guatemala, and Costa Rica and the Chinese Central American community more broadly were instrumental. Individuals and whole families whom I cannot name here embraced my research, brought me into community events and conversations, and provided me with vital contacts to advance this project. This work is deeply indebted to their contributions, and I hope that this analysis does some justice to our collaboration. Finally, I want to thank individual members of the Central American business community who were willing to speak with me on a confidential basis to share their experiences and perspectives.

Beyond the field, my next dilemma was finding a community of scholars who conducted transregional research and could thus engage the dilemmas of work across spaces rather than being located in one geographical area or disciplinary approach. Luckily, my movement within those spaces and beyond was facilitated by two groundbreaking colleagues. The first, Evelyn Hu-DeHart (my namesake, although we share no relation), is the matriarch of Chinese diaspora studies. I was lucky enough to enjoy her expertise, guidance, enthusiasm, and tough questions across multiple collaborations. The second, Lok Siu, opened the way for my study with her early work on Chinese in Panama, providing what is to this day one of the few ethnographic engagements with the questions of geopolitics, race, and culture on the ground there. Her work is germinal to the field, and her friendship and intellectual camaraderie throughout this project have greatly fortified my analysis.

I presented this work and received productive feedback at many different conferences over the years, including the Association for Asian Studies (AAS), Latin American Studies Association (LASA), American Anthropological Association (AAA), International Society for Studies of Chinese Overseas (ISSCO), and just about everything in between. Within that mix, the Asia and the Americas section of the LASA offered itself as an especially rich space of conversation and collaboration. Composed of social scientists and humanists, it offered exactly the kind of interdisciplinary and transregional conversation I needed, bringing together area studies and ethnic studies approaches. During my time as a member of the

Executive Council of the section beginning in 2012 and then as co-chair from 2015 to 2019 (with the wonderful Adrian Hearn and Vladimir Rouvinski), the section provided endless panel presentations, workshops, informal conversations, and community for this project. I am eternally grateful to Ariel Armony, Enrique Dussell Peters, and Gonzalo Paz, as well as Pedro Henrique Barbosa, Ignacio Bartesaghi Hierro, Benjamin Creutzfeldt, Shoujun Cui, R. Evan Ellis, Alicia Girón, Nehemías Jaén Celada, Yrmina Eng Menéndez, Matt Ferchen, Junyoung Verónica Kim, Teresa Ko, Ignacio López Calvo, Genevieve Marchini, María Montt Strabucchi, Sebastian Naranjo, Tom Narins, Anna Pertierra, Cynthia Sanborn, Rosario Santa Gadea, Leonardo Stanley, Julia Strauss, Zelideth Rivas, María Mercedes Vázquez y Vázquez, and Peter Winn, along with countless others.

Within this group, I want to especially acknowledge the important role played by the innovative historians whose contributions provided a crucial frame and foundation for the field of contemporary Chinese–Latin American circulations. That they happen to be close friends and partners in crime makes my appreciation for Jason Chang, Fredy González, Isabelle Lausent Herrera, Kathy López, and Elliott Young that much more profound. Overlapping with my valuable ISSCO interlocutors, including Madeline Hsu, Yoon Jung Park, and Huamei Han, their work has been especially generative for me.

Another important venue for the development of this work and the collegial relations that sustained it was provided by Enrique Dussell Peters through the Centro de Estudios China-Mexico and the Latin American-China Network (Red ALC), whose conferences brought together amazing scholars from across Latin America and provided a crucial venue for conversation and evolving research. Similarly, I benefited immensely from colleagues doing important policy analyses of trends in Latin America. I extend special thanks to Margaret Myers at the Inter-American Dialogue, as well as to Kevin Gallagher and Rebecca Ray at the Global Development Policy Center at Boston University. Their research and friendship over the years made my work quantifiably easier and better.

I was lucky to be able to develop many of the ideas and arguments in this book through close engagement with a wide range of talented colleagues at small symposia. In particular, Juliane Muller and Rudi Colloredo-Mansfield's "Entrepreneurship, Artisans and Traders: The Remaking of China-Latin America Economies" at UNC, Chapel Hill, included the great minds of José Carlos Aguiar, Florence Babb, Adrian Hearn, Rosana Pinheiro Machado, Gordon Mathew, Josephine Smart, Alan Smart, and Don Nonini; and the Migrant Knowledges Symposium at the University of California, Berkeley, organized by Lok Siu, Alfred Manke, and Andrea Westerman, offered me the opportunity for excellent conversation with Ana Paulina Lee, Eiichiro Azuma, and Vivek Bald. "Roles and Impacts of China's Involvement in Latin America" at Renmin University, co-organized with the University of Pittsburgh CECHIMEX, was graciously hosted by my much-esteemed friend and valued colleague Shoujun Cui. The "China-Latin America in the Age of Trump" symposium at the University of South California, convened by Carol Wise, enabled very formative dialogue with Gustavo Oliveira, Victoria Chonn Ching, Nicholas Albertoni, and Yanran Xu. Finally, the "Transregional Studies Symposium" at Michigan State, organized by Jamie Monson, has brought me into contact with an even broader group of Africanists, Middle Eastern studies scholars, and Asianists (too numerous to mention all here) who continue to fuel my thinking on the epistemological and methodological dimensions of transpacific work.

Along the way, invited talks to Latin American studies and Asian studies audiences at the University of Washington, Seattle and Tacoma, were made possible by my gracious colleagues María Elena García, Tony Lucero, Ariana Ochoa Camacho, and Will McGuire. I thank Tamara Williams at the Wang Center at Pacific Lutheran University, and Gerald Figal, Avery Dickens, and Ted Fischer at Vanderbilt University, where I had the great fortune to trade infrastructural insights with Ashley Carse. At the University of Puget Sound, my colleagues John Lear and Andrew Gomez were interlocutors whose hemispheric expertise brought much to my approach, as did the expertise of the China studies specialists Suzanne Barnett and Karl Fields, and the wonderful Mandarin language training provided by Lotus Sun Perry. Emelie Peine's Brazil work piggybacked nicely on mine and was great fodder for our transpacific course. Robin Jacobson provided crucial reads on drafts along with valuable intellectual and personal fortification throughout.

In the world of anthropology, I am forever in awe of the fierce, wonderful women of Stanford—Kathleen Coll, Arzoo Osanloo, Anu Sharma, and Mei Zhan—all of whom have been the best interlocutors and friends one could hope for along this journey. Their collective brainpower, wit, and professional savvy has truly sustained me over the years. Similarly, my longtime Guatemalanist colleagues and friends simultaneously anchored me in familiar territory and accompanied my foray into Chineseness. I am eternally grateful to Walter Little, James Loucky, the electrifying and inspirational Diane Nelson, Kevin O'Neill, Deborah Rodman, and Kedron Thomas. John Collins graciously hosted a workshop on Chinese diaspora at SUNY and has been a wonderful interlocutor throughout this project. I also benefited from many conference panel conversations with Kimberly Chong, Nicole Fabricant, Lynne Milligram, and Robert Oppenheimer.

Several much-admired colleagues and friends have supported this project over many years, reading and offering especially productive feedback on the entire manuscript. Carol Wise's own amazing work on China in Latin America and her strong commitment to creating interdisciplinary communities of conversation across borders and generations were an especially valuable gift. She has been a wonderful model for what true collegiality and intellectual collaboration can look like. Ted Fischer has been the source of ongoing inspiration over the years, serving as a trusted friend, generous reader, thoughtful interlocutor, and excellent dining partner. I have learned so much from his patient, capacious read of all things Guatemala, academia, and life, and I am forever grateful for his insights on this project and his encouragement to experiment with it. Finally, my dear friend Priti Joshi has accompanied me through the tedious tasks and exciting discoveries of fieldwork, the arduous analytical quandaries it produced, the erratic professional paths along which it evolved, and the painstaking process of writing; she has also been a crucial source of friendship, intellectual stimulation, support, and humor. Over wine, food, new glasses, books, and long conversation, she has buoyed, cajoled, and sustained both me and the work. The cocoon has given us both new wings.

My longtime writing partners, Jennifer Hubbert and Lisa Hoffman, get credit for all of the best parts of this project; indeed, they inspired it. Our twenty years of thick collaboration was founded in part on our diverse areas of specialization— mine Latin America and theirs China. Therefore, this project reflected my pivot toward an even more robust field of shared intellectual terrain. Every page of this book bears the mark of the sustained conversation, learning, debate, commiseration, and celebration that has defined our partnership. We've seen each other through multiple books, professional hurdles, and life-changing events. We've plotted, written, and griped together at roadside diners, conference check-ins, and long writing retreats. They bear no responsibility for the failures of this book, but, thanks to their brilliance and generosity, its completion represents a collective endeavor in more ways than one.

The ultimate enablers of this work were, of course, my family, who put up with many summers of my absence and distraction as this project developed. My parents and parents-in-law, my amazing siblings, and their wonderful families have all rooted for me on this marathon, despite its sometimes confusing and seemingly endless route. My partner, Josh, has time and again taken over operations and encouraged my research even when it might have seemed to be at his expense. This book doesn't quite approximate the art he produces, but hopefully its material existence in the world justifies the sacrifices he has made to support it. My incredible daughters, Nayana and Ella, always made my time away feel a little too long, but inspired me repeatedly along the way with their curiosity and enthusiasm for my labors.

A final thanks to the Cornell editorial team who buoyed this project throughout its long journey. An early supporter, Jim Lance was willing to cross area studies borders to see it to safe harbor. Eric Levy smoothed out the many rough patches, and Susan Specter navigated it through production. My excellent student assistant, Ana Cordes, helped plug any holes along the way. Earlier versions of some of the work included here have previously appeared in other scholarly venues. Some of the ethnographic material in chapter 2 appeared in "Costa Rica's Chinatown: The Art of Being Global in the Age of China," *City & Society* 27, no. 2 (2015): 183–207. Some of my analysis on infrastructure in chapter 4 appeared in "Chinese Costa Rica Infrastructure Projects," in *Building Development for a New Era: China's Infrastructure Projects in Latin America and the Caribbean*, ed. Enrique Dussel Peters, Ariel C. Armony, and Shoujun Cui (Pittsburgh: Asian Studies Center, Center for International Studies, University of Pittsburgh; Red Académica de América Latina y el Caribe sobre China, 2018), 3–23. Elements of the anticorruption background in chapter 6 appeared in "The Impact of Chinese Anti-corruption Policies in Costa Rica: Emerging Entrepreneurialisms," *Journal of Latin American Geography* 17, no. 2 (2018): 167–90.

Abbreviations

AFECC	Anhui Foreign Economic Construction Company
AIIB	Asian Infrastructure Investment Bank (PRC)
BRI	Belt and Road Initiative (PRC)
BRICS	Brazil, Russia, India, China, and South Africa Consortium
CCCCG (4CG)	Cámara de Cooperación y Comercio China Guatemala (China-Guatemala Chamber of Cooperation and Commerce)
CCPIT	Chinese Council for the Promotion of International Trade (PRC)
CELAC	Community of Latin American and Caribbean States
CHEC	China Harbor Engineering Company (PRC)
CICIG	Comisión Internacional Contra la Impunidad Guatemala (International Commission against Impunity in Guatemala)
CMNC	Chinese Machine New Energy Corporation
HCEC	Huanqiu Construction and Engineering Corporation (PRC)
HKND	Hong Kong Nicaragua Canal Development Investment Co. Ltd.
ICDF	International Cooperation and Development Fund (Taiwan)
OECC	Overseas Engineering and Construction Corporation (Taiwan)
PRC	People's Republic of China
PROCOMER	Promotora de Comercio Exterior (Office for the Promotion of Foreign Commerce) (Costa Rica)
RECOPE	Refinadora Costarricense de Petróleo (Costa Rican Petroleum Refinery)
SINOPEC	Chinese National Petroleum Company (PRC)
UFCO	United Fruit Company (US)
USAID	United States Agency for International Development

MAPPING MULTIPLE CHINAS ON THE DEVELOPMENT LANDSCAPE

In 2007, the People's Republic of China (PRC) consummated its newly established diplomatic relationship with Costa Rica by gifting the nation a new stadium. Because all other Central American nations maintained official relations with Taiwan at that time, Costa Rica's abrupt turn to Beijing seemed momentous in both local and geopolitical terms. A PRC government-sponsored firm imported over six hundred Mainland Chinese laborers and equipment, housed in a camp adjacent to the construction site, to construct the new thirty-five-thousand-person stadium. That structure replaced an older, wooden stadium to take on all the trappings of what one Costa Rican fan called a "true First-World" establishment. Locally, the stadium's modern profile earned it the moniker "Nido Tico" (Costa Rican Nest) for its resemblance to the famous Bird's Nest stadium in Beijing, built for the 2008 Summer Olympics. Upon its inauguration, the stadium broadcast its newfound global significance by hosting friendly international soccer matches and concerts by global talents like Shakira.

While the stadium was meant to showcase the benefits of partnership with Beijing, it immediately referenced a much more complex set of Chinese actors. To begin, many Costa Ricans I spoke with evaluated the benevolent gift of the stadium and its modern contours in relation to the treatment of the "other" China—that is, their "friend" Taiwan—which, to their minds, had been callously cast aside by Costa Rican president Oscar Arias Sánchez in his pursuit of the status and opportunities offered by Beijing. Those critics would shake their heads in frustration as they recounted the long history of partnership with Taiwan and

1

the many forms of development support it had offered, only to be traded for the PRC. Others raved about the amazing construction feat performed by the industrious Chinese workers who, to invoke a longstanding racialized image, "worked like ants, moving back and forth over the structure" night and day to complete the stadium a whole month ahead of schedule. Members of the local Chinese diasporic community expressed ambivalence about the structure, wondering whether Beijing's arrival would bring more commercial opportunities or problematic politics that would reflect badly on their community.

Costa Rican narratives about the stadium thus illuminated not only the multiple forms of China present in Central America but also what these meant for regional development. For example, many expressed their admiration for the Chinese engineering prowess that produced the "state-of-the art" stadium and what it portended for future projects. Some observers were more skeptical of what this iconic structure boded for the future. Indeed, several identified the stadium as something of a Trojan horse, implying that the "gift" might come back to haunt them in the form of the invasion of Mainland Chinese commodities or PRC political demands that would ultimately be harmful to Costa Rica's future. A more pragmatic contingency simply read the stadium in terms of what PRC-sponsored development might mean for them as working-class Ticos (slang for Costa Ricans): given the high ticket prices for stadium events, they worried about being locked out of the future if the cost of development was one they could not afford. In this sense, it was not only which China that mattered but also how Chinese involvement might impact Costa Rican national identity, sovereignty, and development goals.

Despite the fact that Beijing's growing influence suggests to many a future in which the PRC might replace both Taiwan and the United States as Central America's strategic development partner, I argue that focusing on a single state regime and its perceived interests is insufficient for understanding the current and future effects of China in the region. Instead this book illuminates the complex nature and stakes of Chinese development by exploring the multiple Chinas (plural) at work in Central America.

These multiple Chinas include Central American citizens of Chinese descent, some of whose family members came over in the nineteenth century to construct railroads but stayed on to build businesses, communities, and ethnic associations in the region. Over multiple generations of migration across the Pacific and the Americas, these largely Cantonese-speaking diasporic communities have come to embody a history of small business and translocal connections that continue to reflect some of the main ways that non-Chinese-heritage Central Americans have come to know what it means to be Chinese.

Another form of China is composed of the diplomats, entrepreneurs, engineers, and institutions representing Taiwan, the development partner that four out of seven countries in Central America still recognize as the "official China." Often of more elite class status and Mandarin speaking, these Chinese actors reflect the cross-strait economic collaboration that has enabled textile assembly plant production in Central America and expanded the contours of the Chinese diaspora there.

And finally, there are the embassy officials, investors, tourists, and laborers representing Mainland China and the PRC government. These are the newest of the Chinese development partners, and, as illustrated by the stadium example, they represent both powerful new sources of development capital and racialized forms of labor that have incited new development possibilities even as they have inspired new fears.

While locals throughout Central America might refer to all of these various actors and institutions as *chinos* (Chinese) and associate them in some way with Chinese development efforts in Central America, they cannot be reduced to agents of the PRC. Instead, differences between Cantonese and Mandarin speakers, between earlier and more recent migrants, between prodemocracy supporters of Taiwan and Communist Party members from the Mainland are crucial to shaping the everyday politics of China in Central America, but they are not visible through a study of bilateral state-to-state relations. Guatemalan business owners of Chinese descent, PRC state enterprise employees building infrastructure in Panama, Taiwanese assembly plant owners in Nicaragua, and diasporic Chinese Association members in Costa Rica all reflect different ideological positions, generational and class interests, ethnicities, and nationalities. These diverse identities, politics, and practices—what I refer to here as forms of Chineseness—mark people's belonging to one or various of these multiple Chinas, and also reflect the stereotypes that are frequently used to make sense of *los chinos* in Central America. These distinctions thus reveal the fluid and often entangled connections and affiliations that map different Chinese actors in relation to one another and to the hispanized Central American culture in which they are embedded.

This book explores these politics of China and Chineseness in Central America, a place where their presence and implications are especially pronounced. Central America has not featured prominently in studies of China–Latin America dynamics to date because of the region's lack of the commodity exports, like petroleum or soy, for which China has shown a high demand. Nonetheless, Central America's development dynamics hold clear geopolitical significance given the region's role as a political ally of the United States, a production platform for North American markets, a hub for global commerce, and a chessboard for cross-strait tensions across the Pacific. Based on field research in three different Central American countries—Nicaragua, Guatemala, and Costa Rica—between 2011 and 2019, I identify which actors, projects, and ideas count as Chinese and how locals in very distinct national and local contexts perceive them in relation to larger development concerns. By analyzing initiatives in one country that has established diplomatic relations with the PRC (Costa Rica) and two that maintain relations with Taiwan (Nicaragua and Guatemala), I am able to analyze diverse forms of Chinese development and public diplomacy efforts, as well as the domains in which they unfold.

This ethnographic approach is central to illuminating the transpacific analytic that I develop throughout the book. Scholarly and policy conversations about China–Latin America relations have focused on the PRC government's "going out" to Latin America as a new kind of encounter among essentially different actors, worlds apart. Tracking a longer history of the movement of people, goods, capital, and politics across the Pacific, I show how China and Central America are by no means strangers; instead I argue that they have been constituted by longstanding circulations through and encounters with each other. By moving back and forth across these diverse spaces of encounter and levels of analysis, my transpacific analytic illuminates the wide range of cultural, political, and economic exchanges that have produced transpacific assemblages of identity, place, race, and development. Approaching China–Central America relations in this way not only highlights important shifts in the global development landscape but also illuminates its continuities. As such, it allows us to reimagine contemporary developments less as a battleground over global hegemony and more as a space for conjuring new worlds defined by different identities, scales of action, and politics for the future.

Shifting Development Landscapes

When I began my anthropological research in Central America in 1995, my work was focused on the cultural politics of economic development. During the 1990s, those politics were defined largely by the development industry's interest in ethnic identity (e.g., ethnodevelopment or indigenous knowledges); community-based, participatory development models; and migration as valuable strategies for addressing both local identity concerns and neoliberal economic goals.[1] Working as I was with indigenous communities and nongovernmental organizations in Central America and Latinx migrants in the United States, China was not on my screen. However, as my ethnographic work in the region continued, I began to see the signs of change. The Central American landscape was increasingly marked by new Chinese products—everything from the inexpensive rubber boots used by rural farmers in the milpas to the knockoff name-brand clothing and cheap plastic containers taking over the local markets. Factories devoted to assembly production for export to US markets proliferated, as did new family-owned Chinese restaurants. Suddenly, signs posted alongside development project sites that advertised their sponsorship by the "Republic of China (Taiwan)" caught my eye in a new way; instead of just marking foreign-sponsored products, they seemed significant as a way of marking *which* China was operative there.

When Costa Rica abandoned Taiwan to establish diplomatic relations with China in 2007, it was clear that something important was happening. Therefore, although a Latin Americanist by training and interest, I found myself studying Mandarin and scanning the Central American landscape for more signs of Chinese influence. Most of my Chinese-heritage Central American friends spoke Spanish, but their home language was usually Cantonese. When I mentioned to them my interest in studying the Chinese language, however, they all instructed me to learn "official" Chinese (*putonghua*)—Mandarin, not Cantonese. Mandarin, they noted, was the language of the future.

Their recommendation reflected changes in a global development landscape that is increasingly defined by different actors, modes of operation, institutions, and issues, China principal among them. That refigured landscape represents the tremendous economic growth and deepening global connections enabled by the new millennium, as well as the widening inequality and vulnerability that have accompanied it. The inauguration of political economic initiatives by actors from the Global South like the BRICS (Brazil, Russia, India, China, and South Africa) Consortium, new regional organizations that do not include the United States like CELAC (the Community of Latin American and Caribbean States), and new banks like the AIIB (the Asian Infrastructure Investment Bank) indexes the importance of new voices in reshaping the international system. Global energy market crashes, climate change disasters, and deadly pandemics have also highlighted crucial challenges to national sovereignty within contemporary global politics. In this context, China has emerged as an important, if controversial, development model and agent whose exceptional politics have been perceived as having the power to redefine the nature and stakes of development.

Perceptions of China's transformative role derive, in part, from the PRC's dramatic economic growth and poverty-reduction strategies at home. The World Bank estimates that the PRC government has reduced poverty from 88 percent in 1981 to below 1 percent in 2018.[2] These transformations have catapulted the

PRC from a developing nation to a development donor purveying major international finance and infrastructure projects throughout the developing world. For example, in Latin America, the PRC has become the region's biggest lender, far outspending Western financial institutions through over $150 billion in loan commitments to the region.[3] Furthermore, at the 2015 CELAC reunion, the PRC government announced that it had $45 billion earmarked for infrastructure investment in the region.[4]

The PRC government's method of achieving this economic success—through its one-party political system, planned economy, and heavy reliance on state-subsidized firms—has also provoked major fears. Critics in the West have often used the terms "Beijing Consensus" and "China Model" to identify central features of the PRC government's development policy at home and extrapolate them to its policies abroad.[5] The PRC government's combination of free-market economics and authoritarian politics rejects the "standard package" of policies promoted by global development institutions and Washington Consensus advocates—such as privatization, deregulation, and democratization, among other recommendations—and thus challenges the liberal foundations of the global system.[6] Indeed, the PRC government's policy of noninterference in its partners' domestic politics has only deepened fears that the PRC government not only condones but supports illiberal politics. The PRC's ability to increase its global footprint through growing investment, trade, and membership in regional and international organizations has thus been read as evidence of the PRC's growing global power and the likelihood that it will create new sources of conflict within the global order.[7]

Even though the 2010s have not borne out fears that the PRC seeks to export its brand of state politics abroad, the idea of China as an exceptional development actor remains.[8] China's creation of powerful new global institutions and initiatives reinforces this perception. Invoking historic connections, the PRC government's "Silk Road Economic Belt" and the "twenty-first-century Maritime Silk Road" project—now referred to simply as the Belt and Road Initiative (BRI)—promised to radically reconfigure global commerce through the construction of new transportation corridors connecting Europe and Asia. By 2018, this initiative had been stretched to encompass new infrastructural developments in such faraway places as Latin America, where nineteen nations had signed on. Therefore, designs to renovate and control central features of the Panama Canal or to build transcontinental dry canals across South America have raised the specter of new Chinese inroads to these areas that were once presumed to be firmly under the influence of the United States and multinational corporations.

The rise of PRC policy banks—the Chinese Export-Import Bank, the Chinese Development Bank, and the AIIB—as the main source of financing for Latin America has added to the sense of the PRC's disproportionate power and potential threat to sovereignty.[9] By lending to countries that have been rebuffed by traditional international lending institutions or adopting more agile lending practices, the PRC has destabilized what were once some of the major power-brokers in the region, such as the Inter-American Development Bank and the World Bank. However, these Chinese loans and their corresponding projects have sometimes placed valuable national resources at the apparent disposal of a new regional power.[10] The fact that a large portion of China's loans in Latin America has gone to countries that are unable to access traditional international financing (such as Venezuela or Bolivia) has underlined fears that PRC government lending ultimately might weaken democratic advances in the region.[11] The PRC government's practice of pursuing closed-door bilateral negotiations with nondisclosure agreements, coupled with the reputation of Chinese firms for violating local labor or environmental regulations, has accentuated that worry. In the end, however one views the normative impact of PRC presence in the region, its potential material impact seems all too real.

Nonetheless, when I began asking everyday Central Americans about *el impacto chino* or *la influencia china* (the Chinese impact or influence), I was most often met by quizzical expressions, rather than recognition. People weren't sure if I was talking about the Korean factory up the way, the local Chinese family restaurant, ancient philosophers like Confucius, or the growing economic juggernaut flooding their local market with plastic toys and shoes. I learned quickly that I had to clarify which Chinese I meant, and that, even then, my explanations didn't always yield clear responses. Moreover, when I began trying to identify and assess specific Chinese development projects in Central America, I was quickly struck by the contradictions I saw. Contrary to Western rhetoric about Beijing exporting a threatening socialist model to the Global South, what I saw were infrastructure projects and export production in special economic zones—practices that seemed like continuations of the region's historical development strategies rather than major departures from it. The type and degree of change implied by Chinese development definitely could not be taken for granted.

The question of who or what counted as China in Central America was not simply an ethnographic problem for me but a political problem for China as well. Indeed, the PRC government has worked hard to consolidate various and even competing Chinas through official policies such as the "One China" policy vis-à-vis Taiwan or the "One Country, Two Systems" arrangement in Special

Administrative Districts like Hong Kong. Similarly, the Office of Overseas Chinese has shifted its efforts from simply recruiting remittances from Chinese overseas to promoting sustained citizenship and/or nationalism among its diaspora.[12] While these policies seek to promote particular ideas of China and Chineseness, their subjects may just as often define themselves in opposition to those formulations as through them. For example, in Central America, Taiwanese diplomatic personnel have often established deep bonds of friendship and association with their respective local ethnic Chinese community members. In the wake of diplomatic changes in Costa Rica, Panama, and El Salvador, new generations of representatives from Beijing have occupied local embassies and instituted more formal and distant relations with those same diasporic communities. In addition to this notably chillier relationship, some local Chinese community members chafed at their community being represented by the PRC government and its socialist politics, rather than by the democratic ideals of their Taiwanese antecedents. These examples remind us of the aspirational quality of state sovereignty; conjuring a singular, legitimate China requires constant labor.

Instead of taking for granted the monolithic interests of the PRC and its ability to unproblematically expand its influence through its development partnerships in Central America, I argue that we have to look more closely at the people, practices, and perspectives that constitute Chinese development and ask different questions of them. For example, what exactly is *Chinese* about these projects in terms of what they are and how they are designed, funded, and executed? How different are they from other forms of development cooperation in Central America? And how do Central Americans feel about them in relation to their own ideas of national identity, sovereignty, and development? Getting a sense of what China means for Central America requires that we explore not just trade and policy agreements, but also the complexities of geopolitics, racial formations, class relations, and local history to see how these factors influence both contemporary development relations and expectations for Chinese development in the future of the region.

From this vantage point, I argue that despite its perceived differences, Chinese development embodies many continuities with its Western forerunners and similarities with its contemporary peers. What's more, the combination of a long history of Taiwanese development collaboration, diasporic commercial connections, and hemispheric Orientalisms that stigmatize Chineseness make the meaning and outcomes of Chinese development quite contentious and tenuous, rather than assured and transcendent.[13] To grasp these important nuances, however, requires analytical tools that build on ethnographic research to situate international relations within grounded cultural analysis.

Locating Transpacific Worlds

Explanations of China's global ascendance provided by both PRC representatives within China and the nation's critics in the West often invoke civilizational narratives about Confucian culture, the PRC government's socialist politics, and its unique brand of capitalism to explain the country's intentions and policies. This rhetoric posits the PRC as an essentially different kind of international actor in ways that either legitimize its goals for "harmonious" domestic and global relations or fuel fears of its threat to the liberal political economic order. In doing so, these discourses gloss over similarities between Chinese development and the forms that have come before it, and they also erase the important ways that Chineseness has been constituted through modernization processes in the Americas. My analysis intervenes in these conversations about the nature and significance of Chinese development in Latin America by articulating an analytical approach centered on the concept of the "transpacific."

A transpacific analytic starts by asking, rather than assuming, who and what represents China in Central America. Instead of seeing China as a distant and essentially different place or actor relative to Latin America, it looks to a long history of circulations across the Pacific and the respective "areas" that frame it to illuminate how they have shaped each other. As such, this inductive approach highlights the different forms of encounter and exchange, past and present, that have helped to constitute what we know of China and Latin America today. I follow these flows across scales to discern how translocal exchanges between families, communities, regions, and nations have enabled economic, cultural, and identity formations that are central to development but may not correspond to the borders or policies of nation-states. In doing so I trace movement, networks, and the infrastructure (material, political, and cultural) built to orient and sustain them.[14] I argue that these assemblages of identity, place, and race give us a more nuanced sense of the changing development landscape and how ideas of China and Chineseness matter within it.

For a Costa Rican or Nicaraguan of Chinese descent, for example, China may be located in family villages in Guangdong, in shifting embassies throughout Central America, and in the Chinese diasporic communities that have come together within the Central American Federation of Chinese Associations. These various Chinas are assemblages born of historic political agreements that enacted coolie contract labor in the nineteenth century, the system of Central American railroads constructed by Chinese migrant labor, years of diplomatic relations and development cooperation with Taiwan, the formation of Chinese mutual aid associations throughout Central America, the trade expos and commercial agreements that link Chinese merchants across both regions, and, increasingly, the infrastructure projects within Central America built by Chinese firms.[15] The constitutive elements of these assemblages do not all originate in one place or demonstrate a unidirectional flow toward another place, nor are they limited to transregional flows, but also incorporate intra- and supraregional flows. Therefore, Chinese Central American formations—political, cultural, and economic— have been forged through migrations from Canton to Canada to Costa Rica, as well as through entrepreneurial initiatives stretching from Taipei to Shenzen to Guatemala. By broadening our analytical horizon to the expansive and fluid Pacific, a transpacific analytic helps us distinguish the range of processes, people, and places that have been formative in constructing China and Central America and the politics that give them meaning.

The Pacific has long served as a site for generating new imaginaries, both imperial and liberatory, celebratory and critical. Whether it is the sixteenth-century commercial route of the Manila Galleon, the eighteenth-century explo-rations of Captain Cook, or World War II battles fought by Japan and the United States, the Pacific has featured as a contentious space of conquest and resistance. During the late twentieth century, the rising economic heft of East Asian coun-tries, including Japan, the Asian Tigers, and China, signaled for many a shift from transatlantic flows to transpacific circulations as the locus for modernity, leading some to rename the twenty-first century the "Pacific Century."[16] More recently, we can see manifestations of that impulse in the ill-fated Trans-Pacific Partnership (TPP) trade agreement that the Obama administration promoted as part of the United States' "pivot toward Asia." The agreement, which the US abandoned in 2017, brought together a coalition of countries interested in low-ering trade barriers and boosting exchange across the Pacific, while also neu-tralizing growing Chinese power in the region. As such, the TPP exploited the concept of the Pacific Rim as an ongoing field of capitalist expansion and geo-political influence.

In contrast, my transpacific analytic builds on critical work in the humanities to illuminate the histories and cultural formations erased from these political economic conversations about the Pacific. Arif Dirlik's *What's in a Rim?* laid the groundwork for this approach by analyzing how geographic constructions of the region—and specifically the economic powers at either edge—have legiti-mized expansionist economic understandings of it. The historian Matt Mat-suda's *Pacific Worlds* further highlights how this space of dynamic encounter, conquest, and cultural formations has been overshadowed by the greater-powers discourse on either side of the Pacific Rim. Matsuda offers an oceanic history focused on connections and flows in which "China with its millennia of dynas-ties, conquerors and grandeurs is not a subject, but the port of Canton with its customs agents organizing the trade of the world." In doing so, he emphasizes "sites of trans-localisms" to bring into view the "interconnectedness of different worlds" rather than borders of difference.[17] Hoskins and Nguyen's *Transpacific Studies* continues to develop this critical approach to excavate the diverse mobilities, spatialities, temporalities, and cultures that have defined the Pacific. Like Matsuda's, their work pushes us to recenter the Pacific—rather than the "areas" constituting its edges—to concentrate on what two of their book's contributors call the "diverse traffics" that constitute its global and supraregional flows.[18] My book does this by mapping the multiple Chinas and forms of Chineseness that emerge through ongoing engagement with the Americas in assemblages of racialized labor, nation-building, Cold War politics, and development that span the Pacific. These transpacific formations reflect what Biao Xiang describes as the "complex structures of engagement, geopolitical calculations, and meaning-making processes" that continue to inform development relations between China and Central America.[19]

In the current global context, this transpacific analytic offers a powerful intervention in conversations that seek to understand China–Latin America relations through the lens of China's "rise," highlighting instead a long history of transregional crossings and affiliations occurring at multiple levels. This approach challenges the formulations of Chinese and Latin American difference and distance propagated through both exclusionary immigration regimes and anti-Chinese racism in Latin America, as well as through traditional area studies epistemologies in academe.[20] Working against the assumption of homogeneous areas or nation-states matters not only for reconfiguring fields of scholarly knowledge production but also for the political realities that they seek to represent and shape. By highlighting the qualitative nature and stakes of transpacific developments, we gain a sense not of whether China is good or bad for Central America but of what "good" might mean and for whom. In other words, what would transpacific development ideally mean for differently positioned Central Americans? How might processes like trade, infrastructure, and corruption shape the particular assemblages of transpacific relations in which they are located? A transpacific analytic illuminates not only much more complex, diverse histories and experiences but also more capacious visions of the future worlds they might engender.[21]

Ethnographic Points of Entry

My research accentuates what an ethnographic approach can bring to what has largely been a debate among political scientists and economists. At its most basic, ethnography requires engaging phenomena as they happen and where they happen so as to elicit local interpretations and form embodied understandings of those phenomena. Prolonged fieldwork pivots on curiosity and critical empathy that allows us to ask basic questions about what things are—such as my starting question: who or what is China in Central America?—rather than taking identities, categories, or meanings for granted. Because ethnography privileges narrative, meaning, interpretations, and the idea of partial truths over universal Truths, and insists on empirical observation, systematic, critical analysis, and "evidence" to make its claims, it is both "the most humanistic of the social sciences and the most scientific of the humanities."[22]

My own ethnographic research involved qualitative interviews with people in different geographic and social locations to get at their diverse experiences, as well as the logics and narratives they use to describe their worlds. In addition to the countless informal interviews and conversations I have had with a wide array of Central Americans on this topic over the last eight years, I have collected 125 formal, tape-recorded, transcribed interviews reflecting the views of people ranging from ex-presidents, state functionaries, and diplomatic personnel to development project administrators, engineers, private entrepreneurs, independent consultants, union representatives, and citizens from across all sectors of society, including ethnic Chinese, recent Chinese migrants, and non-Chinese-heritage Central American. These interviewees represent a broad spectrum of age, gender, ethnicity, ideology, and nationality, encompassing Guatemalan, Costa Rican, Salvadoran, Nicaraguan, Taiwanese, US, and, of course, Chinese citizenship.

Since 2011, when I began the fieldwork on this project, I have spent more than thirteen months on the ground in Central America, mostly in the capital cities of Managua, San José, and Guatemala City, but also traveling to the provinces of those countries, where Chinese projects and communities live. This focused work builds on my previous twenty years of ethnographic research in Central America, a longitudinal engagement with the region that has allowed me to perceive changes in the development landscape and to experience shifting political and cultural regimes firsthand, as well as to understand how these shifts manifest in people's everyday lives.

In standard ethnographic practice, anthropologists maintain the anonymity of our interlocutors in order to ensure their confidentiality and trust. In the case of this fieldwork, you will notice that I identify some of my interlocutors by their first names only—in these cases I am using a pseudonym. I sometimes reference full names, which means I am citing public figures or others who have agreed to have the interview material attributed to them. In still other cases, I do not name names at all, but rather try to situate speakers by virtue of their age, vocation, ethnicity, or position in a way that protects their anonymity, especially in the case of discourses of corruption or in the case of talking about PRC state firms, where one's own views might put one at risk. In those instances, I have privileged the trust of my interlocutors, even though it comes at the expense of some ethnographic specificity. One goal of my interviews was to learn about the nature and dynamics of transpacific collaborations; however, I also sought to discern and interpret the narratives and discourse that people used to describe those experiences and perceptions. Therefore, sometimes I have paraphrased people's words and cited the date of our personal interview in the notes; in other cases, I have included quotations to denote direct quotes.

In addition to interviewing, I have also conducted what anthropologists call "participant observation" in myriad settings that offered insight into transpacific development encounters. These empirical data are crucial to explaining why Central Americans might interpret those development agreements with China as both welcome and suspect, as both a new path forward and also a continuation of a longer history of dependent development. These sites of engagement included trade expos, Chamber of Commerce events, industry conferences, project inauguration events, Chinese association and community activities, other community events, political protests, and even an occasional soccer game in Costa Rica's national stadium. Participation in these events helped me to understand important organizational dynamics and structures, discourses, and power relations that constituted those spaces. I also visited and inspected multiple development projects to get a sense of their contours and how they were being used by consumers.

Ethnography offers the possibility of investigating the material dimensions of different development projects—including their design, negotiation, construction, and reception by diverse constitutions—as they unfold in specific contexts. By engaging policymakers, the construction firms, the laborers, the beneficiary communities, and the actual physical space of a project, I am able to see how it has been imagined, executed, consumed, and negotiated from the point of view of different actors across time and space. From this vantage we can perceive the multiplicity of actors, the diverse practices, the alternative meanings, and the complex politics that surround Chinese development efforts, generating a more robust portrait of China and Chineseness in action. We see how a history of Chinese workers constructing local railroads, a history of Taiwanese soft-power stadium building, and a history of state-sponsored public works are manifest on the landscape, embodied in particular structures, people, and narratives. We also see how the idea of Chineseness is contested and reformulated by different actors who seek to accentuate their affinity with or distance from the PRC government in Beijing. As such, ethnography provides us with a better sense not only of what is distinct about

Chinese development initiatives—how they actually work—but also of their cultural and political significance on the ground.

Charting the Way Forward

I have intentionally written this book to speak to multiple audiences located in different spaces within and beyond academia, within and beyond policy conversations, and within and beyond the field of anthropology. Because few people are experts on both Asia and Latin America, I've formulated my analysis to speak to area studies specialists and nonspecialists alike, pointing to important moments, dynamics, and places in the history of each region and in their intersections; however, I've tried not to let the analysis in each chapter get bogged down in dense details that only specialists might care about, or to assume knowledge that a broader audience might not have. I've also tried make my analytical foundations clear, while avoiding dense theoretical arguments that would be inaccessible or irrelevant to a larger informed readership less interested in cultural critique.

Instead, my goal has been to offer a clear narrative that provides a situated analysis of these dynamics in particular places, while also keeping an eye on the broader implications that they have for development relations. To that end, I've avoided extensive in-text citations in favor of referencing most of my sources in endnotes. Those notes not only include additional information about the evidence on which I base my claims, but also point to the more traditional academic work that I've done on this topic elsewhere. In approaching the text in this way, my hope is that my analysis manages to shift the terms of scholarly, policy, and popular conversations by situating contemporary China–Central America relations in a longer historical trajectory, across multiple scales of engagement, and embodied by diverse actors with often very different ideas about the meaning of Chinese development and its utility for Central America.

To clarify which of those diverse actors I am referring to, and to avoid the conflation of China with the PRC government in Beijing, I have varied my use of terminology to refer to the various Chinas and Chinese actors present in this text. When speaking of geopolitics and the nation-state, especially in relation to diplomatic issues, I use the term "PRC." To reference specific policies and politics of the Chinese Communist Party in Beijing, I specify "the PRC government." Simultaneously, I describe state-affiliated enterprises as "PRC-sponsored," "PRC-subsidized," or "PRC-based" to distinguish them from firms or actors that do not receive PRC government support. Finally, to speak to people and processes located on the Mainland, as opposed to in Taiwan, Hong Kong, or other locations of Greater China, I use the term "Mainland Chinese."

The remainder of the book is divided into two parts: the first addresses the various actors and practices that constitute the multiple forms of China and Chineseness in Central America, and the second engages the domains that have come to define contemporary transpacific relations, including infrastructure, trade, and corruption. The chapters build on varying degrees of ethnographic, historical, policy, and discursive analysis to illustrate the multiple meanings of Chinese development and the distinct forms in which those meanings are embedded.

To unpack the various actors and forms that China and Chineseness have taken in the region over time, chapter 1 begins with a panoramic overview of the kinds of transpacific historical flows and encounters that have defined the relationship between China and Central America. Intended especially for readers without a specific area studies background in Asia or Latin America, it explores the essential moments of both Chinese and Central American development that have constituted contemporary relations, and also sets out the foundation for the transpacific analytic that is central to this book. Chapter 2 then fleshes out the first of the Chinas present in Central America—the Chinese diaspora. It highlights how contemporary Central American development efforts to connect to a globally ascendant China have rooted themselves in the history of transpacific migrant flows and their role in Central American national development. Furthermore, I show how nineteenth-century Orientalist discourses applied to Chinese railroad workers, referencing their industriousness and yet perniciousness, have come to frame discourses about contemporary Chinese development labor.

Chapter 3 examines Taiwanese Cold War affiliation and development assistance to explore the particular kind of development model Taiwan has pursued in the region. I show how that history defined certain norms for local labor arrangements, skills transfer, and patronage as the standard for successful South-South development relations that have come to shape local expectations for regional development. In all of these chapters, I triangulate the various forms of China and Chineseness to highlight how each shapes the others and how all of them work together to constitute the possibilities and also the limits of the PRC's development cooperation in Central America.

The second part of the book turns to the fields of action that have catalyzed ideas about Chinese development in the Americas. I highlight how infrastructure, trade, and corruption constitute three processes that both analysts and locals have used to gauge their impression of and engagement with transpacific developments. Specifically, chapter 4 takes up the material work of development by comparing infrastructure projects pursued by the PRC and Taiwan to highlight the similarities and differences between these development agents. I juxtapose their respective road-building efforts to infrastructure building by foreign entrepreneurs in the nineteenth and early twentieth centuries as well as to each other, thus interrogating the uniqueness of this particular dimension of transpacific developments. I also highlight how debates about infrastructure have served as a crucial space for redefining sovereignty and national identity.

In chapter 5, I look at the other side of the trade numbers frequently highlighted by economists to tell a story about transpacific relations. Specifically, I show how diplomatic relations have not hampered burgeoning economic relations among Central American economies and the PRC. I also, however, illuminate how various stakeholders have struggled to cross the cultural and generational boundaries necessary to make a deal that would offer more authentic development. And in chapter 6 I explore the consistent association between China and corruption amid the development landscape in Central America. I show how a combination of Orientalist readings of the history of local Chinese communities, Taiwanese textile factories, and PRC government politics has worked to solidify the association between corruption and Chinese development efforts. This association taints local politicians involved with the PRC and limits the possibilities of future development collaboration from all sides. It has also catalyzed a variety of anticorruption efforts in Central America that span different scales and refigure questions of sovereignty.

Finally, in the conclusion, I explore the implications of these transpacific developments in terms of their impact on ideas about development, sovereignty, and identity. These effects point to the conjuring of new worlds that work across traditional scales of politics to imagine new development landscapes.

Part I

WHO OR WHAT IS CHINA IN CENTRAL AMERICA?

1

TRANSPACIFIC ASSEMBLAGES

Tracing Development Encounters
over Space and Time

My use of the term "transpacific" speaks not to just a geographic space, but rather to the long history and multiple forms of engagement that have produced the actors that we presume to be the protagonists of China–Central America relations today. In contrast to an international relations or area studies approach that would frame the contemporary China–Central America relation as a "new" encounter between strangers, the transpacific analytic I develop throughout this book destabilizes those ideas of distant, different entities, and instead suggests how different encounters have produced assemblages of ideas, people, practices, and commodities that are essential to understanding Chinese development in Latin America today.[1]

The transpacific analytic that I deploy here is inspired by work that has tried to move beyond the nation-state or culture areas to think about spaces of inter-action and cultural production that have been crucial to the formation of our modern world system. Paul Gilroy's *Black Atlantic*, for example, paved the way for studying what Boelhower has called the "uniquely circumatlantic flow of peoples, goods, and cultures" that produced both Western modernity and resistances to it.[2] In doing so, Gilroy spawned a generation of transatlantic studies that have helped us to envision the formation not just of a single Anglophone empire across the Atlantic, but the multiple cultural, political, and economic worlds that it engendered and which also transcended it. Transpacific theorists have been inspired by that work to examine the Pacific as another strategic "zone of con-tact" that, according to Hoskins and Nguyen, "both in terms of how it has been imagined and experienced, is central to the problem of how Americas, Asians, and Pacific Islanders know themselves and each other."[3] In that sense, scholars have focused on a complex network of connections, operating at multiple scales across the Pacific, that have been constitutive of Asia and the Americas.

Building on this idea of networks, my transpacific approach thinks about the crisscrossing flows and relations that have constituted China and Latin America in terms of assemblages, a concept originally articulated by the theorists Gilles Deleuze and Felix Guattari and further elaborated by Manuel DeLanda.[4] Although other recent works in this tradition vary considerably in whether they posit assemblage as what McFarlane and Anderson label a "descriptor, ethos, or concept," they share a focus on "emergence, multiplicity and indeterminacy."[5] In other words, rather than imagining the global landscape in terms of rigid structures that (over)determine the nature and significance of certain identities, relations, or encounters, the idea of assemblages helps us to imagine how diverse agents, logics, values, and practices come together to produce provisional forms that hold together without completely solidifying. Instead, the interaction of an assemblage's constituent parts shape both the whole and also the constituent parts, thus creating the capacity for new forms, or the process of endless "becoming."[6]

In the case of transpacific relations, for example, we can imagine how processes of British colonialism, racialized labor hierarchies on Caribbean plantations, the construction of national infrastructure in Central America, and family-owned businesses came together to shape what China and Chineseness meant in Central America during the late nineteenth and early twentieth centuries. That assemblage not only produced a specific idea of the global and the place and identity of different territories and people in it, but wrought changes on the very elements that constituted it. In other words, as Chinese migrants transformed the nascent Central American nations through their labor on national railroads, the Chinese themselves were transformed from residents of the Canton region into alien residents or citizens of Central America. These particular formulations of identity and international relations give way to other assemblages as different actors (e.g., Taiwan), values (anti-Communism), and global relations (Cold War) reconfigure the elements and the meaning of Chineseness over time and space. In each of these configurations, assemblages, according to Anderson and McFarlane, reflect the "agency of wholes and parts, not one or the other," thus producing a sense of "power as plurality in transformation."[7]

This formulation of assemblage is especially useful for a transpacific analytic, as it helps us to see both shifts and continuities played out over time and space as different political, economic, and cultural forces have come together to (re)produce Latin America and China in relation to one another, rather than in isolation. Furthermore, it draws our attention to how these emergent processes—migration, anti-Communism, and development, to name just a few—have helped to construct the scales (i.e., local, national, global) that we often take for granted as the sites on which these transpacific relations play themselves out.[8]

To illuminate the specific processes and forms that have helped to assemble the actors—China and Latin America—that constitute the basis for contemporary transpacific relations, this chapter offers an analytical and historical orientation to China–Central America relations by focusing on distinctive moments and practices of "Chinese development" as they have manifested and mattered in Central America. In particular, I delineate three distinct dynamics that have brought Chinese development home to Central America and positioned it as formative to nation building and modernization in the region: the history of Chinese diasporas, cross-strait tensions between Taiwan and Mainland China, and the PRC government's "going out" politics. Next, I explain why Central America offers an important place to study these dynamics, especially in relation to its history with the United States, its geopolitical significance, and its global trade implications. In excavating these diverse histories and processes of mutual imbrication that have defined transpacific developments, I illustrate why the focus on a monolithic Chinese state is insufficient for us to understand the past and the future of transpacific developments. In the subsequent chapters, I explore these multiple Chinas and forms of Chineseness in more depth, as well as linking them more centrally to contemporary development processes.

Making Multiple Chinas

Diasporic Dispersions

To speak of China in Latin America, we have to acknowledge a long history of movement and exchange that began centuries before the emergence of modern nation-states in China and Latin America, but inaugurated specific forms of China and Chineseness that have produced both integral and durable formulations of regional identity. Beginning in the sixteenth century and lasting for two and a half centuries, Spanish trade ships circulated silver and luxury commodities from China through the Philippines and Acapulco to Spain on a route known as the Manila Galleon. The Spanish Crown structured the terms of this first transpacific engagement as part of its efforts to profit from commerce between Europe, Acapulco, Manila, and Southeast China, monopolizing the route and limiting trips to two per year from each port. Spanish traders introduced residents of the Spanish colonies of New Spain to highly coveted forms of Chinese textiles and art, not only creating demand for their consumption but inspiring spin-off industries within New Spain. The *china poblana* traditional dress style and *talavera* type of pottery are two examples of globally renowned Mexican folkloric and artisanal production whose roots trace back to Chinese silks and Ming Dynasty painted porcelains that local artisans sought to reproduce locally during this time. Not limited to their products, by the late 1600s, Chinese merchants and tradespeople such as barbers, cobblers, and musicians also established a stronghold for themselves within the *parian*, or Asian market, in Mexico City's Plaza Mayor. When the Galleon disappeared along with the fight for Mexican independence from the Spanish Crown, the legacy of Chinese trade, commerce, and artistic production in the Americas was already well established.[9]

A century later, Chinese labor and enterprise again proved foundational to the consolidation of modern Central American nations. As part of the Opium Wars between the United Kingdom and the rulers of the Qing Dynasty, British forces subordinated Chinese territories to their (and other foreign powers') control and forced China open to trade. First from Hong Kong and then from other treaty ports such as Macao, local and foreign brokers recruited and signed thousands of "coolie" laborers to eight-year labor contracts in the Caribbean to supplement and then replace slave labor on plantations in the Western Hemisphere. By 1853, these Chinese workers were being recruited to Panama to help build the railroad, thus making vital infrastructure another important site associated with Chineseness in the region. As I detail in chapter 2, when railroad construction ended, many of the original Chinese laborers and a new generation of transpacific migrants set up small grocery and supply businesses along the railroad lines throughout Central America, along with hotels, restaurants, and laundries. Therefore, both the infrastructure itself and the pattern of Chinese commerce and small family businesses that came with it became another landmark of Chinese presence in the Americas that has continued to the present.

From the late nineteenth century onward, the Chinese ethnic communities that have emerged throughout Central America have been defined as much by their internal diversity as by the ethnic homogeneity attributed to them by locals. Of those original coolie laborers and sojourners that came to the Americas, the majority were Cantonese speakers from the Pearl River Valley of Guangdong Province in southeastern China. Over time, these migrants were joined by a generation of Chinese fleeing Mainland China in the wake of the 1949 Communist revolution, by wealthier entrepreneurs from Taiwan in the 1970s, by Mainland migrants fleeing the political crackdown of the 1980s, and in even more recent waves by migrants from Macao, Hong Kong, and Beijing. Having long moved to the capital cities to pursue other economic opportunities, these ethnically Chinese community members, many of whom have residency or citizenship in Central America, are thus of diverse national, linguistic, geographic, and even ideological persuasions, a demographic fact that becomes important when we think about changing diplomatic relations in the region in the postwar period.

Diplomatic Deployments

The history of Central American collaboration with Taiwan as a democratic peer and development partner has served as an important force shaping how Central Americans think and talk about China and how they frame the questions they ask about the potential of Chinese development in the future of the region. Therefore, Taiwanese connections constitute not only one of the multiple Chinas in the region but also a primary element in the assemblages of Chineseness that have shaped transpacific relations.

The triumph of the Communist Party in 1949 ended the Chinese Civil War and provoked the exile of nationalist forces to Taiwan, and thus further proliferated the forms of Chineseness constituting transpacific relations. Central American nations recognized the Republic of China—Taiwan—in or just after 1949 as part of this era's anti-Communist politics in the West. And despite Nixon's visit to China in 1972 and the subsequent rapprochement between the PRC and most of the Western Hemisphere, Central America has remained a holdout for Taiwan. Taiwan's many decades of partnership with nations of the region have resulted in free trade agreements with its Central American affiliates and have been the source of important development cooperation, infrastructure, and humanitarian aid, thus making continued diplomatic recognition of Taipei, rather than Beijing, worthwhile for Central American nations. Indeed, in 2020, four of the fifteen countries that still recognized Taiwan were located in Central America, representing half of the region.

Sharpened cross-strait tensions over Beijing's One China policy have slowly begun to chip away at that regional affiliation, beginning with Costa Rica's diplomatic switch in 2007, followed by Panama in 2017 and El Salvador in 2018. However, the legacy of both Taiwanese diplomatic support for Chinese communities and cultural institutions in Central America and Taiwanese migrants to Central America has had powerful political and economic repercussions that shape contemporary expectations for what "Chinese development" should look like and accomplish. For example, Taiwan's tradition of bilateral development cultivated relationships with local communities, whereas Beijing's so far has not. Taiwan defined its development cooperation in terms of South-South partnership, much as Beijing does, but enacted that through the promotion of reciprocity and skills training for local workers, in contrast to China's preference for imported Chinese labor. The role that diplomatic representatives from the Taiwanese embassies in Central America have played in both participating in local Chinese community events and advocating for their interests vis-à-vis Central American governments has also cultivated particular expectations for what an embassy's relationship to the community might be.

Globalizing Goods

PRC government policies have formed another element of transpacific development assemblages, manifesting in the flow of commodities and new forms of market competition as well as in the promise of infrastructure and investment. While the PRC's national development policies at home have shifted since the 1980s from building an export economy to fomenting a domestic consumer base, the PRC government has also extended some of those development strategies to partners within the Global South. China's contemporary development model emerged after 1979 as part of Deng Xiaoping's efforts to enact incremental economic reforms without relinquishing state control over politics or the economy. The reform period was defined by state-directed experiments with market opening to foreign investment and export production in special economic zones along China's southeastern seaboard. Building on foreign investment, cheap labor, subsidies to state firms, and the export of inexpensive commodities, China's own domestic development gained fame as the factory to the world.

This early form of the PRC government's contemporary development strategy had important material reverberations in and for Central America. Where markets and local stores had previously sold mainly US imports or locally produced goods, Chinese imports quickly began to take over, creating a surplus of abundant, inexpensive plastics, toys, household items, shoes, and textiles. These initial commodities, followed by electronics, phones, and increasingly cars, small-scale manufacturing parts, and computers, have become ubiquitous in Central America, representing both the PRC's global reach and the accessibility of its products for residents of the Global South. But the price and convenience of these goods have also been accompanied by suspicions about their dubious quality, due to the perceived lack of regulation surrounding their production.[10] Furthermore, because companies in Mainland China were producing and exporting the very same shoes, plastic toys, and textiles that were the centerpiece of Central America's light manufacturing sector, China was increasingly dominating the US market in these sectors, squeezing Central America out of one of their main export markets.[11] Therefore, although the period from the 1990s through the beginning of the new millennium introduced Central Americans to a whole new generation of Chinese goods, this relationship brought no guarantee of friendship or a win-win relationship between China and Central America when it came to the division of global labor and free-market trade.

These market-based transpacific encounters were embellished and given concrete platforms for regional cooperation and policy making in 2008, when the PRC government published its first policy paper on Latin America. That declaration underlined the PRC's interest in pursuing peaceful development with the region, highlighting principles such as noninterference, respect for sovereignty, equality, and mutual benefit.[12] The PRC government updated that policy in 2016 with a statement outlining specific sectors of strategic cooperation, such as infrastructure, energy, and logistics, all coinciding with China's own national development programs of "going out" to invest abroad and shoring up economic prosperity at home.[13] Those policies have resulted in "strategic partner" designation for ten countries in Latin America (Argentina, Bolivia, Brazil, Chile, Costa Rica, Ecuador, Mexico, Peru, Uruguay, and Venezuela), and free trade agreements with Costa Rica, Peru, and Chile.[14] More recently, nineteen Latin American countries have signed on to China's Belt and Road Initiative, thus solidifying transpacific collaborations and giving them formal, bilateral parameters.[15]

PRC presence in Latin America has also materialized through new regional institutions, such as the 2015 establishment of the China-CELAC forum between China and the Community of Latin American and Caribbean States. The forum committed the PRC government to collaboration with Latin America on regional issues such as security, infrastructure, agriculture, and commerce, through mechanisms including both special and concessional loan programs.[16] More concretely, Beijing also committed to doubling trade with Latin America to reach $500 billion by 2025, and to investing $250 billion in Latin America over the next decade. The combination of these various state-to-state and regional initiatives has meant the proliferation of PRC government policies, institutions, and agents in Latin America, to include Chinese development banks, state-owned or state-subsidized enterprises, construction firms, and diplomatic representatives, among others.

The implications of this latest wave of transpacific development cooperation have been widely debated because of their diverse effects on the nations of the region. The way the PRC government has manifested in Latin America since the 1990s has provided the region with an important alternative source of finance, with much-needed infrastructure projects, and with a massive new market for its commodities. Furthermore, because the PRC government professes a politics of noninterference, its development cooperation has offered a powerful counterpoint to the United States' political and economic dominance in the region. For large economies like Brazil, the PRC not only replaced the United States as the country's top trade partner but also signaled Brazil's arrival as a global economic player and member of the BRICS Consortium. For more developed nations of Central America—such as Costa Rica and Panama—partnership with the PRC was perceived by many locals as a means for those countries to reposition themselves as global logistics hubs and regional players, rather than simply Central American ward states. These developments hint at how PRC policies might recenter the region in geopolitical and political economic terms through its development of infrastructure and trade in the region.

Critics, however, have pointed to the negative impacts of this current configuration of PRC government engagement in the region. They have emphasized how the PRC's nonintervention policy has provided the economic support to bolster authoritarian populist regimes in Venezuela, Argentina, Ecuador, and Bolivia. The spike in commodity exports from South America—soy, iron ore, copper—while beneficial in terms of raising the growth of GDP, was unsustainable, given how it was based on extractive and primary good exports, and thus undermined local efforts at industrialization. Alarmists forecast that by 2050, the PRC would essentially dominate the region as its major trade partner, owner of major firms (i.e., agroexport) and industry (e.g., telecom), and controller of major port infrastructure, petroleum, mining, and energy markets.[17] The implications of this transition would be a massive restructuring of global trade through the Pacific; however, any benefits this shift would offer to Central America as a logistics hub would be mitigated by severe encroachments on sovereignty by Chinese firms that would own and run much of the transport infrastructure. Therefore, Chinese development cooperation would not promote long-term development in and autonomy for the region but would simply reposition it as a pawn of another global hegemon—this time China.[18]

As this brief overview makes clear, Chinese development has involved a long history of transpacific engagements with Central America that have proliferated the number of Chinas in the region and the forms of Chineseness they represent. For example, even just the PRC government's increasing presence in Central America includes official embassy staff in Costa Rica, Panama, and El Salvador; executives from Chinese state-owned companies (like the China Harbor Engineering Company and Sinohydro); and agents of Chinese finance. The PRC also encompasses intermittent constituencies of Chinese workers brought in to work on infrastructure projects, although they tend to remain quarantined at special camps and have limited visas, meaning that they interact little with society at large. Increasingly, Chinese private business representatives and tourists also circulate through Central America, in search of investment and commercial opportunities. Chinese technology products (especially telecommunications equipment from Huawei), as well as Chinese transport vehicles, have quickly come to occupy a central place within local markets. While there are clear convergences between some of these actors, they embody diverse interests and represent distinct benefits or challenges for Central America.

Local perspectives on these transpacific exchanges build off decades of experience with the Chinese diaspora in Central America, a community seen to embody industriousness and commercial success but also insularity and racial difference. They also come from decades of cooperation with Taiwan, whose soft-power diplomacy and capacity building have fueled understandings of South-South solidarity. Finally, they come from recent experience with PRC government policy, which has produced inexpensive and potentially dubious commodities but also infrastructure loans and Chinese tourists. Therefore, China and Chineseness represent multifaceted, ambivalent, and shifting ideas that derive from the multiple actors and commodities that Central Americans have come to associate with China. We must come to terms with this multiplicity to appreciate the promise and challenges that Chinese development represents for Central America.

Constructing Central America

Located just south of Mexico, Central America has historically been an important regional ally for the United States, a supplier of goods for the US economy, and a crucial logistics hub of global trade due to its ability to link the Pacific with the Atlantic. In all of these dimensions, transpacific relations have played an important role in structuring the region's strategic importance. Nonetheless, Central America rarely figures in conversations about Chinese development because the region is materially and symbolically of a different breed than South America, so its relationship with the PRC has been qualitatively different from the start.

The nations that Central America comprises—Guatemala, Belize, Honduras, El Salvador, Nicaragua, Costa Rica, and Panama[19] differ vastly from those of South America in their size, wealth, political regime strength, and history with the United States. Overall Central America boasts a total population of about 44 million, relative to South America's whopping 422 million, with Central America's most populous country, Guatemala, registering approximately fifteen million people, and its smallest, Belize, less than a half million. In terms of resources, the commodities Central America has to offer are hardly the stuff of major commodity booms: sugar, coffee, cotton, pineapple, bananas, meat, and textiles. The economies of the region are similarly disproportionate. In South America, Chile rules with a per capita GDP of approximately $14,896 in 2019, compared to the average per capita GDP across Latin America of $8,869. Central America's largest economy, Guatemala, by contrast, totaled a per capita GDP of $4,620.[20] In material terms, Central America is much smaller and poorer, with fewer resources and lower levels of industrialization than most of China's major trading partners in

South America. For this reason, economists have tended to see Central America as poorly equipped to maximize the possibilities of trade with the PRC.[21]

Academic and journalistic analyses of China in Latin America to date have mainly focused on the large economies of South America, where the volume and stakes of commodity exports like soy from Brazil and Argentina or minerals from Chile and Peru are substantial. The PRC's growing role as South America's main trading partner, and the positive effect this has had for these countries' growth, is often juxtaposed against the negative consequences it may have for long-term sustainability and modernization. South America, moreover, has been the site of some of China's largest and most controversial projects, such as the Coco Coda Sinclair Dam and a proposed transcontinental railway running through Peru, Bolivia, and Brazil. These two initiatives, one completed and the other still in the proposal stage, suggest the powerful way that the PRC's money and domestic development needs may be literally reconfiguring the infrastructural landscape of the region. As such, these projects offer powerful cautionary tales about the debt, environmental degradation, and labor rights violations that Chinese partnership might bring.[22] The potential security concerns posed by the PRC government's technological incursions in the region via its telecommunications juggernaut Huawei or through collaborative space programs like the one that helped Bolivia launch its first satellite add an additional element of distrust to this equation.[23] Finally, the PRC's relationship with petroleum states like Venezuela illuminate other political challenges. On the one hand, the PRC has been accused of propping up authoritarian regimes like that of Nicolás Maduro with loans. On the other hand, Venezuela holds China in a "creditor trap," as the PRC government can ill afford for Venezuela to default and instead must resort to pressuring Maduro to resume its "loans-for-oil" repayment schedule. Rather than a win-win relationship, these developments bode the possibility of a no-win situation.

In order to fully understand the significance of formative transpacific encounters in Central America, however, we must also bring into view Central America's historical struggle to define its sovereignty vis-à-vis the United States, whose interventionist economic, political, and military policies have indelibly shaped the region. Any conversation about Chinese development cooperation and its impact on national identity and sovereignty must take this history into account. For example, what is new or unique about Chinese presence in the region? How does it differ from a history of US intervention there? In what follows, rather than elaborating a comprehensive history of US–Central American relations, I distill three main moments in Central America's development trajectory that explain why the region is so important to global analyses of Chinese development.[24] Taken as snapshots, they seek to contextualize the terms of earlier relations in ways that bear on how Central Americans make sense of Chinese presence today. These snapshots are thus important not only for revealing what is new or different about the current era of transpacific developments, but also for explaining why the region's development fate holds such important consequences.

United Exploits

Chinese development is often associated with the infrastructure and extractive work undertaken by state-owned or state-subsidized firms around the world. However, in Central America, the PRC is only the latest foreign power in a long history of blurring the line between private and public, domestic and foreign actors and goods.

The countries that now constitute Central America declared independence from Spain in 1821. But as early as 1823, the United States had asserted itself as the region's handler, issuing the Monroe Doctrine to warn European powers that the US would not tolerate foreign efforts to exert control in its self-designated sphere of influence. Therefore, as incipient Central American nations began to build their coffee and plantation economies and consolidate national territory, the United States and various multinational firms would play an important role in laying the groundwork for that development and shaping the political economic fate of the region. This history constitutes the foundation on which both the physical work of Chinese development projects unfolds and the political and cultural significance of transpacific development is read.

The story of one man highlights how private capital, multinational firms, infrastructure, and interventionist politics defined this early phase of Central American development. Minor Keith was the nephew of Henry Meiggs, an American businessman hired by the Costa Rican government to construct its railroad from the capital, San José, to the Caribbean port of Limon. Minor Keith took over the railway line construction after his uncle's death in 1877 and shortly thereafter went on to assume construction of the Guatemalan railway. Keith agreed to build the Costa Rican railway in exchange for eight hundred thousand acres of tax-free land surrounding the rail line and a ninety-nine-year lease on the operation of the line. In Guatemala, a similar arrangement bought him a ten-year lease and fifty-seven thousand acres of land.[25]

Two elements of this arrangement are notable for thinking about Chinese development efforts in Central America today. First, Keith drew on imported Chinese and Black laborers from the Caribbean to build these rail lines, resulting in the formation of some of the first Chinese communities in Central America. Second, he utilized land adjacent to the railroads to plant bananas, a venture that proved to be much more lucrative than the railroads themselves and allowed him to form his own company, Tropical Trading and Transport. He later merged this firm with rival Boston Fruit to create the infamous United Fruit Company (UFCO), which by 1930 owned 3.5 million acres of land in Central America and was the largest landholder in Guatemala.[26] The size of its landholdings, the breadth of its control over railroads, ports, and freight transport, and its monopoly over telegraph infrastructure through its company Tropical Radio and Telegraph were just a few reasons why the company was given the nickname "the octopus"—it had its tentacles in everything. In this way, multinational firms acquired control over four essential sectors in Central America: bananas, roads, ports, and electricity.[27]

The active role of US private capital and state policy cannot be overlooked as we contemplate the perceived uniqueness of the PRC's use of state-owned enterprises to conduct development work in the region and its stance of nonintervention in relation to domestic politics. Indeed, US foreign capital, landholdings, and monopoly on transport and media were only one part of the control that private companies like UFCO had over Central America's development. Throughout the beginning of the twentieth century, UFCO's economic interests directly informed US foreign policy toward the region. US secretary of state John Foster Dulles's law firm, Sullivan and Cromwell, represented UFCO, and his brother, CIA director Alan Dulles, was a board member.[28] Therefore, when, in the 1950s, reform leaders like Jacobo Arbenz Guzmán in Guatemala tried to expropriate UFCO's land for redistribution and national development, their efforts were undermined by way of a CIA-backed coup.[29] Indeed, the history of UFCO and its enclave economies in Central America deeply informs local memory of regional dependency and the politics of foreign imposition. PRC officials will readily point to this history to highlight their distance from the neocolonial model represented by US intervention in the region.

Global Logistics

Central America's geographic positioning as a strategic global transport route offers another reason for foreign involvement in the region, explaining why Central America's strategic value has greatly outweighed its size and has made it a contentious site for transpacific relations to unfold.

Because the Central American isthmus offered various possibilities for linking the Pacific with the Atlantic, the region was the focus of bitter nineteenth-century feuds between the US and the French over who would construct a trans-isthmus canal, and where. With the start of the Gold Rush in 1849, the US real estate and transport magnate Cornelius Vanderbilt sought to capitalize on the heightened demand for quick shipment of people and cargo to and from the Pacific coast of

California by proposing the construction of a canal across Nicaragua. While that effort was thwarted by lack of financing, Vanderbilt still built a heady business offering transport by boat via Lake Nicaragua and the San Juan River to cut travel times and cost. The appeal of a true canal led France to begin construction on a canal in Panama in 1881.[30]

Construction of the canal, like construction of the Central American railroads, was executed in large part by migrant labor brought from the Caribbean, including Chinese coolie and free labor. Indeed, as I detail in chapter 2, it was Chinese construction of the Panama Canal that led to the first Chinese communities in Central America. Although the French were not able to complete the canal, by 1903 Panama granted the United States the right to build and administer the canal in perpetuity. In 1977, the United States and Panama signed the Torrijos-Carter Treaty, which allowed for the canal to be handed back over to Panama by 1999. Since 1999 the canal has been administered by the Panama Canal Authority.

Over time, globalizing trade and the increasing volume of imports from Asia have only increased the strategic importance of a trans-isthmus canal. Facing increasing traffic and also larger ship sizes, in 2007 the Panama Canal Authority began work on expanding and updating the canal to increase its capacity, and additional updates are planned for the future. In the meantime, the Hong Kong–based Chinese firm Hutchinson Whampoa acquired the contract to operate the ports located at the Pacific and Caribbean outlets of the canal.[31] That China might control that important transit route and be able to link it to a growing global network of commerce through its Belt and Road Initiative suggests to many a recipe for global hegemony made possible, in part, by asserting power over infrastructure in Central America.

Deepening these worries is the prospect of a second canal in the region. In 2013, the Hong Kong–based entrepreneur Wang Jing and his firm HKND signed a contract with Nicaragua's president, Daniel Ortega, to begin construction on a trans-isthmus canal that would pass through Vanderbilt's initial route across Lake Managua. And while the PRC government has denied involvement in the agreement, many have presumed that PRC government interests lie behind the project, despite its Hong Kong origins. Construction on the canal has not made considerable progress, although the concession did grant HKND fifty-year rights to develop and administer the canal territory, even in the event that the canal is never built, with the option to renew for another fifty years—a concession not so different from the type Guatemala granted to Minor Keith back in the nineteenth century or that Panama granted to the US in 1903. The PRC government's current efforts to build infrastructure in Central America must thus be read in the context of a longer history of US hegemony and geopolitics, in which the ability to control transoceanic shipping routes confers important global economic advantages and raises crucial questions about racialized migrant labor and national sovereignty.

Anti-Communist Arrangements

The strategic place of Central America as the site of anti-Communist proxy wars and its role as a political ally of the United States offer additional reasons why Central America matters for an understanding of Chinese development today. The twentieth-century Cold War context heightened the region's geopolitical importance and threw into question the physical integrity of the Central American nations, their development practices, and their diplomatic affiliations. The region's embrace of Taiwan as an affirmation of Western democratic values and a source of solidarity in the face of its own civil strife has had a lasting impact on the formulations of China and Chineseness present in Central America.

The 1947 Truman Doctrine underscored the United States' intention to contain Communism and protect the free world, especially policing Communist incursions into what US politicians deemed America's backyard. Although both private US citizens and US military forces had occupied parts of Central America at various times throughout the early twentieth century, the Cold War brought new intensity to US regional dominance, especially after the successful Cuban revolution in 1959.

To "shore up" the Western Hemisphere, the US supported Central American dictators who promoted US interests against nationalist reformers and guerrilla insurgents. The Somoza dynasty in Nicaragua, the violent authoritarian rule of Ríos Montt in Guatemala, and Robert D'Aubuisson in El Salvador were just a few of the reactionary regimes propped up by US policy, and threats against them were crushed through the use of local military troops and paramilitary contingents that benefited from US military training, arms, and capital.[32] Violent civil conflicts between military forces, paramilitary units, mercenaries, and local insurgencies not only ripped asunder the social fabric in countries like Nicaragua, Guatemala, and El Salvador but, in the case of Guatemala, unleashed genocide against indigenous citizens, razing villages, displacing communities, and destabilizing the economy.

Although many Central American nations originally recognized the Republic of China in the early twentieth century prior to the civil war that resulted in the Communist takeover of Mainland China in 1949 (Panama in 1912, Guatemala in 1933, Honduras in 1941, Costa Rica in 1944), Central American nations continued to support Taiwan over its Communist counterpart, the PRC, as the Cold War set in after World War II. This unflagging support for Taiwan was impressive in the face of rapprochement with the PRC by many other Latin American nations, such as Mexico, and the United States' own eventual establishment of diplomatic relations with the PRC in 1979. Central American nations have often justified their seventy-plus years of friendship with Taiwan through a discourse of the shared values of democracy and liberalism; however, Taiwan also played an important material role in funding and arming Central American armies in their battles against "Communist" insurgents.[33]

The Cold War battle in Central America played out mainly through military incursions and political intrigue in the region, but it was also articulated through the creation of new kinds of development cooperation. These programs sought to invest in human capital, training individuals and communities to engage directly in development rather than offering material resources with which to foster that development.[34]

John F. Kennedy, in particular, realized the importance of "winning hearts and minds" rather than simply engaging militarily, and, to that end, he enacted development programs like the United States Agency for International Development (USAID) and the Alliance for Progress to promote economic development so as to neutralize the possibility of Communist revolution.[35] During the 1960s and 1970s, cooperatives and "capacity training" became important facets of both US foreign policy and Central American local development practice. Toward the end of the long era of armed civil conflicts in Central America, development work was increasingly taken up by nongovernmental, humanitarian efforts and local, community-based agencies. These connections shifted development work away from bilateral state-to-state efforts to more vertical collaborations between state agencies and local partners, while also creating the sense that communities themselves (rather than the state) were responsible for development. Furthermore, this generation of development initiatives abandoned infrastructure projects for more qualitative human-development goals such as community-based, participatory models, microfinance, leadership, and self-esteem training.[36] Foreign funding for infrastructure as a central dimension of national development waned, becoming an important area that Chinese development efforts in the region have sought to address.

Central America figures not as a peripheral "backyard" for global development politics, but rather as a central node for the coming together of diplomacy, geopolitics, infrastructure, and trade. The countries of the region bring to contemporary transpacific relations a strong need for development but also a long, complex history of economic and political dependence on and intervention by the United States. National development efforts in the region were largely enacted by foreign capital, with the actual infrastructure work executed by migrant labor, including a significant number of Chinese workers. Central America's strategic geographic location in relation to Pacific-Atlantic trade and the United States made it a volatile site of US military intervention and a battleground for Cold War anti-Communist conflicts. Finally, contemporary development efforts have followed the neoliberal policies defined by Western lending institutions and have focused more on market-based, human-capital-building efforts that have frequently been tied to antidrug, anticorruption, or pro-austerity goals more than to providing material infrastructure. It is against this larger historical context of geopolitics and development policy that we have to evaluate the significance of the PRC government's growing presence and its emphasis on South-South, win-win development partnerships; a politics of nonintervention; and infrastructure-focused development. Furthermore, we must read into that history the traces of transpacific politics as a formative feature of Central American modernization.

The history of transpacific relations is one composed of associations among enterprising individuals and foreign governments, colonial powers and private contractors, multinational corporations and migrant communities, all stretched across dense transnational hubs. In the next two chapters, I flesh out in more detail the nature of the different Chinas and forms of Chineseness that have emerged from this long history of encounters taking place at multiple levels of engagement and by different kinds of actors representing a variety of interests. From those assemblages, we can begin to understand the multivalent nature of Chinese development in Central America's own development trajectory.

2

CHINESE DIASPORIC COMMUNITIES

Migration and the Making of Central
American Modernity

In December 2012, residents of Costa Rica's capital, San José, came out to witness
the inauguration of the region's newest Chinatown. The event was trumpeted
on China's official state-run media source, Xinhua, for adding to the hundred-
plus already-existing Chinatowns throughout the world, and for making China's
presence known in the capital of one of its newest development partners, Costa
Rica, with which it had established diplomatic relations just five years earlier.
Following the inauguration, Costa Rica's national newspaper, *La nación*, devoted
a special supplement to Chinatown in which China's ambassador to Costa Rica
described the project as "a new architectural referent for the friendship between
China and Costa Rica."[1] As such, the inauguration publicity advertised San José's
Chinatown as an emergent site of transpacific development.[2]

Locally, project promoters emphasized the multicultural dimensions of the
Chinatown, underscoring how the zone would recognize Chinese immigrants'
contributions to Costa Rican national identity while also creating a more cosmopolitan city.[3] For many Josefinos (San José residents), however, institutionalizing
an iconic space of Chinese culture in the downtown could not be read simply as
an act of historical commemoration or urban renewal. Instead, the location of
the project, the financing from the PRC, the use of Mainland Chinese construction workers, and the timing of the project all contributed to the sense that this
urban initiative embodied both the perils and the promise of a new development
partnership with the PRC. For these residents, the project provoked the question of what it meant to be Costa Rican at a moment when China was taking

FIGURE 1.   San José's Tang Dynasty arch at the entrance of its Chinatown.

on an increasing material and symbolic presence both within their nation and in the global political economic landscape. For members of the historic Chinese community in Costa Rica, the project raised other questions. Would San José's Chinatown visualize and valorize Chinese contributions to Costa Rican nation building, or would it reify their ethnic difference anew? How would the Chinatown link the China of Costa Rica's past with its aspirations to be connected to the global China of the future?

The story of Costa Rica's Chinatown brings to the fore one of the multiple Chinas present in Central American development politics—namely, Chinese diasporic communities. Their history illuminates the crisscrossing flows that have laid the foundation for contemporary transpacific developments, accentuating the importance of the historic migration circuits between China and the Americas, the national infrastructure Chinese diaspora here helped to build, and the foundational ideas about Chineseness that their presence generated.[4] I chronicle this history to show the material and symbolic contributions that multiple waves of Chinese migrants to Central America offered to the region, while also analyzing the legal and cultural mechanisms by which their existence and diversity have been erased by national regimes across Central America. I end by highlighting how Costa Rica's Chinatown experience makes visible not just the history of Chinese presence in the region but also how that history gets reactivated in contemporary conversations that simultaneously praise and elide past Chinese contributions to the nation, while using past ideas about Chineseness to frame expectations for relations with a global, "rising" PRC.

China in Costa Rica

When the San José Chinatown was originally conceived, Chineseness was both everywhere and nowhere in the city. Located in the central valley, with approximately 1.5 million urban residents, San José features architecture that does not bear many visible signs of its colonial past or its multicultural heritage. Instead the city center boasts a series of well-maintained public parks and plazas that have been revamped over the years to give the city a more modern look. In this space, signs of Chinese culture and commerce are visible but somewhat randomly distributed. You could find ethnic Chinese restaurants, supermarkets, and specialty stores that ply Chinese ethnic products (tea sets, fans, silk clothing) and bear Chinese names such as Super Hansan, or Da Xing Supermarket, or, one block over, the upscale restaurant Tin-Jo. Nonetheless, the district also houses generic retail stores (selling inexpensive import goods from Mainland China) as well as indoor skateboard parks and burlesque theaters; a beloved Catholic church, Nuestra Senora de la Soledad; and historic high schools. Therefore, unlike in global cities such as San Francisco, Lima, or Havana, where concentrated Chinatown enclaves are readily marked and institutionalized on the landscape, Chinese presence in San José's downtown was much more diffuse.[5] Indeed, Josefinos were just as likely to describe the area that the mayor had designated for the new Chinatown as a "shady" part of town or a sentimental site of cultural patrimony as they were to identify it as a Chinatown.

The Chinatown project was set in motion by San José's ambitious, enterprising mayor Johnny Araya Monge—a longtime politician (serving as mayor from 1998 to 2001, and then again from 2003 to 2013 and 2016 to 2020) and a member of the ruling National Liberation Party as well as a presidential candidate in 2014. Recounting the project's genealogy, Araya described to me how he visited Beijing in 2005 in order to initiate conversations with his municipal counterparts about the idea of creating a sister-city connection between the two urban metropolitan spaces. As Araya proudly explained, "The Chinatown was my idea. It was an idea that emerged long before the diplomatic relations with China."[6] Because Costa Rica was the first Central American country to recognize the PRC in 2007, Araya presented himself as a visionary, one who understood the importance of China before its global presence had become clear and who saw this local project as a global one.

Given the diffuse Chinese presence in the downtown, Araya claimed that the Chinatown project was designed, in part, to make visible and give coherence to Chinese contributions to Costa Rican history and national identity:

> The Costa Rican Chinese colony . . . is very important in Costa Rican nationality. On the other hand, I think China, the Chinese culture has increasing weight in the world; it is a flourishing, influential culture. It is a rising influence. . . .
>
> . . . [The Chinatown will] . . . combine that which is Costa Rican with decorative elements that echo Chinese millenary culture such that it creates a cultural nexus between both people and both countries.[7]

As this narrative indicates, rather than simply invoking a distant, foreign past, Araya expected Chinese cultural artifacts to construct the architecture of a modern multicultural national identity. What is more, he hoped to use Costa Rica's ethnic Chinese community to make a claim on an ascendant China and its material and symbolic power within the global imaginary.

The Chinatown initiative commenced in earnest in 2011 as a collaborative effort between Beijing and San José. The mayor of Beijing donated $1 million, including both money and a team of expert builders to construct the Tang Dynasty archway at the Chinatown entrance, while the San José municipality provided additional workers and funds with the goal of transforming what were once arterial bus routes into colorful pedestrian thoroughfares, lined with Asian-style red roofs and traditional lamps. Indeed, during the summer months of 2012, I would walk by the emerging archway structure on a daily basis to track the Chinese team's progress, while also watching the lead engineer indulge in late-afternoon mah-jongg games with his Chinese coworkers. The fact that the archway to the Chinatown was being erected just in front of a local bakery owned by a Chinese couple who formed a central part of the local Chinese ethnic community made the construction area something of a Chinese cultural hub throughout the course of the construction process; however, there was little to no interaction between the PRC state engineers working on the archway and the diasporic Chinese Costa Ricans who conversed in Cantonese over Costa Rican coffee.

Soon after the project's groundbreaking, however, local high school students and nearby neighbors came out to protest the initiative. One protester commented to the press, "Chinatown doesn't exist, that's a Chinese myth. Here what exists are Barrio La Soledad and Paseo de los Estudiantes. And then there are four Chinese markets, [and] three or four Chinese restaurants. That is not enough reason to erase the country's history."[8]

FIGURE 2.   Chinese laborers take a quick break for mah-jongg.

For protesters, the Chinese presence in the area did not constitute an ethnic zone worthy of the title Chinatown. Buttressing their claims, an opinion piece in *La nación* recounted the development of Chinatowns in Los Angeles and San Francisco, where Chinese workers lived in downtown neighborhoods and established independent businesses. In those places, concentrated Chinese communities meant that their presence could not be denied; however, in San José, the author noted, "what [the mayor] wants is the opposite—a Chinatown without Chinese."[9]

In these critiques of the project, opponents of the Chinatown rendered the history and presence of Chinese immigrants in the San José downtown not only irrelevant to national history and its hispanized identity, but a threat to the cultural significance of iconic landmarks such as the Paseo de los Estudiantes and the neoclassic Soledad church located alongside its northern edge. For them, rather than institutionalizing a new chapter in Costa Rican history and identity, a Chinatown represented the displacement of local history through foreign imposition.[10] To drive home this point, just one week after the student protest, neighborhood residents and historical preservationists gathered in front of the historic church before marching on to protest at the Legislative Assembly building, carrying banners reading, "History yes, Chinatown no!"

So how are we to reconcile Mayor Araya's claim of the centrality of Chinese contributions to the Costa Rican nation with the protesters' allegations that a Chinatown, and the local history of Chineseness it referenced, represented a myth and cultural invasion? To answer this question, we have to revisit the history of Chinese transpacific flows to Central America to understand their foundational role in Central American modernization efforts. By providing both the physical labor and the ethnoracial difference to reinforce the material and symbolic boundaries of the nation, Chinese actors in Central America could be simultaneously valued for their "industrious" labor and rejected for their "pernicious and menacing" difference.[11] Moreover, I argue that many of the same needs and fears that marked the Chinese diaspora's integration into Central America in the nineteenth century constitute the terms through which Central Americans have come to articulate contemporary assessments of PRC presence in the region.

Chinese Foundations in Central America

The history of Chinese migration to the Americas cannot be told simply as the movement of people from one region to another; instead, from the beginning, these flows were the product of complex, overlapping political, economic, and cultural arrangements playing themselves out across diverse sites on both sides of the Pacific. As the Pacific studies historian Matt Matsuda has argued, these assemblages of different histories, practices, and relations "take on full meaning only when linked to other stories and places."[12] In the early nineteenth century, when modern transpacific labor flows commenced, those assemblages included mercantilist trade, intersecting colonial and imperial structures, emergent national legal regimes, and globalized racial hierarchies.

On the Central American isthmus, independence from Spanish colonialism in 1821 inaugurated the construction of today's autonomous nations, with the Federal Republic of Central America—a single, sovereign state composed of the five contemporary Central American nations of Guatemala, El Salvador, Honduras, Nicaragua, and Costa Rica—a quick, and ultimately unsuccessful, postcolonial experiment.[13] This early nineteenth-century moment in Central America was defined by the rule of local Spanish criollo elite over a hetereogeneous population of mestizos, indigenous peoples, Afro-descendant slaves, and combinations of all of the above, organized into strict social hierarchies that also informed racialized divisions of labor.[14] Most economic production was oriented toward agriculture, often in large landholding patterns.[15] Therefore, the recruitment of labor, the construction of national transport systems, and the cultivation of agroexport industries were crucial next steps to consolidating and developing the fledging Central American nations. Chinese labor entered this context as both a welcome antidote to those labor needs and yet, increasingly, a worrisome threat to the national homogeneity that these early elites hoped to craft.[16]

Across the Pacific, instability and shifting regimes also shaped the ninteenth-century Qing Dynasty, which faced pressures from both within and beyond its borders.[17] Colonial aggression from the British during the first Opium War meant that the Qing Dynasty was losing control over its own trade and sovereignty. That aggression escalated toward the end of the century as the British were able to mandate that China cede control of Hong Kong and the treaty ports from which the British and then the French controlled trade. Internally, the Qing Dynasty faced challenges from its own subjects on the basis of population growth, famine, and war. Therefore, although the Qing Dynasty had banned emigration, local labor brokers sometimes facilitated and more often deceived desperate young men into contracts, working with those Europeans in control of the ports of Hong Kong and Macao to ensure a steady flow of labor to colonial outposts in the West.[18] Abolition movements in Europe were increasingly limiting the supply of slave labor to the region, and even nations committed to ending the slave trade seemed glad for the opportunity to substitute Chinese contract labor in its stead. These overlapping systems of global, regional, and national politics linked to trade and labor set the terms for Chinese labor flows to the Americas.

The original Chinese arrivals to the Americas in the early 1800s were largely from the Canton and Fujian regions of Southeast China, and they identified with their villages of origin in the Pearl River Delta rather than with a Chinese state. These men arrived as coolies brought to the Americas under eight-year contracts to work in sugar planations or in mining. Whether landing in Cuba via the Atlantic or Peru through the Pacific, they were contracted to work alongside slaves or (after most European and many Latin American nations abolished the slave trade in 1821) as their substitute, and were forced to renew their contracts with little hope of freedom or return to China. Because of the political vulnerability of the Qing Dynasty, the regime was not capable of effectively advocating for its subjects' rights on the other side of the Pacific, so the deplorable conditions of the coolie trade meant high fatality rates during the sea passage and high rates of suicide among laborers once in the Americas.[19] Even when the coolie system was banned in 1874, those original migrants were forced to pay off the terms of their contracts before becoming truly free. Furthermore, subsequent waves of "free" migrant labor generally continued to work in slave-like conditions in Latin America, despite their independent status.[20]

The first documented Chinese laborers to Central America, specifically, arrived in Panama in 1852 and Costa Rica in 1855. These early arrivals were indentured labor recruited by brokers in China; they originally traveled to the Caribbean and were later redistributed out to an expanding network of local contractors in the young Central American nations to help construct national railways. The historian Lucy Cohen offers a sense of this process in her chronicle of Chinese labor agents in the Pearl River valley of Canton who recruited two thousand Chinese laborers for the work on Panama's interoceanic railway in 1853.[21] The Panama Railroad Company purchased coolie services from the Canton labor contractor, to whom it agreed to pay twenty-five dollars a month per man, and then made financial arrangements with each individual coolie, offering each a few dollars a month in wages and retaining the remainder as payment for ocean passage and food.[22] Five hundred of these Chinese contract laborers were brought over to help expedite completion of the railway, working alongside black and indigenous as well as European (mostly Irish) laborers.[23] However, these first experiments with Chinese railroad workers were not entirely successful, given that substantial numbers of the laborers fell ill. More Chinese workers were recruited for the construction of the French Panama Canal in 1880–89, although as free migrants. When the French canal company went bankrupt, Chinese laborers whom they had recruited were left unemployed and remained largely in Panama or moved to Costa Rica.[24]

Guatemala authorized the entry of Chinese migrant labor in 1872, albeit with much popular opposition and shifting forms of regulation. As in Panama, the Chinese entered the country by way of individual local contractors who assumed responsibility for their labor. For example, in 1877 the Guatemalan government gave the landowner Don Manuel Arteaga Borrero a dispensation of four years during which he could contract Chinese migrants for employment by local farmers, plantation owners, and others who sought Asian labor. After that period, individuals were able to contract Chinese labor only for themselves.[25]

In the case of Costa Rica, landowners brought a few workers up the Pacific coast from Panama following completion of the railroad to work as domestics on private lands. Six hundred fifty Chinese migrants arrived in Puntarenas, Costa Rica, in 1873 and were assigned to work on the construction of the Atlantic railroad, or consigned to agricultural or domestic work.[26] Although the Costa Rican government rejected many local landowner applications to import Chinese labor, Chinese immigration continued to grow due to its profitability.[27] After 1874 (when the coolie trade was banned), Chinese immigrants filled the ranks of railroad construction and commercial expansion in their new home.[28]

From the beginning, Central American society both embraced and shunned Chinese labor. On the one hand, fledging Central American governments wanted cheap, exploitable labor to do the backbreaking mining and construction work needed to develop the nation. While original accounts of Chinese labor in the Americas highlighted the physical deficiencies that Chinese workers exhibited and their vulnerability to disease, Chinese labor in general quickly became renowned as *laborioso* (hardworking), a quality that became both desirable and also threatening in relation to other migrants. After all, as part of their modernization campaigns, Central American governments generally embarked on a campaign of "whitening," attempting to recruit migrants of European stock, free of miscegenation with "undesirables." Therefore, as the historian Lara Putnam notes, "Chinese immigrants, as one of the main sources of nonwhite labor, were simultaneously promoted as efficient workers for progress and prosperity and criticized as harmful to the physical and moral well-being of the nation."[29] As we will see, this tension between embracing Chinese industriousness and rejecting its racial otherness did not fade with national modernization, but rather continues to be a central frame through which contemporary discussions of Chinese development in Central America unfold today.

With time and the inflow of new generations of migrants, these waves of Chinese migrants created communities that spread throughout the region and took on new forms of social and political significance. In doing so, the Chinese shifted from working as laborers on national infrastructure projects to crafting the terms of their own integration into the Central American nations. They established themselves alongside the railway, usually forming "nuclei" of groups with the same last name. These workers eventually shifted their small-business skills into more profitable industries such as laundries, hotels, commerce, and food service.[30] Therefore, whereas Chinese communities originally formed mainly along the Caribbean and Pacific coast railway lines, those communities gradually moved inland toward the capital cities.

Chinese assimilation into the local economy, however, was not accompanied by a more inclusive sense of local identity or belonging; instead, as historians have argued, Chinese immigration and the communities of difference it produced catalyzed the formation of exclusionary immigration regimes that became central to defining national identity throughout the Americas.[31] In Mexico and Central America, one way these exclusionary politics manifested was through efforts to follow what appeared to be the legal status quo in North America. The United States' 1882 enactment of the Chinese Exclusion Act, the only immigration law to single out a specific ethnic group, was, thus, a flagship model. As Lara Putnam observes, Central American nations "surveyed foreign legislation before formulating policy, seeking the principles put into practice in the matter by the most advanced nations."[32] This emulation of North American immigration policies meant that many Chinese migrants pursued a trajectory of remigration throughout the Americas during the nineteenth century, often arriving in San Francisco only to be shipped to Mexico and then Central America. Therefore, Central American Chinese grew not only from the descendants of coolie labor but through new migrations or remigrations of free migrants through the United States, Mexico, and the rest of Central America.

Because of this history of exclusion enacted at multiple sites, Chinese diasporic communities in Central America reflected and consolidated new forms of transpacific networks. Henry Yu has called these migration circuits and their constituent communities parts of a "Cantonese Pacific," to reference the particular originary localities (Canton), cultural forms, and notions of time and space that structured migrants' sense of identity and community.[33] He distinguishes this dynamic from "Chinese" migration because of its cultural specificity, as well as the way that it stretched back and forth across the Pacific.[34] Nonetheless, the patterns of racialization and exclusion that these Chinese migrants faced in their various destinations in the Americas have led scholars such as Erika Lee to speak of "hemispheric Orientalism" as a foundational dynamic of the region.[35] Therefore, as I detail below, emergent Chinese transnational connections and ethnic communities built on small-business enterprise quickly provoked new xenophobic responses by both locals and the state. These exclusionary efforts pivoted on narratives of Chinese otherness, highlighting how assemblages of legal regimes, racialized hierarchies of citizenship, and local commercial practices worked together to either erase Chinese presence or mark it as permanently outside the bounds of the nation.

Exclusionary Nation Building and Ethnic Erasures

If Chinese labor was central to building the material and economic bases of Central American modernization through both infrastructure and petty commerce, so too was Chineseness symbolically central to defining Central American identity. As noted above, Central American citizens often lauded the industriousness of Chinese workers, but they feared their racial mixing with local populations, worrying that it would degrade their young societies rather than improve them, as whitening through the import of European migrants was thought to do.[36] The racist xenophobia that characterized the "yellow threat" movements in the United States also permeated Chinese experience throughout Mexico and Central America. Indeed, by 1911 there were violent attacks on Chinese communities in Torreon, then Sonora, Mexico, and the expulsion of these Chinese from the country.[37] Central America's history of anti-Chinese mobilization is distinguished as being much more benign, not reaching the point of collective physical violence despite strong, if somewhat erratic, anti-Chinese sentiment.[38] Nonetheless, Chinese residents had to navigate exclusionary laws, obligatory registries, and public threats as part of their residence in the region, based on the assumption that Chinese posed moral and racial threats to the integrity of the new nations.

As early as 1870, regional newspapers began to speak publicly of the Chinese as a *raza degenerada* (degenerate race) whose tendencies toward vices such as opium and gambling, whose lack of hygiene, and whose corrupt, monopolizing business practices would be the ruin of the nation.[39] Indeed, it was often the confluence of these factors—physical, moral, and commercial—that would mark Chinese individuals and communities as threatening to the white or mestizo Eurocentric societies that Central American nations sought to cultivate. Newspapers characterized the Chinese as "un pulpo que chupa y chupa y nada mas" (an octopus who consumes and consumes, nothing more) and as a social group "aislado del centro social y fuera de los demas razas" (isolated from the social core and outside of the other races).[40] Chinese miscegeneation with local women was condemned as polluting and maligned for creating a race of sickened, vulnerable citizens. While this level of racist discourse does not persist today, the ideas of difference that underlie it do continue to play a powerful role in shaping ideas of China and Chineseness.

As Chinese communities became more established in Central America, locals disparaged Chinese business owners for being unscrupulous and pernicious, despite the fact that they provided crucial goods, sold on credit, and often maintained strong relations with consumers. These perceptions were exacerbated by allegations of Chinese commercial exploitation and monopoly in many of the places where Chinese did business, creating ongoing tensions over the centrality of Chinese business to daily life, as well as resentment about unfair practices that undercut local businesses. As just one example of how these tropes are resurfacing in the present, in talking with Costa Ricans about Chinese labor's role in constructing Costa Rica's national stadium, I was repeatedly told how impressed people were at the "industriousness" of Chinese workers. However, in talking about Chinese restaurants or goods, the dubious quality or, worse yet, contaminated inputs—usually the suggestion of rats or dogs in the food—of Chinese goods were a taken-for-granted frame for not only understanding the difference of the Chinese but also reinstating their danger to the nation.

Based on these claims that the Chinese were "dangerous to the progress and well-being of the Republic," Central American nations pursued exclusionary legal regimes to police Chinese presence in the region.[41] For example, in 1897, the Costa Rican government issued an explicit prohibition of Chinese migration into Costa Rica. Although lifted in 1906, the ban was soon replaced by a required registration process for all Chinese migrants. These prohibitions helped to keep Costa Rica's population fairly segregated, with Afro-descendant and Chinese populations quarantined on the Caribbean coast. In 1911, the Costa Rican government put in place a registry and obligatory census to limit the mobility of Chinese through the otherwise porous borders of the country.

In Guatemala, the government issued the Law of Foreigners of 1894, requiring foreigners to register themselves in a book with the secretary of external relations or the chief of police in their respective department of residence. By 1920, the government issued an executive decree ordering Chinese residents in particular to register themselves with the seretary of external relations, making Chinese residents hypervisible to the government and subject to scrutiny over their livelihoods, kin relations, finances, and travel.

And while not an overwhelming trend, expulsions did occur in Central America. In Nicaragua, an 1895 law prohibited Chinese immigration, and in 1897, Chinese businesses on the Atlantic coast were expelled and their business licenses revoked. Nonetheless, by 1909, Chinese were brought back in to help construct the Atlantic railroad there. Similarly, in Panama, a 1904 and 1913 law prohibited the immigration of Chinese citizens, along with Turks, Syrians, and other "orientals."[42] As in the other cases noted above, these laws often allowed residents previously in the country to remain, but simply barred the entry of new migrants. Despite strong Chinese presence in Panama due to the construction of the railroad and then the canal, by 1940, the Chinese were expelled as "prohibited races."

Although these efforts sought to segregate, regulate, or even expel Chinese residents, Chinese communities throughout Central America grew and flourished over time. Indeed, Chinese residents deployed various strategies to outlast blatant state exclusionary politics. By 1892, Costa Rican census figures showed that Chinese residents represented 2.8 percent of the Costa Rican population and that San José was a growing site for Chinese community.[43] However, perhaps because of the strong anti-Chinese sentiment across the region and the more lax government controls, Chinese migrants took up the practice of establishing their small businesses and communities in the peripheral areas, and only slowly moving toward the capital cities.[44] In addition, many Chinese Central Americans took on Latinized last names to smooth their integration, often becoming "Leon," "Sandino," or "Lopez."[45] These tactics, designed both to facilitate everyday engagement and assimilation and to evade state surveillance and persecutory politics, had the effect of making ethnic Chinese citizens harder to identify and communities also harder to track, at least on paper.[46]

Changing census categories and politics of self-identification have also made current estimates of Chinese communities throughout Central America fraught. Costa Rica is one of the few countries in the region that includes the term *población china* (Chinese population) as a possible ethnoracial category in its census. By that count, in 2011 the Chinese population in Costa Rica amounted to just 9,170 people, or 0.2 percent of the population.[47] In Guatemala, the National

Statistics Institute tracks ethnicity only in terms of *indigena* or *no-indigena*, highlighting the country's emphasis on indigenous-ladino relations to the exclusion of other ethnoracial categories. Similarly, in Nicaragua and Panama, statistics count Afro-descendant and indigenous communities, but not Chinese, thus making an official estimate of Chinese diaspora difficult to establish.

The invisibility of ethnic Chinese citizens within Central American census norms has been compounded by porous borders within Central America, allowing for fairly fluid movement back and forth across the region by many Chinese migrants as they adapt to sometimes volatile political situations or economic declines. Indeed, during my interviews with many members of the Chinese diaspora, I heard frequent stories of family trajectories that not only traced to China but also included long periods of family residence in other Central American countries, the United States, and Canada.[48] The fact of high levels of undocumented Chinese migration to the region further accentuates why official population records cannot capture the size and type of Chinese communities in the region.

In addition to the lack of tools that elicit self-identification, the changing composition of the Chinese diaspora in Central America over time has also caused other complications for counting the community. After all, who or what counts as *la población china*? Throughout the region, the original generation of indentured and free labor from the Guangdong and Fujian regions has produced up to four generations of ethnic Chinese who are citizens of their respective Central American nations and are fully assimiated into local culture. Some of these later-generation community members may have non-Chinese parentage as well, but they can tell the story of Chinese migration to Central America as the family history of their grandfathers or great-grandfathers. This constituency has been joined by more recent Cantonese-speaking migrants from Southeast China who came to Central America in waves around 1949 and 1989, often in response to political repression in China. Now in their sixties or eighties, this segment of the Chinese community is older and has not assimilated as much into local culture, continuing to speak Cantonese with varied levels of Spanish. The original Chinese migrants and these more recent arrivals mostly reflect Chinese from rural, peasant backgrounds who have made their way economically in Central America through small businesses such as restaurants or groceries. Another wave of migrants from Taiwan in the 1970s is much smaller in number but, as I explain more fully in the next chapter, represents more middle-class, educated businesspeople. A final wave of migration since the beginning of the twenty-first century represents Mandarin-speaking Chinese from the Mainland who have come to work for Chinese firms or do diplomatic work in the embassy, as well as businessmen from Hong Kong and Macao looking for private enterprise opportunities. Therefore, while all would insist that they are Chinese based on a common culture, the Chinese diasporic community in Central America represents a vast range of age (old-timers versus young, assimilated youth), language (Cantonese versus Mandarin), national/ethnic affiliation (Han, Hakka, Taiwanese), and ideological persuasion (liberals versus Communist Party members), which affects how they identify in relation to the larger national space in which they are embedded.

These diverse community members often come together in different community associations, some organized around home village or clan in China, others around regional distinctions such as Taiwan versus Canton, and others around artistic forms, such as dance groups. In each Central American nation, official Chinese associations were formed as early as the early 1900s and as late as the 1940s as mutual aid societies. As national-level associations now, they tend to be located in the capital city of each country and function as the umbrella organization under which many of the smaller groups are organized.[49] These are the groups that manage the community buildings or schools that I describe below, and they tend to be run mainly by the older guard of the local Chinese community. The associations are organized regionally under the Central American Federation of Chinese Associations, which holds annual conventions to do networking, weigh in on regional issues facing the Chinese community, hold beauty pageants, and engage in cultural activities.[50]

These generational politics, to which Chinese community members are well attuned, nonetheless make a precise accounting of the Chinese community difficult and, thus, explain some of the highly variable numbers found in scholarly and popular accounts of the same. Fabio Lau Sandino, a member of the Chinese Association of Nicaragua and a longtime scholar of Chinese migration to Central America, calculated the Chinese communities of Central America in 2016, including with his count a footnote that specifies that his numbers "include fourth and fifth-generation descendants," to provide a more reliable estimate. Compare, for reference, Lau Sandino's estimate of a population of 53,000 Chinese community members in Costa Rica with the census data above, indicating only 9,170 Chinese, and you can see how widely these estimates vary and how much of the community they miss (see table 1).[51]

I include this present-day portrait and address the problem of measuring the Chinese community as a way of highlighting how, over time, Chinese migrants to Central America have negotiated the economic opportunities and also the anti-Chinese attitudes, laws, and practices they have encountered in their new home. Despite those challenges, they have become a part of that landscape in ways that are elided both by official statistics and also by conversations about

TABLE 1   Chinese communities of Central America in 2016

COUNTRY	CHINESE POPULATION
Panama	226,500
Costa Rica	53,000
Guatemala	20,000
Honduras	4,000
Nicaragua	2,300
El Salvador	2,000

Source: Lau Sandino 2016, 11.

national identity. The questionable accuracy of population numbers and the relatively small percentage of the total population represented by Chinese communities in Central America obscure their social significance in both the past and present. By approaching this history from a transpacific frame, however, we can look across the various levels of analysis in order to discern shifting forms of Chineseness as they are expressed through translocal migration circuits, national census statistics, and local community demographics. In doing so, we grasp a much more robust picture of the overall numbers, histories, and heterogeneity of communities understood as "chinos" in Central America. Therefore, while Chinese diasporic community members have been persecuted, invisibilized, and eventually integrated in many Central American nations, they have been increasingly revisibilized as part of national efforts to connect to a "global China." To illuminate these dynamics and their implications, I return to the Costa Rica Chinatown story.

Which China's Chinatown?

Given the elusive numbers of the Chinese communities in Central America, it is perhaps no surprise that Chinatowns—presumably a recognizable, ethnically marked feature of the built landscape—remain one of the most potent signs of Chinese presence in the region. Architectural evidence of contemporary ethnic Chinese presence in much of Central America is harder to locate than it is in other more famous Chinatowns in the Americas.[52] For instance, in Guatemala, a large building in the historical downtown, known as the Salon Chino, functions as the main headquarters for the local Chinese community's big community events, Chinese language lessons, dance practices, and museum. Other Chinese restaurants are dispersed throughout the larger downtown, and Chinese merchants dominate a section of the Eighteenth Avenida street market, but no more stable Chinese presence is visible on the built landscape. In Panama, Taiwan donated the arch that serves as the entrance to the city's Chinatown, and the Chinatown itself consists of four streets that host traditional restaurants and shops. In Nicaragua, the Chinese Association built its Salon Chino outside of Managua on a more rural site off the main highway so as to allow for a larger venue and more varied activities, including a primary school and sports fields.

In the case of the Costa Rica, most Chinese community members acknowledged that the 2011 initiative was "the mayor's project," rather than an effort by the Chinese community to carve out a space for themselves in the city. While they generally expressed an interest in seeing the space succeed, they feared its failure. Therefore, when the construction was completed but the imagined flow of eager pedestrian consumer traffic didn't materialize, local businesses began leaving the area. One local Chinese couple involved in several enterprises within the Chinatown space said, "We agreed to buy here because we thought it would be good business, but that has not been the case. For us, Chinatown has been only headaches. No wonder no Chinese businesses want to stay here."[53]

One vocal opponent of the project was a charismatic, well-respected member of the community, Ricardo, who had come to Costa Rica from Macao in the 1980s. After moving to Canada for several years with his wife and children (a very typical trajectory for many of the immigrants arriving in Costa Rica at that time), he returned to Costa Rica to build a growing empire of businesses, including grocery stores, retail stores, restaurants, and real estate investments. Ricardo was always dreaming up new business opportunities, both local and transnational. One afternoon over lunch, we had a long discussion about the Chinatown. Ricardo's take on the project was unique, and I was intrigued to hear him invoke the PRC's global rise as a lens through which to analyze its significance. In his mind, the growing global power China merited a more dignified and expansive concept of Chinatown than the outdated image promoted by San José's Mayor Araya. Indeed, Ricardo became visibly agitated as he explained his take on the project to me: "What they want is to make it like other Chinatowns, but these Chinatowns were made like fifty years ago and why do we have to reproduce that experience? They're diminishing us; we're limiting ourselves with this project."[54]

Scrunching up his shoulders into his neck, raising his voice to a high-pitched squeak, bowing forward, and clasping his hands in a performative show of humility, Ricardo then enacted the portrait of the self-deprecating Chinese immigrant to whom the project was supposed to appeal: "Thank you very much for this little bit, thank you," he mocked. Then, returning to his normal voice and leaning back in frustration, Ricardo continued: "We don't have to repeat the experience of the Chinese throughout the Americas. China [the PRC] is no longer small; it's now big and we should also do something big. . . . We need a Chinatown that is as modern as we are, not a Chinatown of the past."[55] As this quote makes clear, Ricardo saw an increasingly important PRC as reframing the significance of the local Chinese community, but in a way that signaled a dramatically different relationship than Mayor Araya's plan entailed. Indeed, Ricardo critiqued Araya's project as an effort to diminish and minoritize the Chinese community, rather than as an authentic effort to grant it new significance in Costa Rica.

This critique was echoed by another well-known, highly educated community member, Irene, whose extended residence in the United States informed her take on the project: "Chinatowns are ghettos in most places; they are places where minorities had to live because of poverty. It's only the fact that they have nice little stores and food that make them palatable to people today. . . . Who is to say [the San José project] won't end up like the Chinatown in Washington, DC, with drunks lining the streets?"[56] Like Ricardo, she worried not only about the problematic global Chinatown model to which the San José project aspired, but also about the way that it might reflect negatively on the Chinese community, were it not to be successful. Irene's concern was echoed by business owners within the Chinatown zone who worried that the construction of the Chinatown in a downtown area that was already known for crime would institutionalize the area as the place of illicit business and vice—the "shady" space described to me by some Josefinos. They worried that the Chinatown's failures would bring negative attention to their ethnic identity, reinscribing racial stereotypes and social stigmas often associated with Chinatowns rather than celebrating Chinese culture.[57]

As an alternative, Ricardo described a model more befitting of the contemporary identity of China and its diasporas. As I listened, he animatedly outlined his own plans to build a large, modern Chinatown campus on the edge of town, approaching the suburbs. Rather than being constrained by the traffic and the small lot sizes in the downtown, this Chinatown would be a destination for families (both Chinese and non-Chinese) in search of a day of leisurely consumption and entertainment, groups looking for event facilities, or businesses offering high-end products. The architecture would be decidedly modern and spacious, the grounds immaculate and aesthetic, and the products ranging from traditional Chinese goods to expensive global brands. Ricardo's model smacked of a theme park, yet it offered a vision of Chinese culture that was not the exotic, millenary culture of ancient China, but rather a glossy, cosmopolitan culture like that projected for visitors to and/or potential investors in cities like Shanghai and Dalian.[58] This was a vision that catered to an upper-class, Chinese transnational elite as well as other tourists. In this sense, Ricardo invoked the prosperous, global China of today, rather than the historic Chinese immigrant experience of the nineteenth century, as the ideal on which Chinatown should be built. His vision also reflected an astute awareness of the diversity of Chinatown forms globally, reiterating aspects of the ethnoburb phenomenon that characterizes Los Angeles or Vancouver. As Wei Li observes, "Unlike ghettos, the creators of ethnoburbs choose their potential locations with their economic strength."[59]

In San José, by contrast, while the Tang Dynasty arch donated by the Chinese government provided an imposing physical gateway to the zone's pedestrian boulevard, by June 2013 the area was defined more by vacant buildings, sparse foot traffic, and quiet business fronts than by the Chinese red lanterns, Orientalist aesthetic, or bustling tourist presence promised by the project blueprints. Locals universally complained about how the project had diminished rather than stimulated local business, removing major bus stops and driving out many longstanding business owners (both Chinese and non-Chinese) due to rising property values. Just a few months after the area's inauguration, only a handful of the shops bore signs of Chinese culture, marked by red lanterns, Chinese characters on the red awnings, or Chinese surnames on the signs. And while Araya had argued that twenty-one of the sixty locales in the district were owned by persons of Chinese descent, the potential Chinese provenance of these locales was often identifiable only by their densely packed, widely varied plastic toys, containers, and inexpensive import goods that Costa Ricans, like consumers in the United States, have come to identify as "made in China." At the southern end of this pedestrian zone, the only physical landmark denoting the Chinatown identity was a bronze statue of Confucius in the middle of the walkway. The few tourists that perused the boulevard usually stopped to take pictures near the archway before asking local passersby, "Where is the *rest* of the Chinatown?" and then abandoning their stroll of the remaining three blocks of the district. As a disparaging article in *La nación* put it, this space was "ni tan barrio ni tan chino" (neither very Chinese nor much of an urban district).[60]

Because the project invoked Costa Rica's present and future relationship with a global China just as much as its historical relationship with a local Chinese immigrant community, the ramifications of the project's failure were far reaching. Indeed, one local resident explained to me how when China's president, Xi Jinping, visited Costa Rica in July 2013, the Chinese government had sent an advance team to scope out the Chinatown as a potential location for a publicity event and advised against it. So, ironically, when China's highest leader came to visit Costa Rica, he did not step foot in the Chinatown, but rather spent the afternoon sipping coffee at a nearby coffee plantation. While Xinhua had trumpeted the project as yet another of the hundred-plus Chinatowns around the globe, apparently it was not a place where the Chinese president wanted to be seen.[61]

Perhaps, like Ricardo, the San José Chinatown did not fit the image of contemporary China or Chinese culture that Xi's entourage had in mind.

The mayor's Chinatown strategy was grounded in an understanding of the symbolic power of China within the global imaginary and a desire to lay claim to some part of it through Costa Rica's historical relationship to its local Chinese diaspora. Nonetheless, while Araya perceived the performative aesthetic features of a Chinatown as the way to do that, diasporic community members like Ricardo constructed alternative ideals of Chinatown that, in Ricardo's mind, were more befitting the PRC's standing in the contemporary geopolitical order. Ironically, a similar appreciation for the PRC's global power informed preservationist fears of a menacing, foreign culture erasing an idealized, Eurocentric past, and even Chinese community members' worries about how the Chinatown might reinscribe ethnic difference and return them to a racialized past. All of these formulations conflated notions of China as past and future, intimate and distant. The fact that representatives of the visiting PRC government would not sanctify the Chinatown with the president's presence indicates that the meanings built into the San José Chinatown held important stakes not only for Costa Ricans but also for their Chinese counterparts. In this sense, the Chinatown project is important not just as a space of local or even national politics, but also as a place for imagining and playing out the significance of shifting global power.

That said, the Chinatown debates highlight how the presence of early Chinese migrant workers in Central America and the generations of Chinese migrants that followed them provided the forms, practices, and relationships on which local ideas of China and Chineseness in the region were crafted. As they laid the physical groundwork for nation building, Chinese migrants also became the source of local understandings of Chinese labor as industrious and necessary for national development, as well as suspect and potentially undesirable in terms of its ethnoracial and cultural difference from a hispanized Central American identity. The largely Cantonese-based Chinese diasporic communities that took up residence in Central America embodied forms of Chineseness that may have been ethnically and historically specific, but which have since been embellished by and/or conflated with other types of Chinese migrants, state actors, enterprises, and institutions, informing local understandings of Chinese culture and entrepreneurism. For this reason, Mayor Araya could recruit historical Chinese cultural artifacts to connect with a rising global China, while Ricardo could call on a rising global China to validate a much more modern space for the local Chinese diaspora. For other Costa Rican citizens, those same connections could be embraced as a valuable legacy or recast as a foreign threat.

Moving forward in our understanding of transpacific relations, then, we must appreciate the important and yet often invisible role of historic Chinese ethnic communities in Central American development and their increasing entanglement with the PRC, both in the eyes of local Central American residents and also in their role as business and diplomatic gatekeepers to China. In subsequent chapters, I describe in more depth how individual Chinese community members and the official Chinese Associations in the region have negotiated the way they have been alternately conflated with foreign PRC government influences and ignored by local state efforts to forge business ties with Mainland China. For now, however, I step from the historic Chinese community to introduce another form of China in Central America—Taiwan.

3

TAIWAN

Diplomatic, Economic, and Cultural Associations with the "Other China"

When I arrived in San José in 2011, Costa Rica was the only Central American nation to have abandoned Taiwan in favor of Beijing. My goal was to look for evidence of the switch, a task that turned out to be much more difficult than one might imagine. After all, other than the embassy, where and how would I see material signs of these shifting diplomatic relations? Would they be evident in the types of development projects unfolding and the way they were executed? Would their influence extend into the dynamics of the local Chinese community? It was not at all clear to me what signs I might see of Taiwan's legacy or continued presence.

With these questions in my mind, it is no wonder that I stopped in my tracks the first time I spotted the sign marking the Asociación de Taiwan's headquarters in downtown San José. The faded, retro-looking plastic sign barely drew notice to the nondescript commercial locale over which it hung on the busy Second Avenue thoroughfare. Because I was already acquainted with the local Chinese Association's large, recently renovated Casa China restaurant and event locale just down the way, the Taiwanese Association's neglected facade seemed a telling indicator of the changing faces of China in Costa Rica. This sign seemed to corroborate the offhand comments I'd heard from several local Chinese community members who mentioned that, with the diplomatic switch, a large number of Taiwanese families had left Costa Rica fearing the new Beijing regime. Nonetheless, these same community members had quickly waved off the suggestion that

FIGURE 3.   The Taiwanese Association headquarters in downtown San José.

cross-strait tensions had any impact on their world, adding, "We are not a political organization, just a cultural organization. We're all Chinese."[1]

Costa Rica's surprise diplomatic switch from Taiwan to the PRC in 2007 seemed to many like a major geopolitical event given that, except for Nicaragua's quick postrevolutionary recognition of the PRC from 1985 to 1990, Taiwan had long functioned as the de facto China in the region. Given Beijing's One China policy, which made recognition of one or the other China mutually exclusive, Central America's political affiliation with Taiwan was a logical reflection of their shared democratic, liberal traditions and their alignment with the US policy that defined those traditions. That said, even when the United States made its historic recognition of the PRC in 1979, the Central American nations stayed with Taiwan, rather than following suit.

The decision to stick with Taiwan reflected not just politics, but also the important economic ties that Central America had cultivated with Taiwan over the years. Taiwan's own path from agricultural foundations to industrialization and export-led economic growth made it a compelling model and generous collaborator for Central America's development process. Indeed, Taiwan offered Central American nations liberal grants and loans, lucrative trade quotas for their exports, much-needed infrastructure, and technical assistance designed to foment local industry.[2] These development contributions materialized in projects such as Panama's Chinatown arch, Nicaragua's presidential executive offices (known as Casa de los Pueblos), Costa Rica's "Friendship Bridge" over the Tempisque River, and Guatemala's Transoceanic Highway, among others. What is more, Taiwanese diplomatic personnel in Central America often figured as both prominent sponsors of and intimate participants in local Chinese cultural events, offering opening statements, sitting at the head tables, and conferring an air of authority to the local community celebrations. At the political, economic, and cultural levels in Central America, Taiwan was China.

The PRC-Taiwan debate in Central America has both reflected and shaped larger geopolitical conversations. After Costa Rica's diplomatic switch in 2007, six of Taiwan's seventeen remaining allies—El Salvador, Nicaragua, Honduras, Guatemala, Belize, and Panama—were located in Central America; therefore, the region's importance to these global politics cannot be diminished. Indeed, on the heels of Costa Rica's change in 2007, Taiwan and Beijing negotiated a diplomatic truce by which they committed to refrain from influencing further shifts among their respective allies. The election of the nationalist Tsai Ing-wen of Taiwan's Democratic Progressive Party in 2016 disturbed this peace and brought Central America back into the limelight, making Panama's and then El Salvador's diplomatic switches in 2017 and 2018, respectively, indicative of a new phase of cross-strait standoff. Tsai Ing-wen has visited Central America at least four times since 2016 to reiterate the value of these regional partnerships and offer new aid packages to Taiwan's remaining regional allies. The fact that her last two trips to the region also included two-to-four-day stopovers in the United States—much to Beijing's ire—highlights just how closely entangled the US and Central America are in these cross-strait tensions.[3]

Central American decisions over which China to recognize also reflected and impacted local values and identity. For example, when Costa Rica abandoned its ties to Taiwan to become the first Central American nation to recognize the PRC, many Costa Ricans criticized this switch for its apparent ideological contradictions.[4] How could Central America's strongest, most progressive democracy opt for the PRC government's authoritarian politics over Taiwan's shared liberal foundations? Others rationalized the switch through economic pragmatism, noting how the "new" China offered Costa Rica not only a massive new market for trade, but also access to important new investment opportunities. When Panama and El Salvador followed suit, the presidents of both countries gave similar explanations for their willingness to abruptly terminate relations with Taiwan in favor of the lucrative prospect of doing business with Mainland China. Indeed, Panama's president, Juan Carlos Varela, summed up Panama's choice in one sentence: "As a country, China [the PRC] represents 20 percent of the world's population and the second-largest economy in the world."[5] What other justification did one need?

In the wake of these shifts, Taipei has publicly lamented the loss of its Central American allies in intimate, affective terms that Taiwanese state representatives often echoed to me—for instance, "How could our friends treat us this way after so many years of friendship?" After all, hadn't Taiwan been a doting, generous development partner? While the economic choice might be obvious, Taiwanese representatives felt that the ethical, political, and even personal rationales were not, given all that Taiwan had done for its Central American partners. For them, even though the need for allies was political, the approach to bilateral relationships was very personal in terms of how they were framed and executed.

Because of Taiwan's significance within Central American development politics, I was less interested in speculating about which would be the next nation to switch recognition to the PRC or why; instead I wanted to know how Taiwan's seventy-plus years of development cooperation had shaped the region. How did the two Chinas differ in terms of their development policies and practices in Central America? How did the two Chinas intervene within local diasporic community relations? And how did these differences inform local conceptions of what Chinese development collaboration is or should be?

Over my years of research on this topic, I came to find that even Central Americans who were apprehensive but hopeful about the PRC's global status tended to harbor a fairly positive view of Taiwan and use it as a yardstick by which to measure the PRC's difference. Furthermore, while local Chinese diasporic communities were clearly impacted by the diplomatic affiliations of their respective Central American nations—one day China was represented by representatives from Taipei, the next day from Beijing—how community members related both to the changing embassies and to one another certainly did not fall simply along nationalist or ideological lines. Instead, both Taiwan and the PRC were deeply entangled in national- and community-level politics in ways that the mutually exclusive One China policy and ongoing cross-strait tensions elided.

In this chapter, I explain how Taiwan's legacy in the region has established the standard against which many Central Americans have formulated expectations for and evaluated the significance of the contemporary era of PRC state development cooperation. Specifically, I show how the language and practice of bilateral development efforts, the history of Taiwanese private industry and investment in Central America, and the role of the Taiwanese embassy in local Chinese community associations in Central America have created particular ideas about what China and Chineseness mean for local development. I further demonstrate how, although the discourse of South-South, win-win development partnerships and soft-power diplomacy are concepts associated with the PRC government's contemporary development politics, in Central America it was Taiwan that revolutionized these concepts, giving them concrete meaning in collaborative, participatory initiatives. Therefore, even in the nations that have more recently switched sides and recognized the PRC, Taiwan's legacy in Central America remains central to local interpretations of Chinese development, setting the normative standard for how PRC state-sponsored development cooperation should play out today.

State-to-State Development Partnerships

Taiwan has generally concentrated its efforts in Central America on development aid and investment that reflect Taiwan's own areas of development experience and expertise.[6] Since 1991, those efforts have been the work of Taiwan's International Cooperation and Development Fund (ICDF), supervised by the Ministry of Foreign Affairs. That agency works mostly through bilateral relations with governments, rather than nongovernmental organizations, although it also partners with multilateral organizations to achieve larger development goals. The ICDF characterizes its programs as (a) facilitating social and economic development; (b) promoting better economic ties; (c) cooperating with international organizations; (d) providing humanitarian assistance; (e) providing technical and human resources training; (f) operating overseas missions to develop and improve agricultural, industrial, economic, medical, and educational sectors; and (g) promoting other initiatives to bolster international cooperation and "foster good relations with partner countries."[7] The ICDF's 2019 report listed initiatives in Guatemala and Nicaragua that took on major agriculture, public health, and education issues, among others.[8] While projects in all of those countries included overseas missions, technical/humanitarian assistance projects, and lending and investment projects, most also included some form of participation by the Taiwan Overseas Volunteers program or the Taiwan Youth Overseas service, thus hinting at how a combination of both economic and people-to-people connections have defined Taiwan's approach. In what follows, I highlight how Taiwan has cultivated these principles in practice and how they have come to shape what many Central Americans expect from Chinese development.

South-South Collaboration

Following the Kuomintang nationalist party's defeat by the Communists and exile to the island of Formosa in 1949, the Taiwanese government initiated a process of national development that took it from an agricultural society to an industrialized economic powerhouse. By the 1980s, this successful strategy placed Taiwan among the much-lauded "Asian Tiger" economies of East Asia. Taiwan's experience of moving from domestic agricultural provisioning to a successful export-oriented economy also defined its relations with its Central American allies, shaping its development cooperation strategies and solidifying efforts to legitimize its autonomous political status.

From the beginning, bilateral relations with Central American partners reflected Taiwan's desire to share its own experience and technologies for development, as well as to maintain strategic partnerships that ensured its political survival. Nonetheless, Taiwan pursued those goals in a way that foregrounded Central American needs. Taiwanese diplomatic personnel that I interviewed stressed how, rather than exporting a certain model of economic development, they worked with the Central American states to elicit ideas about local needs and to fund projects that reflected those priorities. Building on local resources and industries—such as agricultural production extension, bamboo cultivation, aquaculture technology, and seed supply—and executed through technical missions, these projects usually sought to transfer Taiwanese development expertise and tools that would help Central American constituencies cultivate sustainable industries and livelihoods appropriate to their local resources and level of development. For example, projects in Nicaragua included the enhancement of common bean production in areas experiencing frequent drought, the cultivation of seed banks, and the development of more resilient rice-growing practices in the face of climate change. In Guatemala, where export agricultural production was more deeply entrenched, development aid included training agribusiness leaders, building information platforms (e.g., phone apps) that enabled instantaneous access to data on market conditions, and providing education on product packaging for export.[9] Therefore, in terms of both the goals and the structure of its development assistance, Taiwan approached its relations with the Central American partners as a collaboration between developing nations jointly struggling with shared challenges—natural disasters, a transition from agricultural to industrial production, and a reliance on export-driven development. The fact that Taiwan could offer expertise from its own experience made this kind of South-South collaboration that much more meaningful.

Taiwan's brand of South-South development can be attributed, in part, to its active promotion of capacity building and investment in human capital alongside the construction of material infrastructure. For example, an initiative commenced in 2009 offered Nicaraguans the scientific and technological tools necessary to improve disaster-prevention efficiency and strengthen emergency response by training both technical personnel at the national level and local government leaders at the grassroots.[10] More recently, Taiwan subsidized the creation of a Center for Entrepreneurism in Guatemala, designed to support small and medium-sized businesses. Therefore, by following the Western development model of investing in the cultivation of human capital, these efforts sought to create new capacities and share knowledge through collaborative projects where and how individual Central American countries needed them.

Taiwan's focus on capacity building has not been limited to initiatives centered on the development of particular skill sets, such as entrepreneurism, but has also defined its larger public infrastructure works projects, which have been structured so as to communicate a sense of partners working together. For instance, in early 2003, Taiwan donated $27 million to construct the Puente de la Amistad (Friendship Bridge), a modern, cable-stayed bridge over the Tempisque River connecting the Costa Rican mainland with the Nicoya Peninsula. Construction for that project was led by the private Taiwanese firm MAA but executed by a team of approximately ten Taiwanese engineers with the help of a handful of civil engineers from the Philippines who worked as foremen. All of these supervisors lived on a campus near the site. They hired approximately one hundred local Costa Ricans to execute the work, recruiting them from nearby communities and busing them to and from the site each day. Reflecting nostalgically on the project in 2013, one of the project's foreign engineers described this collaboration as "harmonious." A local Costa Rican translator for the project echoed that sentiment by describing how, throughout the project, "everyone ate at the same table." Local workers reportedly felt well supported due to the commendable salaries, the compliance with labor laws, and the provision of overtime. By living near the community itself rather than directing the project from a cosmopolitan city far away, foreign technicians demonstrated their commitment to the project. After it was completed, some of the engineers even stayed in Costa Rica, rather than returning abroad. Therefore, for technical staff involved in the bridge project, what left a lasting impression was not only Taiwan's development largesse but also this more collaborative model of infrastructure work, which provided local jobs and developed relationships among foreign technicians and locals.[11]

This connection between foreign and local counterparts explains in part why, after 2007, many Costa Ricans renamed the bridge "Backstab Bridge" to critique the instrumental economic motivations that they felt drove Costa Rica's decision to abandon Taiwan in favor of the PRC. And while these views may reflect a degree of nostalgia given that people had readily acknowledged and critiqued the corruption that had defined earlier relations with Taiwan (see chapter 5), they also represented experiences of Taiwanese aid as an informed partnership between developing nations (South-South mutual support) rather than a top-down China Model associated with the PRC government, one based solely on state-to-state negotiations, the use of foreign state-owned firms, and the application of standardized techniques (a point to which I return in my discussion of infrastructure in chapter 4).

Rhetorically, Taiwan has couched this concern for local needs and capacities in terms such as "win-win" and "mutual benefit," language that bears an eerie resemblance to the discourse deployed by the PRC government as a signature feature of *its* development philosophy. In its 2009 white paper on foreign aid policy, Taiwan's Ministry of Foreign Affairs articulates how, "through specialized and effective bilateral aid programs, Taiwan will continue to draw on its own development experience and the resources at its disposal to help its diplomatic allies develop their economic infrastructure and to further boost its diplomatic ties, creating a *win-win* scenario" (emphasis added).[12] Reinforcing these principles, the 2017 ICDF report also includes subtitles like "Aligning with Government Policy, Creating a Win-Win Situation."

Despite these ostensible similarities in development discourse between Taiwan and the PRC government, Taiwan sought to distinguish its brand of South-South, win-win relations through an emphasis on personal attention to its respective partners and building relationships of friendship. In part, this individualized attention was made possible by the small number of countries that recognize Taiwan—in other words, Taiwan could afford to and in fact had to dote on them individually in a way that the PRC government could not and would not. And while Taiwan represents this style of development partnership as characteristic of a deeper principle, the dramatically smaller scale of Taiwanese development aid also offers another explanation for this rhetorical emphasis on the personal. During a 2018 visit to Taiwan by Guatemalan ex-president and Central American Integrative System representative Marco Vinicio Cerezo, Taiwanese president Tsai Ing-wen distinguished her government's approach from Beijing's by noting, "We are not like a factory that can mass-produce clothes of predetermined measurements, but rather, we are like a highly-skilled tailor who can discuss requirements with our client at every step of the way, perfectly tailoring clothes to meet their needs."[13] Through this metaphor of the personal tailor, Taiwan thus highlighted its efforts to get to know its partners and to cater to their specific needs in a way that a large company (or nation) engaged in mass production could not. Taiwan's emphasis on making development initiatives appropriate and personalized thus sought to capitalize on what might be read as a deficiency—namely, the significantly smaller scale of Taiwan's resources and projects—relative to the massive resources of the PRC government. Even though PRC state-sponsored initiatives might have more to offer in material terms, Taiwan highlighted its own brand of personalized development partnership as superior to the more modular, one-size-fits-all approach associated with Beijing.

Taiwan's strategy of emphasizing the personal and promoting appropriate development that built local capacity mattered for how Central Americans evaluated the similar discourses of the two brands of Chinese development. Indeed, Taiwan's emphasis on South-South collaboration rang true to many in a way that the PRC government's did not. For example, Central Americans often raved to me about Taiwan's legacy as a development partner, especially in relation to the PRC.[14] As one Costa Rican Chinese community member and scholar explained to me, "Taiwan had a theory of development. . . . They were cognizant of how Central America was. They knew the difference between Costa Rica and Africa and they brought in projects at the stage of development they thought we could use."[15] To her mind, Taiwan cultivated authentic development partnerships based on the specific needs and capacities of the particular nations with which it collaborated, rather than seeing them as part of a generic Third World. And while these views occlude the instrumental diplomatic interests that were driving Taiwanese intervention, they matter for how Costa Ricans evaluated and made sense of the PRC's development collaborations after 2007.[16] The top-down, modular development engagements offered by the PRC government did not measure up to the personalized attention that Central American nations received from Taiwan.

Soft Power

Taiwan's relationship to all of its partners, including the Central American nations, reflects a long history of checkbook diplomacy through which Taiwan has sought to sustain its allies with economic gifts and favors. Joseph Nye has described this process as "soft power," or the ability to persuade others based on attraction and appeal rather than force.[17] These policies include attractive aid packages with few strings attached and informal perks offered to individual politicians or influencers that ultimately seek to increase the status and appeal of the donor and sustain its legitimacy. In Central America, my interlocutors listed things like all-expense-paid "familiarization" trips to Taipei, construction of baseball stadiums, sumptuous banquets in the home of the Taiwanese ambassador, and university scholarships as just a few examples of how Taiwan sought to curry and sustain favor among its partners. Indeed, the premiums for diplomatic friendship were so widespread that one veteran Costa Rican politician recounted that, for a whole generation of politicos, a trip to Taipei was a rite of political passage.[18] These soft-power practices took place in spaces ranging from intimate dinner parties to high-level public meetings between heads of state.[19] Not just symbolic show, these encounters imparted the important material benefits of friendship, including lines of credit or new projects, and produced material legacies of Taiwan's legitimacy in the form of new fleets of cars for local police or new buildings. These economic incentives complemented Taiwan's rhetoric about the democratic, liberal ties that served as the foundation for its transpacific collaboration, thus seeking to cultivate Taiwan's appeal on both ideological and strategic terms.

As a political practice, checkbook diplomacy has a negative reputation because of its perceived goal of buying friendships and its reliance on a lack of transparency. In its most benign form, these practices included giving governments discretionary power over aid money so that those funds could be spent however local officials saw fit. As one might imagine, local politicians that I spoke with tended to interpret these practices as a show of "respect and trust," rather than an effort to buy their allegiance; however, the two outcomes often go hand in hand. For example, Taiwan donated to Nicaragua $30 million toward the construction of the Dennis Martínez baseball stadium, but when I asked Nicaraguans about the stadium, several complained that in 2014 Nicaragua's president, Daniel Ortega, used that money for humanitarian disaster relief following major flooding. While these critics of Ortega were quick to cite that as an example of corruption, when I asked the Taiwanese state officials about this diversion, they confirmed that Taiwan had approved its reallocation.[20] They admitted that they intentionally designed fluidity in these funds so that they could be used for emergencies of this kind. And indeed in 2018, Taiwan handed the besieged Ortega a check for $100 million (in the form of a twenty-year loan) to "re-build" the Nicaraguan economy based on humanitarian interest and the hope that "social order can return to normalcy and stability."[21] In response, the Ortega administration, according to Taiwan's foreign ministry, "promised to use this loan appropriately in the aforementioned areas."[22]

A generous read might interpret the practice of providing individuals rather than institutions discretion over funding as a testament to Taiwan's respect for the autonomy and sovereignty of its partners; however, at their most extreme, these practices have also produced corruption in the form of bribes or illicit campaign contributions. Indeed, several Central American politicians have been caught up in corruption scandals that include money from Taiwan. For instance, Costa Rican president and Organization of American States secretary Ángel Rodríguez was accused of receiving money for his personal benefit from Taiwan in a Panamanian bank account. Former Costa Rican president Abel Pacheco similarly acknowledged receiving Taiwanese donations to his political campaigns, an illicit practice given the ban against foreign contributions to national politics. And Guatemalan president Alfonso Portillo pled guilty to receiving $2.5 million in bribes from Taiwan in exchange for maintaining diplomatic relations.[23] Interestingly, while many Central American citizens in Guatemala and Costa Rica vividly recalled these political campaign scandals involving Taiwan, most did not seem to perceive them with the same severity with which they regarded other forms of corruption. Instead, local critics just as often interpreted them as a negative reflection on their own politicians, rather than on the Taiwanese. As I detail in part II of this book, however, this tendency did not necessarily follow in local characterizations of PRC-government-sponsored projects, where lack of transparency was seen as reflecting the possibility of corruption by PRC agents specifically.

In recognition of the thin line separating diplomacy from corruption, Taiwanese representatives were quick to reassure me that the history of checkbook diplomacy and its correspondent potential for corruption had been pointedly rejected in 2008 in favor of a much more transparent aid protocol. As one diplomatic representative explained to me, "There is no checkbook diplomacy. That died in 2008. Any project that our allied countries need always requires that we sit down and talk about the details and evaluate it. We then send the proposal to Taipei where councils evaluate the project to see about its feasibility. Sometimes they send teams to study the project."[24] Taiwanese representatives highlighted how they had adopted this policy of transparency not only in funding, but also in their work on public projects. In particular, they emphasized how the effort to undo the perception of backroom dealing had changed how they participated in local concessions, noting, "We respect the local legal process. . . . It has to be a public bidding process and transparent for anticorruption."[25]

Most often, citizens' critiques of Taiwanese development efforts were directed not at Taiwan's soft-power efforts but at the limited scale of those efforts. Many interviewees waved off the material importance of Taiwan as a development partner, noting that it simply did not have enough money to engage in the kind of big projects that would have a major impact locally, especially in relation to the prospects offered by the PRC. People were generally well aware of the big infrastructure projects that Taiwan had undertaken, such as Nicaragua's national palace, Costa Rica's Friendship Bridge, or Guatemala's Transoceanic Highway. Nonetheless, their critiques focused on the paltry size of Taiwan's aid relative to the PRC government's perceived resources and the prospective megaprojects the latter could sponsor. Indeed, if anything, the Guatemalan and Nicaraguan governments were doing all they could to *promote* Taiwan's checkbook diplomacy so as to maximize the resources they might acquire from Taiwan following the 2016 renewal of cross-strait tensions and the subsequent diplomatic switch of two Central American neighbor states (Panama and El Salvador). Guatemalan president Jimmy Morales, accompanied by his wife and two children, visited Taiwan in May 2019 at the invitation of Tsai Ing-wen. There, Morales reiterated the historic ties and friendship between the two countries as they discussed efforts to deepen bilateral trade and cooperation.[26]

Central Americans from a wide range of social positions spoke highly of Taiwanese development efforts, be they in Costa Rica (which now partnered with the PRC) or in Guatemala and Nicaragua (which remained with Taiwan). Therefore, while they recognized that Taiwan engaged in checkbook diplomacy to woo and sustain political recognition and they critiqued the corruption it had wrought, the instrumental goal behind those practices seemed straightforward and relatively benign. Over the many decades of development partnership, people seemed to have internalized Taiwan's representations of a relationship built on ideological affinity, respect, and trust. Thus, while they might have critiqued Taiwan's practices, they didn't harbor the same kinds of worries about Taiwan's intentions that characterized their views of the PRC.

In conclusion, while many observers have watched with interest the PRC government's efforts to cultivate soft power in Africa and Latin America in order to extend its global influence, in Central America, checkbook diplomacy has long served as a function of the diplomatic tension between Taiwan and the PRC, with Taiwan the far more diligent practitioner.[27] As a result, while people generally harbored a more positive image of Taiwan's development policies, distinguishing them from the potentially dubious interests of the PRC government, Central Americans that I interviewed still viewed these strategies as the hallmark of *el desarrollo chino* (Chinese development)—that is, a universal practice marking all forms of Chinese development. This understanding of "Chinese development" as in many ways synonymous with checkbook diplomacy thus shaped one of the local critiques that I heard repeatedly about the new era of transpacific development relations—namely, that Central American nations imagined their partnerships with the PRC as defined by a system of patronage in which the region's strategic economic and logistical location could be bartered for development resources. Indeed, the scandal that followed El Salvador's precipitous change in diplomatic relations was linked by many to Taiwan's refusal to take on the renovation of the La Unión port facilities; both locals and US observers feared that the PRC, upon establishing relations with El Salvador, would take advantage of a new free trade zone established there to gain control of strategic territory.

Playing the two Chinas against each other was an important means by which some Central American governments felt they could acquire the resources they needed for development. However, the strategy of relying on Chinese soft-power efforts to acquire development resources also threatened to become the default position from which countries with diplomatic relations with the PRC negotiated their fate. As I detail further in later chapters, this practice diminished the possibility that Central American countries deliberated on and articulated their own development priorities vis-à-vis the PRC before sitting down at the table to negotiate. By approaching development negotiations with open hands and an empty agenda, local governments thus ran the risk of accepting projects that ultimately favored PRC interests over their own. The PRC-sponsored infrastructure projects in Costa Rica that I detail in chapter 4 provide some examples of this dynamic, alternately highlighting the perceived differences between Taiwan and the PRC—one as longtime friend and the other as dubious newcomer—and also conflating the two as benevolent sources of capital defined by particular cultural stereotypes.

Assembling Taiwanese Private Influence

During the 1980s, Taiwan and its Central American partners represented opposite sides of the development coin. Taiwan was in the midst of the export-led development miracle that placed it among the so-called "Asian Tiger" economic powerhouses of East Asia. The Central American nations (except for Costa Rica), on the other hand, were experiencing an especially difficult and tumultuous moment, defined by political conflict and violent insurgencies, economic austerity programs, and massive social dislocation. The Central American countries desperately needed new avenues for economic development, and Taiwan needed global strategies to sustain its economic growth and to feed the growing demand for small-scale manufactured goods and textiles in northern markets. Therefore, the establishment of strategic partnerships between Taiwanese private industry owners and Central American governments marked a new chapter of transpacific production and exchange. Taiwanese businesses set up maquila production alongside Korean and US counterparts in export-processing zones throughout Central America, and a new generation of Chinese migration emerged, this time from Taiwan rather than the Canton region.

While addressing important economic challenges, Taiwanese private industry in Central America has left an ambivalent legacy, including memories of economic opportunity as well as substandard labor practices and factory exploitation. In this sense, for many non-Chinese Central Americans, Taiwanese private enterprise in the region affirmed longstanding stereotypes of dubious Chinese business practices, even as it contributed to local development. For members of the Chinese diaspora, this same period expanded and diversified local Chinese communities, adding new sources of growth and tension.

In Taiwan, growing garment and factory production peaked in 1987 and began to diversify through offshore investment and production. The industry needed new sources of cheap labor and sites for low-cost production for export into North American markets. While Taiwanese industry owners looked to Mainland

China and other places in Southeast Asia for that labor, Central America offered an important destination for the assembly of textile inputs that would eventually flow north.[28] Even before the implementation of the Central American Free Trade Agreement in 2005 and the lowering of trade barriers associated with it, Nicaragua and Honduras's status as poor nations qualified them for exemptions under the Agreement on Textiles and Clothing. Taiwanese textile maquilas established there were thus able to import textile inputs to the export-processing zones and then reexport garments directly to the US, bypassing trade barriers.[29]

Multiple governments participated in structuring this new form of globalized textile production.[30] International aid actors like USAID actively encouraged the Central American nations to abandon experiments with import industrialization and regional trade to pursue export-oriented development strategies through foreign investment from US, Korean, and Taiwanese firms.[31] Because offshore production was central to Taiwan's continued national development, and because Taiwanese business owners feared the growing rapprochement between the US and the PRC, the Taiwanese government promoted the emigration of private business owners in order to stimulate investment abroad. Meanwhile, Central American governments used creative strategies to woo Taiwanese investment, playing not only to investors' economic interests but also to their cosmopolitan desires.

Many of my older interviewees recalled how the administrations of Rodrigo Carazo in Costa Rica (1978–82) or Vinicio Cerezo in Guatemala (1986–91) tried to entice Taiwanese business owners to Central America through opportunities for enhanced visa or passport status. In the Costa Rican case, the offer stipulated that Taiwanese entrepreneurs who paid $5,000 and committed to buying property in Costa Rica would receive a Costa Rican passport. Similarly, in Guatemala, there have been allegations that Cerezo signed an agreement with Taiwan that waived visa requirements for Taiwanese investors who opened businesses there that created at least seventy jobs, but I have not been able to verify this claim with official sources. The incentive for these investors was the promise of documents that identified them as legal residents of Central America, with which they could more easily obtain visas to travel in the United States and Canada, which many stressed was the ultimate goal of moving to Central America.[32]

The economic impact of Taiwanese factories in Central America was substantial. In Nicaragua between 1992 and 2004, Taiwanese garment production firms became the largest textile investors in the country, employing 49 percent of the labor in the export-processing zones.[33] In practice, this impact reflected the presence of a handful of large employers, rather than many small businesses. In 1992, Fortex Exporters Ltd., one of Taiwan's largest exporters of clothing, was one of the first Taiwanese firms to enter Nicaragua's industrial market, with an investment of $1 million and a working capital of $3 million, to create one thousand jobs.[34] Like all Taiwanese maquila initiatives of this period, the firm operated out of Las Mercedes export-processing zone. By 1994, Nien Hsing Company, a Taiwanese jeans production firm, set up the first of its garment factories in Nicaragua, expanding to include two more by 1998, and then expanding to casual-wear factories in 1999. In 1997, the Taiwanese firms represented 27.8 percent of the firms operating in the export-processing zones and accounted for almost 50 percent of employment in that space.[35] However, whereas at the height of the Central American maquila boom seventeen different Taiwanese businesses provided employment to no fewer than 30,000 workers, by 2016 that number had dropped to seven distributors providing employment for 6,500 people and an over $250 million investment.[36]

Although Taiwan figured prominently in these maquila strategies, its global business model relied centrally on Mainland China, laying the groundwork for what has now become an intimate relationship of economic interdependency between the PRC and Taiwanese commerce. In the early maquila phase, Taiwanese businesses relied on labor and production in Mainland China, such that Taiwanese firms became the conduit for inputs from Mainland China to Central America, to be reexported to North America. Taiwanese private business enterprises that specialized in imports were also responsible for opening the door to cheap, Chinese-made goods in Central America, even where Mainland Chinese representatives were not yet officially present. Therefore, contemporary entrepreneurs engaged in transpacific commerce frequently cited the early days of Taiwanese production in Central America as crucial to inaugurating the current state of affairs in which Chinese goods have saturated the local markets. As one Guatemalan businessman put it, "Taiwan was a model. In terms of business, it went to [Mainland] China and created a fusion between its innovative business and [Mainland] Chinese cheap labor."[37] Central American entrepreneurs were now looking for a way to do the same thing.

While Taiwanese investment may have boosted regional GDP in terms of economic output in the special economic zones, Central American citizens were ambivalent about the legacy of that investment on the ground. Memories of the significance of Taiwanese private business in Central America in the 1980s and 1990s differed greatly between non-Chinese citizens who worked at or read about the Taiwanese maquila factories and local Chinese diaspora members of whose community the Taiwanese became a part. For non-Chinese citizens, Taiwanese firms quickly earned a reputation for inhumane, exploitative labor tactics in their factories, despite the substantial employment opportunities they offered. Workers complained about low wages (between twenty and twenty-three cents an hour), forced overtime, excessively high production goals, harsh treatment of the workforce, and filthy bathrooms, leading many to try and form unions or to strike against the company.[38] Many workers did not distinguish between Taiwanese and Korean employers, referring to all of them as *chinos*, such that the association between Asian-owned factories, Chineseness, and exploitative labor policies became part of local lore.[39] In this way, longstanding Orientalist stereotypes about the Chinese as pernicious, conniving, and exploitative took on new, modern meaning in the Taiwanese textile maquilas.

Within the local Chinese communities, this phase of Taiwanese presence and influence tended to be remembered more in terms of its cultural and class implications for the community itself. For example, local historians and Chinese community members document Taiwanese immigration to Central America beginning in the 1970s and increasing in the 1980s. From the community's perspective, this immigration differed from previous generations of Chinese emigration from Canton, as the immigrants were not poor, rural farmers, but rather businesspeople with capital and connections. Whereas the former worked in restaurants, the latter tended to establish import businesses and garment factories.[40] Despite these class differences and cross-strait ideological differences, Taiwanese immigrants integrated themselves into the fabric of local Chinese communities. As Fabio Lau Sandino notes of Nicaragua, "Beginning in the 1990s, Chinese from Taiwan . . . integrated into the Association, sharing friendship and celebrating traditional activities together."[41] Therefore, within the community, the Taiwanese private business presence was perceived as a useful addition to community, rather than causing a rift.

Indeed, in Guatemala, Laky Men Instant Soup provided an oft-cited example of the power of Taiwanese business in the region. The soup company is Taiwanese in origin, but in 2001 it set up a factory and distribution throughout Guatemala, and it was cited to me by both local community members and Chamber of Commerce representatives as a successful example of Chinese enterprise in Central America. Despite the company's Taiwanese roots, the firm advertised in the Guatemalan Chinese Association's monthly magazine, *Seminario Gua Kio*, and helped to sponsor the annual Central American Federation of Chinese Associations Convention in Guatemala—both organizations affiliated mainly with immigrants from Canton. Therefore, the business was perceived as an entrepreneurial success at the national level and maintained strong roots within the diverse Chinese diasporic community, despite its Taiwanese origins.

To summarize, then, connected to but distinct from the realm of state-to-state development aid, the Taiwanese investors and businesspeople who came to Central America cemented global commercial chains that brought Central Americans into overseas production circuits and helped to lay the groundwork for Chinese commodity penetration of both North American and Central American markets. In doing so, they helped to reinforce ideas about a more advanced, but commercially predatory, "China" through their importation of new business and maquila production for export to the United States. While they represented immigrants of a more privileged class—and, indeed, some came with the hope of becoming even more cosmopolitan travelers through the acquisition of a US visa—they created a new association between Chinese development, business, and commerce but also reinforced some of the stereotypes of the early twentieth century. Industrious and ambitious in commerce, but also infamous for exploiting their employees, Taiwanese investors provided a link between the early Chinese migrants to Central America and the contemporary, while also troubling some of the more generous pictures of Taiwanese development cooperation promulgated through state projects.

Ambassadors of Chineseness

Beyond these official state development and private enterprise dimensions of Taiwan's engagement with Central America, Taiwan also had an important cultural impact on the local community through its embassy. The Taiwanese embassy's approach to cultural relations with the local community crafted a particular image of Chineseness that sits in contrast to but also frames that offered by Beijing. For at least sixty years, Taiwan was the authoritative face of China in most Central American states and an important source of political power, upward mobility, and official Chinese culture for Chinese Central Americans. Through both practice and association, the Taiwanese embassy legitimized particular versions of Chinese culture and state-society relations through its collaboration with diasporic actors. As Central American nations have switched from Taipei to Beijing, changes in their respective embassies have catalyzed new arrangements of Chineseness in Central America, some of which pose challenges to the diasporic community's historic institutions and raise questions about any presumed solidarity between a PRC-government Chinese embassy and Chinese people on the ground. Therefore, I examine how shifting ideas of both China and Chineseness are elucidated through Taiwan's legacy and ask how they might temper the reception of PRC government interventions in the future.

Taiwan as Source of Authoritative Chinese Culture

Despite the fact that the Chinese diasporic communities of Central America largely spoke Cantonese at home and participated in native-place associations connected to actors and processes in the Canton region, up until recently Taiwan

FIGURE 4. Chinese nationalism at the Nicaraguan Chinese Association headquarters in Nicaragua.

served as the main referent for both their political identities and their cultural capital. Every Chinese Association center that I visited in Central America displayed a picture of the nationalist hero Sun Yat-sen in the main hall, and many of those portraits were accompanied by a similar portrait of Tsai Ing-wen, Taiwan's current president. Indeed, Taipei stood as the hegemonic source of Chineseness—the place where students went to learn Mandarin Chinese (*putonghua*), and also the place that embodied "preferred" Chinese politics (i.e., Western liberalism). Therefore, when Chinese embassies switched from representing Taipei to Beijing, the impact on the local Chinese community and cultural institutions was significant, with many of the older generation of Chinese immigrants and their descendants complaining about the lack of cultural understanding, the lack of cultural support, and the lack of intimacy between their communities and the Beijing diplomatic regime.

One reason for the solidarity between Chinese ethnic communities and Taiwan was the fact that a large portion of the diasporic Chinese had left Mainland China in 1949 with the Communist revolution or in the 1980s around the time of the Tiananmen Square massacre. Fleeing Communism, they saw Taiwan as a more humane expression of Chineseness, especially in terms of its complementarity with liberal, democratic, and capitalist ideals. As Lau Sandino notes in his history of the Chinese Associations in Central America, "The majority of Chinese immigrants in America have identified with the Taiwanese government because of its democratic and pluralist ideology, which promotes the market economy that represents prosperity for the people."[42] Another older Chinese community member in Guatemala put it more bluntly: "There is no sympathy for the Communist government here."[43]

Despite this lack of love for the Communists, members of the Chinese community have historically been adamant about the One China policy *not* being the source of animosity within the community. As the general secretary of Guatemala's Chinese Association, Augusto Chang, noted in his opening comments to the Central American Federation of Chinese Associations Convention in 2017, "Currently there are no divisions between Chinese from Mainland China, those from Taiwan, or from any other place. We fight for the benefit of our countrymen [*paisanos*], for a bright future; we work united to maintain peace and harmony, to achieve a prosperous development in both sides of the strait."[44] Therefore, even Cantonese migrants could support Taiwan and include members of the Taiwanese Association into their fold for the joint celebration of activities and community. Indeed, Lau Sandino recounts how the wave of Taiwanese migrants in the 1990s embellished the Chinese Association by two to three hundred people, "sharing the bonds of friendship and celebrating traditional activities together."[45] Older members of the Costa Rican Chinese community highlighted their relationship to the split in terms of an essentialized Chinese ethnic identity: "I am Chinese," one said, "so Taiwan-China doesn't matter to me, my blood. The politics don't matter to me."[46] Therefore, on the surface there was public assertion of solidarity among Taiwanese and Mainland Chinese diasporic communities that clung to the language of common blood and culture as the glue that held them together.

In Guatemala and Costa Rica, the organizational structure of the broader Chinese diasporic community consisted of not only smaller name-place associations from Canton but also a separate Taiwanese Association, all of which would affiliate within the larger Chinese Association. In other words, the Taiwanese Association figured as just one of many more localized identity groups (e.g., the Zhongshan residents) that came together under the larger Chinese Association umbrella. Therefore, what had originally seemed to me to be the important discovery of the Taiwanese Association in San José, Costa Rica, was actually of little consequence and certainly not indicative of any real difference or strain between the two sides of the diplomatic battle. Nonetheless, some signs of tension did exist and spoke to the ongoing importance of Taiwanese origins as something that held people apart, even in the Chinese community. For example, while the Nicaragua Chinese community celebrated the arrival of Taiwanese immigrants in the 1970s and 1980s as a welcome addition to the community, by 2017 an association member reported that there were probably "only sixty to seventy Taiwanese in the group and they keep to themselves."[47]

Interestingly, generational differences—between "old-timers" and assimilated youth, and between migrants from Canton and those from Hong Kong, Macao, or other parts of Mainland China—often trumped ideology as the bigger source of difference within the organizations. In describing to me why the Mainland-Taiwan split no longer mattered within the local Chinese community, Mariá, a thirty-something China Tica of Taiwanese descent, noted, "The political distinction mattered more to my parents. My generation realizes that Taiwan's fate is increasingly tied to China [the PRC]. Since Taiwan is going to return to China [the PRC], the difference doesn't really matter."[48] As suggested by this frank assessment, cross-strait politics made the One China policy inconsequential to some young Central American Chinese, not for reasons of ethnic unity, but rather because of the close commercial connections that already bound Taiwan to Mainland China and the very real prospect of the PRC's eventual assertion of political control over Taiwan. Given that this young woman was a successful entrepreneur with two thriving transnational businesses, it is fair to say that her views reflected her own entrepreneurial ambitions as much as her sense of realpolitik; however, other Chinese Central Americans of her generation often seemed similarly blasé about the idea of the cross-strait standoff, given the deeply intertwined business interests that they saw conjoining Taiwan and the PRC.

In addition to Taiwan's political appeal and commercial connections, its cultural influence in Central America was promoted through its government's longstanding public diplomacy efforts and cultural institutions. Students at Central American universities who studied the Mandarin language largely studied with Taiwanese-born professors and participated in study-abroad programs to Taipei to further hone their skills. Even for language learners outside of Central America, for much of the Cold War Taiwan served as the official site for international Chinese-language study through the Inter-University Program for Chinese Language Studies, created by Stanford University at the National Taiwan University in Gongguan, Taipei, in 1961. In 1997, a new Inter-University Program was established at Tsinghua University in Beijing, essentially moving the seat of Mandarin Chinese learning to China; however, Taipei's many years as the cultural hub for language learning meant that Taiwanese-inflected Mandarin constituted the "educated Chinese" dialect relative to the local prevalence of

Cantonese. Therefore, for a select group of Chinese Central Americans who came of age during the 1970s, the experience of studying Mandarin in Taipei marked them as subjects of "modern" Chinese culture.[49]

Enrique, a forty-something Chino Tico, provided a sense of how political, economic, and cultural relations with Taiwan shaped transnational networks and ideas about China in Central America. Enrique's parents were from the Canton region, but he spent six years in Taipei studying agronomy and Mandarin at the National Taiwan University. Returning to Central America after his education, Enrique worked for six months at a Taiwanese textile factory in Mexico and then another year and a half at a textile factory in Nicaragua. There, he was in charge of overseeing production and quality; however, as the Nicaraguan employees attempted to unionize, the company increasingly fired employees associated with this effort, making it impossible for Enrique to do his job. He finally returned to Costa Rica and continued to work on Taiwanese public aid projects and missions there, using his Mandarin to help with translation and public relations. He now taught Mandarin at a local primary school and at the public university. While he had tried working for a PRC state-sponsored company in Costa Rica, he claimed he didn't like the work conditions. "I don't want to be in a place where they treat you like a subaltern," he said. Enrique contrasted this experience with his work on Taiwanese state projects, where he "liked it because you were friends with the bosses; it was a more comfortable environment and a better environment." Therefore, for him, the formative experience studying in Taipei and working with Taiwanese projects had made it difficult for him to accept the kind of rigid hierarchical relations he encountered in PRC-sponsored firms. This is an important distinction as, when asked about possible tensions between Taiwanese and Mainland immigrants in Central America, Enrique was quick to note, "There's no tension within the community over politics, as we all think of ourselves as the same. It's the politicians who highlight these differences."[50]

Taiwanese Embassy Support

The local Chinese community's affinity with Taiwan was not just a product of distant politics or cultural authority, but was also born of the intimate role that the Taiwanese embassy representatives played within the local Chinese communities of Central America. For example, on a bright sunny Sunday morning in October 2019, I was invited to attend the annual Confucius Celebration in Guatemala's Confucius Park. The park, framed by traditional lion and Confucius statues, was the product of a joint effort between the local Chinese Association and the Taiwanese embassy in Guatemala, with the legacy of that collaboration memorialized in a plaque on the site. The Guatemalan Chinese Association had organized the event for the larger Chinese ethnic community and featured its local Lion Dancers, a martial arts troupe, dragon dancers, and a tai chi group. Plastic chairs for the audience were positioned in eight long rows facing the stage where performances were to take place, so I took a seat in the back to observe the festivities. As the chairs filled in with families, young children, and older community members, I quickly noted that the first row of these chairs was reserved for the older gentlemen, dressed in suits, who represented the leadership of the Chinese Association and its prominent elders.

As was often the case for public events in Guatemala, the ceremony did not start at the designated time. I scanned the preparatory efforts underway for a sense of what was holding up the event. The dancers were all in place and the audience was similarly situated, but something was clearly missing. Approximately twenty minutes after the scheduled start time, a car pulled up and delivered a representative from the Taiwanese embassy. It wasn't until this gentleman was absorbed into the front row of prestigious community members that the event finally started.

At that point, the event MC welcomed the crowd and gave thanks to both the Chinese Association and the Taiwanese embassy for their sponsorship of the event. This introduction was followed by words from both the president of the Chinese Association and the representative from the embassy, who also gave a brief speech in Mandarin. When it was time to make offerings to Confucius, the association president and the embassy representative again were the two main protagonists. Immediately following the distribution of food at the end of the event, the diplomatic representative was whisked away into his official car.

As this vignette indicates, Taiwanese embassies have played a crucial role in the cultural life of the Chinese diasporic community. Diplomatic personnel have actively participated in Chinese cultural events and established themselves as part of the Chinese community. As one China Tica noted, "[The Taiwanese] showed a real sensitivity to the Chinese community needs and the national interests. Diplomats came with their families and they came to stay. The Beijing diplomats come by themselves. They do not bring their families." In these and other testimonies especially from the Chinese community, members like this China Tica reiterated how the Taiwanese embassy cultivated a close relationship with the Chinese community and ingratiated itself with the community through both collaboration and the way they "used their diplomatic skills to support the community."[51]

One way that Taiwan showed this support was through its advocacy for the various Chinese Associations in the region. While these associations were established between the beginning of the twentieth century and the 1940s, Taiwan supported the diasporic Chinese communities in Central America by sponsoring the Central American Federation of Chinese Associations, which brought together all of the national associations under one organizational roof.[52] In this capacity, Taiwan thus underwrote many of the communities' most important cultural activities, including New Year celebrations and beauty pageants—such as the Miss China Costa Rica pageant, which continues to this day.[53] In these events, as in the Confucius Celebration I described above, Taiwanese representatives functioned as authorities, not only financially underwriting the events but also conferring legitimacy on them and, in doing so, cultivating close relations with individual members of the community.

Historically, association members relied on their local Chinese embassy not only to help consolidate the community but to help mediate problems with their respective governments.[54] Indeed, older members of the Costa Rican Chinese Association nostalgically recalled how the Taiwanese-run embassy engaged the Costa Rican government on their behalf, advocating for their interests in the face of discriminatory migration policies. One older Chinese woman deeply involved in Chinese Association politics described with appreciation how the association had a close friendship with Taiwan because Taiwan had worked hard to help Chinese migrants get residency in Costa Rica. She added that when they couldn't do more with state-level representatives, the Taiwanese officials often helped the associations informally, by providing support "under the table." Therefore, when Costa Rica switched diplomatic relations, people were worried that Beijing wouldn't respond the same way, and, seeing that suspicion confirmed, the association had distanced itself somewhat from the PRC embassy representatives.[55]

The diplomatic switch from Taiwan to Beijing thus wrought important changes not only in trade agreements and development projects, but also in the embassy's relationship with the local Chinese community. As Lok Siu notes in her study of the Chinese in Panama, Taiwan "played an active role in shaping notions of Chinese tradition, history and culture. . . . The change in Chinese state representation is not merely a question of ideological difference, but one that is closely linked to established ways of being diasporic Chinese, both in terms of the social organization . . . and [in] the meanings and practices of Chineseness."[56] Indeed, at the 2017 Central American Federation of Chinese Associations Convention in Guatemala, the president of the Guatemalan Association issued a welcome message laying bare the community's affinity with and continued support of Taiwan in the face of changing diplomatic relations across the isthmus: "This is a new opportunity for the unity and the friendship of the Chinese communities of Central America and Panama and the Republic of China (Taiwan) to renew, invigorate, and consolidate themselves. This traditional encounter of friendship and solidarity that exists between our countries and the Republic of China (Taiwan) has historically been very deep in terms of custom and tradition. Because of that, we overseas Chinese located in Central America and Panama have permanently supported [Taiwan] as part of its patrimony, and as a support and impetus for progress and development of the nation" (parentheses in original).[57]

In contrast, members of the various Central American Chinese communities often spoke somewhat derisively of the occupants of the new embassies, which were populated by diplomats from Beijing in those countries where diplomatic relations had switched. For example, one China Tica who had spent many years working with the Costa Rican diplomatic mission in Asia critiqued the PRC embassy representatives' naiveté about how to deal with its overseas communities. She framed her critique in terms of the relative newness of Beijing's diplomatic corps for Latin America, noting that it did not have the necessary experience with the region and thus lacked understanding of the Chinese diasporic community. According to her, the Beijing diplomats would ask, "You're Chinese, why don't you speak Chinese?" She went on to complain, "They don't get what it is to be an immigrant or to live overseas. They're too green, they're too young."[58]

Reinforcing this image, PRC government representatives in Central America did not seem as keen to participate in local Chinese community events as their Taiwanese precursors had been. As one Costa Rican Chinese community member complained to me, "In Costa Rica, the Chinese [PRC] ambassador comes only to the biggest events, and they don't pay for any of them, whereas in a place like Honduras, the [Taiwanese] embassy hosts a New Year's party and everyone is invited. The Chinese [PRC] embassy in Costa Rica does nothing for the community, unlike the Taiwanese embassy, which was very involved in community politics and cultural affairs."[59]

One way of reading this aloofness is to note the challenge that Latin America has represented for a new generation of PRC diplomats less familiar with the region's language or customs. Another read, offered by a Costa Rican Chinese community member, is that this diplomatic distance was a reflection of the PRC's desire to distance itself from cultural institutions—like the Chinese Associations—that Taiwan had constructed. According to this view, Beijing wanted its relationship with the community to be on its own terms, rather than a continuation of Taiwan's policies, especially given that the associations in some countries remained affiliated with the Taiwanese embassy and in others with the PRC.[60]

It must also be said that the PRC embassies did not *need* the Chinese community's support to sustain their legitimacy in quite the same way that the

Taiwanese embassies before them had. For the Taiwanese, the Chinese diaspora was a crucial linchpin in local advocacy for continued affiliation with Taiwan. The PRC embassy's aloofness, on the other hand, signaled the power of the "new China," which, unlike its Taiwanese predecessor, gained legitimacy from its status in the international realm, rather than from the support of local constituencies.[61] Instead, the PRC government could assert an increasingly hegemonic form of Chineseness—articulated through the Mandarin language, hypermodern urban spaces, new consumer markets, and state-led development—that held increasing value in the global landscape. Nonetheless, one astute member of the Costa Rican Chinese community asked, "Isn't Beijing's behavior a bit hypocritical given its One China policy? Shouldn't the embassy be looking out for all Chinese, if that's the case?"[62]

To illustrate the ongoing value of the local Chinese Associations to these broader geopolitical considerations, one young member of the Guatemalan Chinese Association recounted a telling story. Recently the Taiwanese embassy had asked the Chinese Association whether it could install an office within the Salon China in Guatemala City. Simultaneously, however, the neighboring PRC embassy issued a similar request. Given the number of Guatemalans who sought visas to travel to Mainland China, diplomatic personnel from the PRC embassy in Costa Rica would come to town a few times a year to process these visas. The Costa Rican PRC embassy representatives thus asked the Guatemalan Chinese Association if they could set up shop within the Salon China to do this work. Negotiating the politics of which China to allow access to their cultural headquarters, members of the association finally declared, "We are members of a beneficiary organization and we want to stay neutral, without getting involved in politics." With that, they rejected both Beijing and Taiwanese embassy representatives access to the Salon.[63]

Diplomatic and association politics also impinged on regional Chinese diasporic affairs. Each year, Chinese Association members from across the region attended the annual regional convention of the Central American Federation of Chinese Associations. The annual congress rotated among the different Chinese Association headquarters across Central America, giving each association a chance to host the event and to familiarize each national constituency with the broader contours of the Chinese community.[64] One effect of the changing diplomatic relations in Costa Rica, Panama, and El Salvador, however, was increasing pressure by the PRC embassies on their local associations not to attend federation events (which the Beijing representatives apparently associated with Taiwan). Chinese association members got around these prohibitive measures by sending "unofficial delegations" to the federation convention in countries that maintained relations with Taiwan. Some association members also accepted trips to Taiwan but, according to one younger association member I spoke with, "avoided getting their pictures taken so as to avoid reprisals from the Chinese government."[65] Therefore, the switch in diplomatic relations had powerful consequences for the diasporic community's ability to maintain Chinese associations both within their home countries and across the region. Even though the respective associations tried to stay out of politics, the One China policy certainly ended up shaping their local organizations.

As I have described elsewhere, community members have increasingly been reorienting their own forms of Chineseness to correspond to the new global model. While a particular group of ethnic Chinese may once have studied Mandarin in Taipei, the increasingly universal appeal of Mandarin-language skills as a key to global business and cosmopolitan identity was now embraced by both Chinese and non-Chinese Central Americans alike.[66] Nonetheless, within the Chinese community, the history of working with Taiwanese embassy representatives who supported their organizations, participated in them, and offered connections both to Mainland China and to a broader Chinese diasporic community in Central America remained the standard against which they judged the efforts (or lack thereof) of the embassy representatives newly arrived from Beijing. The fact that the Beijing representatives demonstrated neither understanding of nor support for the diasporic experience and even tried to preclude association with the larger regional diaspora marked a breach in what had been, with Taiwan, a synchronicity between the political, economic, and cultural forms of Chineseness promoted within the local associations.

Regardless of diplomatic status, Taiwan's heavy influence in shaping ideas about China as a development partner and authoritative forms of Chineseness on the ground will continue to shape the expectations and mechanics of PRC-led development initiatives in the region for years to come. Many of what have been perceived to be trademark PRC government development strategies—South-South collaboration, win-win partnerships, soft power—are, in fact, well-worn concepts and strategies born of many years of Taiwanese–Central American development collaboration. Therefore, rather than qualitatively "new" policies, many of these represent the continuation of a status quo that Taiwan initiated, albeit at a different scale. As the history of Taiwanese maquila production in Central America further highlights (and as elaborated in more detail in chapter 4), Taiwanese and Mainland commercial influence also have a deeply entangled legacy in the region, based on a complex transpacific triangulation of production and trade. While Chinese ethnic communities in Central America might downplay the significance of cross-strait politics, we can see how changing embassies have reconfigured the politics of Chineseness on the ground. Therefore, instead of seeing the PRC as a distinctly new development actor in Central America, a focus on Taiwan's legacy in the region helps us to appreciate this moment as a proliferation and comingling of different forms of China and Chineseness that have been alternately highlighted or obscured in conversations about the stakes of Chinese development in the region.

Part II
MATERIALIZING TRANSPACIFIC DEVELOPMENTS

4

INFRASTRUCTURE

Laying the Groundwork for Sovereignty
and National Identity

"People here build roads to make money, not to build a road. You get the contract, pocket half of it, and then build half a road or build something of such poor
quality that it requires redoing in a few years." This cynical insight from a Guatemalan colleague responding to my query about a local road project rehearsed
a common refrain in Guatemala, locating infrastructure as a well-worn form of
corruption paved in the guise of development. In this formulation, public works
were understood as a central means of achieving private gain.

This instrumentalist equation translated to politics as well, as Guatemalan
infrastructure often figured as a resource dangled by political candidates in front
of their poorer consistencies. In the late 1990s when I was living in the rural
highlands of Guatemala, I remember many an election cycle when urban politicians would visit these indigenous communities in search of votes. Handing out
election swag, they would pronounce to the rural constituents assembled in the
public square, "Vote for me, and I will pave this dirt road to connect you to the
Inter-American Highway. I will see that you're connected to markets and can
access the fruits of development." While those particular connective roads didn't
materialize for decades, their entanglement with the politics of the future did.[1]
In fact, a common protest strategy for those same indigenous communities
would be to block vital highway intersections to remind politicians of their local
power. Politics was truly a two-way street.

China's Belt and Road Initiative (BRI) offers, perhaps, the best example of
the politics of infrastructure at the global level, representing one of the most

capacious and provocative symbols of the PRC's growing global power. Promising a new silk road and maritime route stretching from Asia to Europe, the initiative would not only build transport linkages, roads, and ports but also construct economic zones along the route, facilitating improved trade and remapping the global economic landscape. As an indication of the scale of the aspirations that undergird the project, the PRC government has publicly declared its commitment of $1 trillion for infrastructure projects built under the auspices of the BRI.[2] The possibilities for the massive project are thus sizeable, with the World Bank estimating that participating countries would see a 12 percent reduction in travel times along economic corridors, a potential 2.7–9.7 percent increase in trade, and up to a 3.4 percent increase in income, thereby lifting 7.6 million people from extreme poverty.[3] While those numbers seem especially optimistic, they highlight the unique scale and reach of the PRC government's perceived infrastructure-building capabilities and the new futures they augur for partner nations, at least at the level of imagination.

Although Latin America did not originally figure within the parameters of the BRI project, the PRC government continues to expand the initiative's possibilities, and by 2019 nineteen Latin American nations had signed memoranda of understanding to avail themselves of its resources and opportunities.[4] The fact that infrastructure is now the main destination for PRC lending and investment in Latin America has made the prospect of regional BRI initiatives not only enticing but concrete to many countries in the region.[5] If and when they ever materialize, ambitious proposals such as a transcontinental dry canal/railway extending across Peru, Bolivia, and Brazil or a trans-isthmus canal and logistics hub in Central America would create vital new connections between the Pacific and Atlantic coasts, augmenting and expediting commercial flows between Asia, the east coast of the United States, and Europe. Like the BRI plans for Eurasia, these Latin American initiatives would also be accompanied by additional roads, ports, and economic zones to encourage more income-producing activity and trade within and between individual nations in the region. In other words, these projects would represent not only long overdue national infrastructure but also the promise of connections to and even centrality within shifting global trade networks.

The PRC is certainly not the first foreign actor to pursue material inroads into Central America through infrastructure; as discussed in chapter 1 and further elaborated below, North American and European actors have played a significant role in building the region's infrastructure toward their own ends. For that very reason, the PRC government has insisted that its policy of noninterference and its willingness to invest in material infrastructure development represent a counterpoint to the history of US imperialist presence in the region. Both international and local observers have also tended to interpret China's contemporary infrastructure proposals based on assumptions about the PRC government's unique character and motives. For some, PRC state-sponsored infrastructure projects, embedded as they are in a discourse of South-South development, seem to offer an important corrective to a history of North-dominated, exploitative regional development dynamics. Others, however, have read the PRC government's efforts in this domain as more dubious, guided not by South-South solidarity but rather by Chinese commercial interests, be they in extractive industries or in proliferating contracts for Chinese construction firms. Critics fear that, rather than creating new avenues for development, the PRC poses a unique threat, potentially exacerbating dependency and vulnerability to foreign takeover of vital national resources.

Through a detailed description of the contours of four different projects, this chapter explores the particular concerns that shape local perceptions of and engagements with PRC state-sponsored infrastructure projects in Central America in relation to other foreign-sponsored projects. Given the controversy surrounding Chinese initiatives and, in several cases, their failure to materialize, what can we learn from them about how infrastructure has functioned as a site for negotiations over sovereignty? And what new development imaginaries do they conjure?

The Road to Sovereignty

Guatemala's Transoceanic Highway

In 1951, Guatemalan's reformist president, Jacobo Arbenz Guzmán, inaugurated an ambitious highway project—the CA-9, or Transoceanic Highway—to enable high-speed automobile travel between the capital city in the center of the country and the nation's Atlantic coast. The project was massive in scope, incorporating five thousand laborers and requiring substantial equipment purchases so as to ensure its completion in three years. But its ambitions were not limited to the technical challenges posed by the highway's construction; instead, the highway's true goal was to compete with the International Railways of Central America railroad, built by Minor Keith and used by the United Fruit Company to support its extractive enclave economy. Therefore, the road project had a pointedly nationalist motive in that, in Arbenz's words, it sought to "establish indispensable physical infrastructure for national development that would break the monopolies of the United States."[6]

The highway's symbolic status was not lost on Taiwan when it undertook the reconstruction and widening of CA-9 in 2006. The project unfolded in four phases over the next thirteen years, with financing apportioned separately for each phase to reach an estimated total of $250 million in donations and $350 million in loans.[7] Although that financing was the subject of continuing negotiation between each subsequent Guatemalan administration and its official Taiwanese counterpart, the contract for each phase went through the requisite public bidding process.[8] At each step, the Overseas Engineering and Construction Corporation (OECC), a Taiwanese firm, administered the project through its offices in Guatemala City, contracting local firms to do portions of the work and hiring largely local labor, with the exception of a handful of foreign engineers.

While I will address the differences between the contours of this road reconstruction project and one pursued by the PRC government in Costa Rica below, I first want to analyze how Taiwanese officials articulated their involvement in the project as well as how Guatemalan citizens perceived the same, especially in relation to the questions of sovereignty and national identity raised by Arbenz in 1951. Just as Arbenz's efforts to build the highway did not happen in a political vacuum but instead spoke directly to a history of foreign presence through the United Fruit Company, Taiwan's efforts regarding CA-9 must also be considered in light of both that same history of US intervention and the contemporary reality of PRC diplomatic overtures and infrastructural initiatives just around the corner.

When I sat down with Taiwanese officials at the embassy in Guatemala in 2018, we discussed the road project as one of Taiwan's flagship efforts in Guatemala, one that they identified as emblematic of Taiwan's development practice and philosophy. For example, the officials described how "the Guatemalans proposed this project because they needed public works. It appealed to us because the construction of infrastructure lasts. . . . So when Guatemalans talk about cooperation [with Taiwan] they mention the highway because it is something concrete. Although the overall highway system is a disaster, the piece of highway that does work well is CA-9."[9] More than just an explanation of the project's background, this response crystallized two important elements of the politics of infrastructure building in Central America today.

First, the officials took pains to emphasize that the project was identified and requested by Guatemalans rather than emerging as a lucrative business opportunity in which Taiwan simply figured as the largest bidder. This reference to building a highway for the public good rather than for private gain sought to distinguish Taiwan both from the corrupt Guatemalan contractors that I described at the outset of this chapter and from the PRC government, which locals perceived to be taking on regional construction projects in the interest of generating business for Chinese state-sponsored construction companies and, thus, supporting the PRC's own development. Second, although Taiwan was involved in myriad development collaborations with Guatemala, it saw infrastructure projects like this one as special because they had a physical, material presence that lasted. Indeed, anyone who drives along the highway system in Guatemala will find that not only are the stretches of good road coveted, but they are usually prominently marked by signs announcing which foreign entity or local politician was responsible for making them so. CA-9 was no exception, boasting signs with pictures of brightly colored, crisscrossed Taiwanese and Guatemalan flags at several key construction points. Posted alongside new bridges, these signs declared the work to be illustrative of a "Friendship Bridge" (Puente de la Amistad). Visually marking Taiwan's role in such a historically important stretch of highway and making it a gleaming example of both engineering prowess and friendship allowed Taiwan to leave a lasting legacy that Guatemalans would appreciate on both material and symbolic levels.

And in fact, everyday Guatemalans did mention the highway when they talked about Taiwan's contributions. When describing examples of Chinese presence in his country, Manuel, a well-established, mild-mannered Chinese community member in his fifties, quickly identified Taiwan's important infrastructural contributions and attempted to locate their significance in time and space. Harking back to the project's origins, he told me, "The road to the Atlantic is one of Taiwan's most important projects. This route is historically important as it serves as an interoceanic canal via the railroads. All of the rail lines had been used by the *bananeras* [banana companies] to export goods from the country, so Arbenz . . . built a road toward the Caribbean as a way of reconnecting the country and allowing it to be independent."[10] This narrative resonated with reports from several other locals I interviewed about where and how they perceived Chinese presence in local development (which in Guatemala meant Taiwan). They affirmed the emblematic link between CA-9 and the nation's sovereignty, while also lauding Taiwan's solidarity in executing this important infrastructural work.

Taiwanese officials also used the CA-9 highway construction to distinguish themselves from their PRC counterparts by highlighting Taiwan's adherence to strict legal process and transparency, thus avoiding any allegations of corruption. As noted in the previous chapter, corruption had been associated with Taiwanese development cooperation in the past, but this was now a quality they deflected onto the PRC. In describing Taiwanese involvement in the highway project over time, Taiwanese officials were quick to insist on the formality of the bidding process and their compliance with it as something that differentiated Taiwan.

In particular, they stated that "all projects require a public tender in order to get the best prices. We also respect the local juridical process. Projects have to be executed under public and transparent bidding to comply with anticorruption measures."[11]

In a similar spirit, the officials emphasized that they did not place proprietary requirements on their infrastructure involvement, again differentiating themselves from both a history of US aid in the region and the norms of PRC state-sponsored construction contracts. In particular, they stressed that while they might give priority to the OECC to manage a given project, the Taiwanese government would not exercise proprietary control over the choice of contractor.[12] "Yes," they said, "we prefer to use the Taiwanese brand, but it's not required. It's not tied aid. We don't do tied aid."[13] Here we can read the Taiwanese officials as addressing the United States' longstanding practice of tying aid to required reforms such as fortifying democratic institutions, implementing anticorruption measures, or, more recently, limiting US-bound migration.[14] Even programs to support agricultural development or food sustainability might require the use of inputs from US agro-industry firms. But just as important as that US reference, these Taiwanese officials were also addressing initiatives in the region where PRC lending institutions mandated the use of PRC construction firms as part of the project contract (see below). The officials seemed to be saying that Taiwanese aid sought to provide true solidarity, rather than the interested investment that both the US and the PRC pursued.

The highly self-conscious performances of transparency and due process enacted in these representations did not prevent Taiwan from becoming embroiled in some controversy over its highway funding; indeed, in 2015, the Guatemalan congress identified irregularities in the approval process for the Taiwanese lending package, thus stalling Taiwanese highway construction. Furthermore, in 2017 the Guatemalan General Control of Accounts presented a claim to the Public Ministry citing anomalies in both the offers used to win the project and the legal status of the OECC relative to origination laws.[15] Nonetheless, if they registered at all in the minds of local Guatemalans, these hang-ups were usually interpreted not as signs of misdeeds on the part of Taiwan, but rather as examples of instrumentalist politics on the part of Guatemalan politicians and institutions. "That's what they always do when new officials take office," one Guatemalan businessman told me. "They blame some other office for not having done its job."[16] Therefore, although this person did not specifically remember these particular controversies, he saw them as indicative of squabbles within the Guatemalan political system, rather than of irregularities by Taiwanese partners. As if reflecting a more generalized sentiment, these controversies quickly disappeared into the rearview mirror as the highway's physical progress seemed to pave over these processual bumps in the road.

To summarize, Taiwanese representatives and local citizens saw the CA-9 highway renovation as an important type of infrastructure project both for its historical status as a nationalist symbol and for the way that it positioned Taiwan as a South-South development collaborator that could, through its engineering prowess, make a concrete, lasting contribution to Guatemala's national development and sovereignty. As I describe below, in addition to these perceived ideological differences, the slower pacing and smaller financing of Taiwanese infrastructural assistance marked its distance from its wealthier PRC counterpart. However, taken together the projects provide important lessons about the future of Chinese development.

Costa Rica's Route 32

As part of the fanfare surrounding his visit to Costa Rica in May 2013, Xi Jinping announced the PRC government's commitment to funding the expansion of Costa Rica's Route 32 highway. Like its Guatemalan counterpart, Route 32 serves as a major artery connecting Costa Rica's capital with its Caribbean coast, a hub for crucial shipping routes and the site of a $1 million port renovation project.[17] The highway initiative promised to widen and construct new bridges along a 107-kilometer stretch of the highway's very difficult terrain, representing a project of significant material scale, distance, and technical challenge. To support that effort, China's Export-Import Bank committed to financing $395.75 million of the roughly $465 million project.[18] In exchange for this funding, however, the project agreement stipulated that the Chinese loan would be tied to a commercial contract with a PRC state-run construction company, the China Harbor Engineering Company (CHEC).[19] This provision distinguished the project from other infrastructure projects in Costa Rica, which required a public bidding process, as well as from the Taiwanese highway project described above.

The Route 32 highway upgrade was originally warmly received by Costa Ricans, who were tired of travel delays for themselves and their port-bound merchandise. When asked about their views on the project, many even embraced, rather than balked at, the prospect of imported Mainland Chinese labor for the project, recalling how efficient and competent the Chinese construction of their national stadium had been.[20] People would regularly point to the ineptitude of the Costa Rican Ministry of Public Works and Transport in its failed efforts to repair highway segments and bridges just outside San José.

In January 2017, a local satirical news site captured this sentiment in a comic piece that announced that Costa Rica's president had arranged to have twenty Chinese workers sent over for one week to accomplish work on another stretch of road whose closure and repair by Costa Rican crews was estimated to last at least two months.[21]

Despite what had looked to be a quick fix, problems with the highway expansion project soon erupted, plaguing its progress and extending it through several administrations. In 2014 Costa Rican legislators stalled approval of the project over allegations by a local group of private-sector associations and engineers that the project costs were inflated, the interest rate too high, and the clause for resolving contract disputes through a PRC-based arbitration body unacceptable.[22] More damning still, the group objected to the obligatory contract with CHEC, whose holding company (the China Communications and Construction Company) had been barred from World Bank projects over corruption charges.[23] In response, five Costa Rican firms submitted a collective proposal to take over the highway project, highlighting that the proposal would allow "a 100 percent national project with Costa Rican labor."[24] As these challenges to the project agreement testify, sovereignty was a major concern here for local firms unable to compete with their Chinese counterparts for control of an important "national project."

Labor arrangements for the project further muddled what had first looked to be a straightforward collaboration. While the project agreement stipulated that CHEC assume management of the project, Costa Rican law requires that 30 percent of the labor used on projects be local, in an effort to connect to or build local value chains. Accordingly, the breakdown of labor on this project included 33 percent Mainland Chinese and 67 percent Costa Rican, offering what many saw as an important concession from the PRC government relative to its frequent use of imported labor. That said, there was no condition of reciprocity in terms of technical exchange or formal capacity building for Costa Rican labor involved in the project—a feature that Taiwan accentuated as a central feature of its own infrastructure projects (see chapter 3). Instead, the PRC-based firm assembled camps along the route to house its laborers apart from the communities in which it was working, a practice in keeping with construction norms in Mainland China as well as earlier precedents for PRC projects in Costa Rica.[25] And while the camps and construction sites were inspected by Costa Rican officials for compliance with environmental regulations, the question of compliance with labor regulations was more ambiguous.

Beyond the question of who would do the work, the project was also stalled by questions about its technical and environmental norms. In 2015, Costa Rican lawmakers balked at what was widely acknowledged to be the project's poorly constructed original technical plan; its lack of detail meant that the cost of construction was likely to rise considerably beyond the original price estimate, as indeed it soon did.[26] The project stagnated again pending the results of the environmental feasibility study, which, when published in 2016, was promptly rejected by the Costa Rican National Environmental Technical Secretary for serious omissions in geotechnical and social impact analyses.[27] Hang-ups like this stoked local fears about both Chinese noncompliance with local norms and the potential for corruption.

PRC and Costa Rican counterparts involved in the project interpreted these stalls in the construction process differently. The Chinese participants became quickly frustrated with the bureaucratic processes that seemed to bind them at every step. For example, the project had originally designated three thousand property expropriations to accommodate the road widening, but that number had to be adjusted as the actual construction got underway. Furthermore, Costa Rican law requires a consultation with the communities that a road will go through, but in this case that process created many problems and extended the delay. In the face of these legal hurdles, the CHEC construction representative Theresa Wu could hardly hide her exasperation from the local press. "We are always here accelerating the projects," she said. "Our main goal is to control the rhythm by which this [project] advances so that once we have the conditions, we can start immediately."[28]

Costa Rican representatives, on the other hand, blamed the Chinese for being disorganized and unresponsive. Following standard practice for its construction contracts in Latin America, the PRC-based construction firm brought in its equipment from other construction sites in the region. Nonetheless, as Guiselle Alfaro, an engineer who served as the vice minister of infrastructure during the Solís administration and now worked with the National Council of Concessions, explained to me, "The Costa Rican government takes strict inventory of all of the equipment brought into the country for these kinds of projects. In this case, China [the PRC] was bringing in equipment from Jamaica, [Mainland] China, et cetera. In addition to this slow start, when we had inquiries, they were not quick in responding. So, where we thought that they would be pressuring us to move faster, the opposite has been true. It's difficult to create credibility when we expected faster, more aggressive action, and we didn't see it."[29]

As a result of these delays, highway construction approved in 2014 did not begin until September 2017 and was only 50 percent complete by August 2018.[30] When I asked Alfaro whether she thought this project had been a success, she answered with a definitive "No!" She said that the time and delays had been a problem, revealing that the negotiation had been especially complex. "It would be a successful project if it was finished, but up to now, that hasn't been accomplished." Sighing deeply in frustration and shaking her head in apparent exasperation, she said, "China [the PRC] is the most complicated country I've ever worked with."[31]

In 2020, the highway project continued to advance, albeit with frequent delays, generating speculation that the project would drag out through at least mid-2021 with an additional cost of at least $65 million.[32] For many Costa Ricans, those delays solidified their ongoing suspicions about the integrity of their PRC business partners, even as they coveted Chinese capital, engineering, and labor prowess as a solution to local transport infrastructure problems. The growing cost of the project and the many technical delays led many Costa Ricans to imagine that the PRC firms were trying to take advantage of the project for their own gain. This led many to question whether it was worth it to be hamstrung by a Chinese firm for this kind of a national project. For their part, PRC representatives critiqued Costa Rica's overbearing bureaucratic and legislative obstacles; however, they had to be publicly accommodating of those delays, lest their impatience be read as disrespect for democratic process and transparency.

Intersecting Chinas

These two road projects represent examples of Chinese infrastructure in the local imaginary, even as they refer to two different development partners—Taiwan and the PRC. Both projects represent crucial infrastructural advances in terms of providing east-west transport connectivity for their respective countries. The financing for both had been negotiated at the bilateral level and largely reflected the use of low-interest loans (augmented by substantial donations, in the case of Taiwan) and proprietary construction firms to manage the process, and both drew on a combination of local and foreign labor for the projects' execution. However, local perceptions of these foreign-sponsored infrastructure projects varied considerably and, thus, reveal important ways that ideas of Chineseness and sovereignty matter for local assessments of them.

First there was the question of how these different Chinas became involved in the two projects. In Guatemala, although negotiations about financing were happening between heads of state through successive regimes, the actual contract went through public bidding, making it compliant with local process and subject to public scrutiny. In Costa Rica, however, the Route 32 project was the product of a high-profile bilateral negotiation with PRC officials, who largely mandated its terms. This fact intensified local worries about the lack of transparency around PRC agreements, stoking fears about whose interests they represented.

Second there was the issue of time. The CA-9 project in Guatemala began in 2006 and, negotiated incrementally, had taken thirteen years to get to its final phase of construction. In part, this trajectory was due to the piecemeal funding for the project, a reflection of Taiwan's smaller financing capability and also its desire to renegotiate the inclusion of donations in the twenty-year loan. Rather than a financial practicality, some local cynics suggested that this drawn-out process also reflected an effort to prolong the *promise* of infrastructure so as to maintain Guatemalan loyalty in the face of the growing diplomatic battle with the PRC. Despite this protracted process, neither local views nor media coverage of the construction painted it as delayed or problematic. Instead, the few short delays in the construction process over time were seen as reflective of problems with the Guatemalan bureaucracy in its approval of the financing or in its verification of the legal details of the project. Taiwan got the benefit of the doubt, and local suspicions of misdeed were, instead, projected onto local politicians.

In Costa Rica, on the other hand, one of the perceived benefits of doing infrastructure with the PRC was not only the attractive financing—issued in one large sum, rather than incrementally over many years, albeit with no corresponding donation—but also the prospect of an expedient construction process resulting in the quick execution of the road. Delays on the Route 32 project were thus perceived largely as the fault of CHEC, the PRC firm charged with its construction. People close to the process described how CHEC had overestimated its ability to do this job quickly, facing serious problems with sourcing sufficient rock material for the project and underestimating the challenges that the tropical climate would present to building in this particular landscape. Despite the PRCs global reputation for efficient infrastructure building, it turned out that the place of construction mattered greatly in both political and topographical terms. Furthermore, because the China Export-Import Bank stipulated that it would extend the loan only for the four-year period outlined in the contract, the project delays became quite worrisome for Costa Rican officials tracking the loan repayment clock. As one Costa Rican official stated, if the PRC withdrew the money without finishing the project, "that would certainly be the last project China [the PRC] ever does here."[33]

Beyond the logistics of financing and time, these projects also highlight the important role of labor in distinguishing different forms of Chineseness and their implications for infrastructure. In both projects, Chinese firms—the OECC for Taiwan and CHEC for the PRC—were the contractors of record. While Taiwanese officials represented the use of the OECC as a "preferred but not required" part of its financing for the CA-9 project, in Costa Rica, the use of the PRC state-sponsored firm CHEC was mandated by the financing agreement. And while the OECC seemed to hold a good reputation in the eyes of Guatemalans, the fact that CHEC's holding company had been banned by the World Bank for corruption allegations did not create good faith in that firm. Indeed, it is no wonder that Costa Rican firms questioned its appropriateness for a national project.

These administrative arrangements and their resulting labor dynamics also mattered on the ground. In Guatemala, the OECC maintained a small office of Taiwanese engineers in the country to oversee the project and hired multiple Guatemalan subcontractors and Guatemalan labor to execute the work. In Costa Rica, CHEC employed the requisite proportion of local labor to foreign labor; however, the fact that it housed its employees in special camps built along the construction route accentuated Costa Rican ideas about Chinese foreignness. Indeed, several people that I interviewed regarding the highway construction process seemed to regard the camps with dismay, both for the squalid living conditions they seemed to represent and for the "strange" cultural norms practiced by the male employees living there. These interlocutors would highlight the huge volume of alcohol and cigarettes that firm representatives occasionally brought from China to reprovision the camp and would cautiously describe the camps in the generic language of "muy raros" (very strange). Nonetheless, these timid assessments were always accompanied by contorted facial expressions that communicated a sense of the camps as otherworldly relative to local labor standards. Indeed, their assessment of these conditions echoed earlier critiques of the Chinese male railroad workers and later small business owners who were seen to embody dubious cultural practices. For many, then, these labor configurations reaffirmed Chinese cultural difference just as much as they manifested the PRC's solidarity and infrastructure-building prowess.

Finally, perhaps just as important as these technical differences between the projects was the way that they were framed by both their donors and their beneficiaries. Taiwan positioned its work on CA-9 as making a lasting contribution to Guatemala's national development in a way that Guatemalans read as supporting the road's original efforts to promote local sovereignty vis-à-vis imperialist North American interests. Taiwanese officials also emphasized their compliance with transparent public-bidding procedures as a way of highlighting their ethics and their rejection of tied aid. These two features sought to distinguish Taiwan from the PRC, for whom infrastructure construction was perceived as a profit-generating business, lacking transparency and benefiting the PRC government more than the beneficiary country.

Taken together, these projects highlight how Central American citizens viewed Chinese infrastructure construction in terms of nuanced distinctions between different forms of China that had important implications for questions of sovereignty and national identity. In other words, it mattered *which* China was doing the work of national infrastructure. Even when the PRC state firms were offering attractive financing and expeditious completion of infrastructure projects, the failure to follow public bidding norms, the tight loan repayment windows, the use of proprietary firms, and the residence of imported Chinese labor in isolated camps all seemed to distinguish PRC initiatives from Taiwan's state-led infrastructure building just up the road. While both were deemed valuable for national development, the models of Chineseness the two experiences communicated and their perceived relationship to national development goals were very different.

Controversial Constructions

While the road projects in Guatemala and Costa Rica showcase the multiple Chinas in Central America and how they are differently positioned within the local development landscape, other projects associated with the PRC in particular have generated intense debate, both for their technical contours and for their political implications. These cases highlight the spectacular scale and promise of Chinese collaborations, and also how the controversies surrounding them have been generative of new local development horizons. At stake in these imaginaries is not just the PRC's global ascendance or dominance, but new formulations of the nature and scale of politics and identity.

Although the PRC government has consistently presented itself as a development partner that respects its partners' sovereignty through a strict policy of noninterference in local politics, the idea of a foreign nation (and potentially imported workers) building and eventually controlling vital national infrastructure has raised some concern. One way this fear has been expressed is through investigative journalist reports that have accused the PRC government of pursuing a policy of "debt diplomacy." In these framings, the PRC's irresponsible lending and faulty projects result in countries defaulting on loans, thus availing the PRC government of vital national infrastructure and leading citizens, local politicians, and nongovernmental organizations to mobilize to retain control of precious local resources.[34] And while Sri Lanka constitutes the only case to date where the PRC has appropriated a major port because the local government defaulted on Chinese policy bank loans, the prospect of irresponsible Chinese lending as a strategy to compel the takeover of national public works has struck fear in the hearts of many. In part for this reason, the PRC government has been actively rethinking its lending strategy and renegotiating its loans to emerging economies to avoid accusations of "infrastructure imperialism."[35]

Another way that infrastructure sovereignty concerns have been expressed is through the suggestion that the PRC government's participation in major port renovations in Panama or elsewhere will result in China's ownership of crucial logistics information that it could use to prejudice not only local shipping but also global trade more generally.[36] These allegations both stem from and reinforce notions that, despite a long history of dubious US involvement in infrastructure construction in Central America, Chinese efforts are distinct from those of its predecessors.

When I began my field research on PRC initiatives in Central America in 2011, my queries to locals about where and how China was present in local development efforts were often met by a quizzical expression and a shoulder shrug. In Costa Rica, people would identify the shiny national stadium that the PRC

FIGURE 5.   A Trojan horse? The Costa Rican national stadium built by Chinese labor.

government had donated and constructed, but other than that, there were few other examples of Chinese construction in the popular imaginary.

By 2018, however, the PRC's growing influence in Central America meant that actors across Central America were quick to list for me projects in which they perceived Chinese involvement. Several local businesspeople working in the field of development described to me how the PRC's China Development Bank, headquartered in Panama, sat ready with a checkbook worth $40 billion with which to fund infrastructure projects that would extend from the Argentine Patagonia to the southern border of the United States.[37] In particular, they spoke of a "Mesoamerican corridor" of rail and roads through which the PRC hoped to facilitate both connectivity within and export from the region. After Panama's diplomatic switch in 2017, plans quickly emerged for a high-speed train in Panama, extending to the border of Costa Rica to be later extended from El Salvador to the US border. This rail project was the first in Central America to be officially tagged as a product of the BRI, and many argued that these roads and railway connections would be augmented by new airports and ports that would further facilitate global transport, crisscrossing the isthmus and facilitating north-south shipments to the US. Whether they were worried about this development or seeking to buy into some portion of it, these locals' sense was that PRC infrastructure initiatives had the power to radically reconfigure the region and its place within global trade networks.

The two projects I describe in this section—the Moín petroleum refinery in Costa Rica and the interoceanic canal in Nicaragua—offer us concrete sites to explore local engagement with Chinese infrastructure. I argue that when we look more closely into these cases' details, such as the terms of their contracts, the structure of their financing, and the politics of their execution, we see, rather than simply PRC government negligence or malfeasance, that responsibility for the projects' failure or threat lies just as much with the local governments negotiating them as with any Chinese predatory spirit. Even in their failure, however, these projects represent crucial signposts within the local imaginary, making concrete Central Americans' ideas about the meaning of sovereignty and national identity in a shifting global landscape.

The Moín Refinery in Costa Rica

Costa Rica's joint venture with the Chinese National Petroleum Company (SINOPEC) to renovate the aging oil production facilities at the Moín refinery on the Caribbean coast emerged as part of the original "Act of Relations between Costa Rica and China" signed by Oscar Arias Sánchez and Hu Jintao in 2007.[38] The expansion of the refinery's production capacity was initially justified as an important means of modernizing Costa Rica's energy sector and increasing oil production to bring down the domestic price of petroleum. Unlike the hydroelectric dam that Costa Rica's state electricity provider designed and executed with traditional international financing, however, the refinery project sought to build on the PRC government's financing and engineering know-how to reflect a new model of Chinese–Costa Rican bilateral cooperation.[39]

In November 2008, the PRC's SINOPEC signed a cooperation agreement with Costa Rica's energy company, the Costa Rican Petroleum Refinery (RECOPE), to take on the $1.3 billion project, with the Chinese Development Bank contributing a loan of $900 million.[40] The goal was to increase production from eighteen thousand to sixty thousand barrels per day, allowing for a savings of $530 million over twenty-five years and producing cleaner fuel.[41] By 2009, SINOPEC and RECOPE formed a fifty-fifty joint venture firm, Soresco, to oversee and finance the renovation, with Costa Rica contributing the remaining $300 million.[42] The project was estimated to create somewhere between one thousand and five thousand jobs annually during the three years of construction, of which 75 percent would consist of Costa Ricans, 10 percent Latin Americans, and 15 percent Chinese.[43] However, despite those optimistic aspirations, the project quickly began to falter.

In June 2011, Soresco contracted the Huanqiu Construction and Engineering Corporation (HCEC) to conduct the first feasibility study.[44] That study was evaluated by Honeywell, whose recommended improvements to the proposal provoked another round of evaluation by the consulting firm Worley Parsons in 2012 to further refine the project plan.[45] Although Xi Jinping's visit to Costa Rica in May 2013 bolstered bilateral commitment to the project, by June of that same year growing public outcry mounted over the revelation that HCEC was a subsidiary of SINOPEC, which sparked a Comptroller General's Office investigation into a possible conflict of interest.[46] Many Costa Rican politicians and members of the public interpreted the use of a PRC-based firm for the feasibility study as evidence of a Chinese effort to exploit the project for its own benefit. Forthcoming revelations about budget irregularities, inflated RECOPE payments to Soresco, and expensive Soresco employee trips to Mainland China seemed to confirm corruption and prompted the June resignation of RECOPE's executive president.[47] Despite several efforts to develop alternative plans, including a new feasibility study and the possibility of incorporating biofuels, the project reached its demise in 2016, when the refinery's modernization was officially and very publicly scrapped.

Long before the project's death knell, however, both local media sources and Costa Ricans more generally had begun to refer to the project as *la refinería china* (the Chinese refinery), using that term as a derisive rather than descriptive label to draw attention to how the initiative might (or might not) align with Costa Rican national identity. Indeed, during interviews as well as in informal conversation, people would often roll their eyes in exasperation as they mentioned "the Chinese Refinery," saying, "This is what we get for doing business with China [the PRC]." As with the Route 32 project, despite initial hopes of a development bonanza, collaboration with the PRC seemed to be underpinned by doubts about the PRC government's potentially dubious motives and the way they implicated local politicians.

During the growing firestorm around the project in June 2013, for example, the opposition leader, Ottón Solís of the Citizens' Action Party, framed public critique of the project in terms of what it communicated about Costa Rica's national identity, asserting that "in this lamentable business, the Chinese decide absolutely everything and the Costa Rican government, in the style of a banana republic, obeys and pays what it is charged."[48] This critique speaks, of course, to the notorious history of the Central American nations as banana republics subordinated to the commercial and political interests of the United Fruit Company and its affiliates in the US government. Indeed, as described in chapter 1, Minor Keith's railroad concessions allowed United Fruit to profit handsomely from its complete control over land and labor within its banana plantations and to utilize the west-east railroads to extract both commodities and profits from Central America. Therefore, in the modern history of US Central American relations, infrastructure stood as a key index of national sovereignty.[49] By rehearsing Costa Rica's historical relationship to nineteenth-century US fruit companies and its role as an outpost of US imperialism, then, Solís's critique suggested that the refinery's cooperative joint venture represented a return to the days of peripheral dependency and foreign exploitation rather than a sign of modernization. And in this critique, the blame lay not solely with the foreign power—the PRC—but also with the local politicians who ceded to Chinese interests and seemingly placed Costa Rica in the position of vulnerable pawn.

Another line of critique reinforced this opposition to the "Chinese refinery" while also taking up the environmental implications of the project and how they represented or betrayed Costa Rica's green, progressive environmental identity. Mónica Araya, a climate change consultant and Costa Rican delegate to the United Nations, was allegedly fired by the Costa Rican government for her public critique of the refinery project.[50] In a controversial opinion piece, she framed the dilemma as follows: "Costa Rica confronts a decisive moment in its relationship with China [the PRC]. We have the opportunity to demonstrate that in the twenty-first century we will consolidate our national commitment to a model of development that protects natural resources and generates low emissions. A refinery is incompatible with the global transition toward cleaner economies. . . . Building the refinery is a step backward."[51]

The oil refinery, rather than simply a material means of modernization, thus became an important site for constructing ideas about national identity and global power relations.[52] The debate singled out the PRC government as a powerful and potentially corrupt opportunist that used its own subsidiaries to construct a favorable business deal based on the extraction of Costa Rica's resources. However, the controversy also implicated the Costa Rican government for its failure to imagine, build, and protect a different kind of development future. In doing so, the scandal spoke to the backward-looking, neodependent, fossil-fuel-based development model that the PRC offered and to the way that local regimes might be complicit in that model. In that sense, the Chinese refinery became the foil against which formulations of a green, autonomous, and progressive Costa Rican nation were asserted.

Ironically, even the Costa Rican legislature's efforts to monitor this project and ensure its compliance with local regulations added to the scandal.[53] In this case, PRC government negotiators endured several rounds of proposed "alternative" plans that kept the project alive between 2013 and 2016, only to see the project eventually canceled. As a representative of the PRC's diplomatic corps explained way back at the start of the project, "Law and democracy are important, but in business there's a problem here in Costa Rica because the functionaries work very slowly and there are many obstacles. . . . For example, right now China is cooperating with RECOPE . . . to construct a refinery to enhance the level of oil production because Costa Rica's technology is not very advanced. China wants to help, but the pace is very slow because different institutions have to investigate and approve. . . . It takes a long time."[54] So, while Costa Ricans would see the intense legal scrutiny of these projects as an important means of ensuring transparency of process and safeguarding local law, Chinese firms saw it as obstructionist and confounding. The process was instructive in that Costa Rican processual norms—objective, third-party impact studies; multiparty approvals; and construction firm selection—would have to be incorporated into PRC state company practices on future public works projects (as we saw happening on the Route 32 project). But it also highlighted how norms that Costa Ricans associated with a democratic, transparent process might actually open the door to corruption by its own politicians.

Taken together, these debates show the importance of local sovereignty concerns in assessing infrastructure joint ventures, even if ultimately Costa Rica and the PRC government were deploying different conceptions of sovereignty that didn't necessarily correlate. While the PRC government promoted its idea of sovereignty as noninterference in the political process, Chinese state actors were perplexed by the overwhelming role that the Costa Rican government seemed to play in arbitrating the terms of this public works project (including feasibility study norms, reporting norms, and so on), which seemed only to frustrate the project's progress. For their part, Costa Ricans were invoking a notion of sovereignty that spoke to control over natural resources—that is, what does our petroleum mean to us and who gets to dictate the terms of public projects designed to exploit it?[55] In this sense, the "Chinese refinery" controversy affirmed how infrastructure worked as a potent expression of national identity whose value could not be measured simply in barrels or kilowatts. Instead it inspired a clearer articulation of a progressive, environmentalist Costa Rica that would not be driven solely by Chinese capital, but rather should be oriented toward greener pastures, a point to which I will return in the conclusion of this chapter.

The Grand Canal of Nicaragua

One of the most provocative Central American initiatives associated with China would, if constructed, constitute the world's largest infrastructure project of the twentieth and twenty-first centuries: the proposed "grand interoceanic canal" in Nicaragua. Not simply a Chinese dream, in many ways this project is the materialization of a dream harbored by Britain, France, and the United States since the 1800s, when each sought to build a canal across the isthmus to open commerce between the Pacific and the Atlantic (see chapter 1). In the current case, the PRC government is not a direct agent of the project, nor is the project set in a country with diplomatic relations with the PRC. Instead Nicaragua maintains relations with Taiwan, and the project was the product of a hurried and covert arrangement between Nicaraguan president Daniel Ortega and a fairly obscure Hong Kong telecommunications entrepreneur, Wang Jing. Therefore, this project points to the problematic way that China and Chineseness get mapped onto regional development efforts, even when the project's actors and interests are not quite so clearly positioned. Moreover, it highlights how the failures of these projects are productive of new development imaginaries.

On the heels of the canal agreement's finalization in 2013, the streets of Managua were abuzz with talk of the project. As I discussed the initiative with Roberto, a working-class Nicaraguan with whom I was working on an NGO project, he offered a surprising assessment that mirrored what I was hearing from many other regular Nicaraguan citizens at the time. In response to my skeptical query about whether the canal would ever be built, he replied, "Yes! Daniel is finally bringing us development!" (Sí, por fin Don Daniel nos va a traer el desarrollo!).[56] He enthusiastically explained that the proposed trans-isthmus canal would include airports, economic zones, and lots of new economic opportunities that his country had been lacking. With these, there would be no more need to migrate to Costa Rica to support one's family, a situation that had described the reality of approximately 4 percent of the Nicaraguan population, including Roberto's own family, and one that made remittances 9.6 percent of gross national product.[57]

But while Roberto's optimism about the project and the economic development possibilities that anchored it was clear, the circumstances of the project led many others to regard it with substantial suspicion, if not downright opposition. After all, Ortega had granted the concession to finance and build the canal—codified as Law 840—to the Hong Kong Nicaragua Canal Development Investment Co. Ltd. (HKND), a private firm run by Wang Jing. HKND's small size and previous lack of experience with projects of this magnitude immediately led many informed observers to assume that the estimated $50 billion canal project was being underwritten by the PRC government.[58] Some sources have even identified PRC state enterprises engaged in the project, although the Chinese international relations scholar Shoujun Cui has speculated that their involvement "seems merely symbolic" and depends on the procurement of investment capital.[59] The absence of a visible PRC economic presence in Nicaragua outside of this initiative made speculation about the PRC government's relation to the concession that much more compelling, intensifying public frustration about the opaque details of the concession agreement. Furthermore, given that the concession ceded control and development of 173 miles of Nicaraguan territory to a private foreign buyer (and his presumed state backers), and introduced those interests into the literal backyard of the United States, the proposed canal raised the specter of serious threats to both Nicaraguan sovereignty and the region's security.

Specifically, the concession promised a canal uniting the Caribbean Sea and Pacific Ocean, ports on both sides, an oil pipeline extending between the ports, a dry canal for rail transport cargo, two free trade zones, an international airport in the free trade zones, and "other infrastructure." The concession was granted for a term of fifty years, with the possibility of an extension of another fifty years, opening up the potential for a century of foreign control, regardless of whether the canal itself was ever actually built. It allowed for the expropriation of any private or communal property within the autonomous regions along the Atlantic coast, and it waived all environmental indemnity costs, making the concession owners free of "any relief or compensation payment damages or other quantity related to preexisting environmental conditions within the project area."[60] This last point was particularly troubling given that the environmental impact study for the project itself states, "All of the economically viable routes for the Nicaragua Canal within the area study would have significant environmental and social impacts as these routes would have to go through protected areas recognized at the international level, legally recognized indigenous territories, and the lake of Nicaragua, all of which would under normal circumstances be considered nonviable."[61]

In exchange for the development rights granted by Law 840, the concession offered Nicaragua rights to 1 percent per year of the canal's financial profits, increasing by 1 percent per year until they reached 99 percent. Many speculated, however, that the real profit was both an immediate bank deposit for Ortega himself and the important publicity and promise of development the project generated for his faltering regime.[62] Further muddying the waters, the concession was approved in the National Assembly after less than three hours of debate, raising major concerns about the legitimacy of the process among local constituencies concerned with due process, environmental impacts, or the land rights of communities in the concession's path.

As outrageous as the concession's process and parameters might have been, they built on a powerful regional precedent of foreign infrastructure investment—namely, the Panama Canal—whose history and significance loomed large in oppositional interpretations of the concession. In that infamous 1903 arrangement, the US purchased rights to the canal concession from France for $40 million, giving the US control over the canal and its surrounding administrative zone for one hundred years. In 1914, the US and Nicaragua signed the Bryan-Chamorro Treaty, which granted the US exclusive, perpetual rights to build an interoceanic canal across Nicaragua, and a ninety-nine-year lease, for $3 million.[63] When US president Jimmy Carter signed the 1977 Panama Canal Treaty and Neutrality Treaty promising to return the canal and its territories to Panamanian control, his efforts were lauded by Panamanians as a step toward regaining sovereignty and derided by conservative forces in the United States for relinquishing a vital asset of US interests.[64] Therefore, in part what made the contemporary Nicaraguan canal project so audacious was not just its size or substance but the fact that it was happening now, in the twenty-first century, and was spearheaded by Daniel Ortega—one of the region's fiercest critics of "Yankee imperialism"—with Chinese backing.[65]

Construction on the canal showed some signs of advancement through 2016, with evidence of soil testing, biodiversity management plans, and civil engineering considerations presented at regional conferences and press conferences.[66] Nonetheless, doubts about whether the project would truly materialize remained constant throughout this period, based on skepticism about the intentions and integrity of its authors, the scope of the project (in material and engineering terms), and its profitability (in terms of cargo shipping volume forecasts).[67] For example, several local critics emphasized not only the PRC's lack of visible presence in Nicaragua prior to this initiative, but also the dubious behavior of Wang Jing and his firm Xinwei for not delivering on the promise to expand the nation's telecommunications system as part of the concession agreement. Summarizing these doubts, the local Chinese community leader and historian Fabio Lau Sandino declared, "Nobody's going to build the canal. No one is going to invest in a man [Wang Jing] with such little resources. . . . These are all lies. The government just says it for posterity's sake . . . to say that they made the agreement."[68] For him and others, the concession represented a publicity stunt meant to prop up Wang Jing's and Ortega's personal profiles and political fortunes, rather than an effort to address the public good.[69]

Therefore, despite the initial optimism the initiative had generated among everyday Nicaraguans, the fact that none of the development goods promised by the concession materialized led to increasing disillusionment, even among previously ardent supporters. Indeed, by 2018, this sentiment seemed to be shared by the majority of Nicaraguans I spoke with about the project. Their doubts intensified in 2019, when HKND's website disappeared and Wang Jing's company abandoned its lease of the prominent Hong Kong office building where it had previously been headquartered.[70] When Panama established diplomatic relations with the PRC in 2017, the logistical ground on which the canal calculations were based shifted significantly. As one Taiwanese diplomatic representative in Nicaragua told me, "With Panama under its belt, China [the PRC] won't pursue the Nicaraguan canal."[71]

Skepticism about the canal's ultimate viability did not stop large constituencies of concerned Nicaraguan citizens from mobilizing against it and turning this major infrastructural proposal into an important focus of debate on national identity and sovereignty. In Nicaragua, the grassroots coalition No al Canal Interoceánico (No to the Interoceanic Canal) emerged under the leadership of Mónica López Baltodano, an attorney and rights advocate for Fundación Popol Nah, and the peasant organizer Francisca Ramírez. They argued that regardless of whether canal construction went forward, the concession itself posed the real threat, as the rights it granted to HKND remained in force whether or not the canal was actually built. Indeed, López Baltodano and other critics expressed the concern that especially if the canal did not materialize, the concession would open the way to a surge in unregulated, illicit speculative investment that would have lasting impacts not only on the rule of law in the country but also on labor, environmental, and human rights. Between 2016 and 2017, No al Canal Interoceánico pursued a series of legal remedies to stop or overturn Law 840, including the Citizens Legal Initiative to Overturn Law 840, presented to the National Assembly with 6,993 signatures; the Recourse for Unconstitutionality, filed with the Supreme Court; and a petition/presentation to the Inter-American Commission on Human Rights, as well as various other lawsuits and legal papers. These formal legal proceedings were complemented by over eighty-six public marches and protests across Nicaragua, each ranging in size from as low as four hundred to as many as twenty thousand participants.[72]

From the grassroots perspective, the Chinese role in the concession politics was an important target of the opposition. López Baltodano described how back in 2014, Ortega contracted people from the census service to go out to the communities to collect census information, and these workers were accompanied by PRC functionaries as well as the police. Although no further Chinese presence emerged in the communities, graffitti there showed locals' assumptions about the relationship between the concession and the Chinese, warning, "Fuera chinos" (Chinese go home). Because the Nicaraguan government has tried to penetrate the communities through "informants" disguised as NGO representatives, researchers, journalists, and so on, protesters saw the canal effort as a largely foreign one, although one mobilized in close coordination with the repressive forces of Ortega. As those forces pursued the "economic asphyxiation" of the rural communities located along the prospective canal route, activists identified the emergence of a "new organizational force" in the country, mobilized around opposition to this infrastructural proposal and its embeddedness in corrupt state politics.[73]

The confrontation over the Nicaraguan canal project was subsumed by larger national politics in April 2018, when Ortega announced a proposed tax increase on social security pensions. A broad spectrum of business community leaders, students, and citizens burst onto the streets to protest the measure, but their opposition was met by a brutal crackdown by the Nicaraguan military that became a protracted policy of government violence against civil society groups and perceived dissidents that continues to this day. An Inter-American Commission on Human Rights report from May 2019 accused Ortega of extrajudicial killings and torture, arbitrary detention, widespread harassment, and threats against people participating in national strikes, and also noted the deterioration of prison conditions for inmates identified as dissidents. All of this resulted in 700 people being imprisoned, 325 killed, and 2,000 injured, with an estimated 62,000 fleeing the country altogether.[74]

Amid this national political crisis and the ensuing economic fallout, talk about the canal construction or plans for the concession have taken a back seat to more pressing issues of rule of law and human rights. Nonetheless, the danger posed by the concession, especially in light of the blatant disregard for the democratic process demonstrated by Ortega and the increasingly desperate economic situation in which the country finds itself, makes this infrastructure project one of ongoing and vital importance to national sovereignty. As activists have been exiled, and remaining opposition leaders face the threat of arbitrary arrest and ongoing persecution, it is unclear whether and how the concession will be developed and who will be able to surveil those efforts. While, on the one hand, the combination of the shift in diplomatic relations in Panama and the widespread political instability in Nicaragua would seem to offer a powerful disincentive to HKND or the PRC government to pursue their economic interests in the concession, the PRC government's policy of noninterference has allowed it to continue to do business with other regional authoritarian rulers, such as Nicolás Maduro in Venezuela, long after local and international backing have disappeared. That said, in the wake of Venezuela's economic collapse, the valuable loans-for-oil arrangement that had underwritten the PRC-Venezuela relationship has shown itself to be a double-edged sword; after all, Venezuela's inability to repay Chinese banks has left the PRC in a creditor's trap in which it cannot afford to cut ties. Therefore, the PRC will likely be cautious about involvement in a canal concession that, like its predecessors, appears too good to be true.

Drilling Down

In the end, the Moín refinery in Costa Rica and the grand interoceanic canal in Nicaragua represent very different kinds of infrastructure initiatives in terms of their contract and legal status, scale, and protagonists, but they highlight several patterns within Central American infrastructure projects associated with China. First, they embody local desires for a new era of national development that the PRC government and its infrastructural capabilities seem, at least at the outset, uniquely positioned to deliver. After all, who else could underwrite a massive global infrastructural system like the BRI or, closer to home, bring to fruition the construction of the largest infrastructure project of the last two centuries? While much of the architecture for Central American modernization was originally built by foreign, mostly US, firms, that history of material development investment from the North has long ceased to be a viable road forward. Therefore, at least at the beginning of the projects I've explored here, Central Americans have imagined Chinese infrastructure as providing both crucial domestic economic opportunities—cheaper petroleum, more jobs—and broader regional and even global significance through collaboration with China. This imagined power of Chinese infrastructure has, however, been mitigated by its perceived difference from the work of other Chinas in the region, such as Taiwan, whose efforts have been read as much more anemic in scale, but far less dubious in intent and execution.

If we drill down a bit into these diverse infrastructure experiences, we can also discern the very different discourses of sovereignty that frame Central American versus Chinese considerations for these projects. Both the PRC and Taiwan came to these development partnerships promoting a discourse of noninterference, sovereignty, and South-South mutual collaboration. As we saw with the road projects, Taiwan distinguished itself from the US by highlighting an anti-imperialist history and a rejection of the tradition of tied aid that benefits the donor more than the beneficiary. Taiwan similarly separated itself from the PRC, justifying its lack of conditionality by virtue of its democratic principles and the democratic tradition of the Central American nations, literally noting, "We cannot tell them what to do. They are democracies."[75] The PRC government, on the other hand, articulated its notion of sovereignty in terms of its emphasis on buttressing the material needs of the nation without getting involved in formal politics, disregarding the importance of the technical details of its contracts (e.g., mandating CHEC as the contract administrator) or the terms of the loan as political instruments in and of themselves. Scholars have noted how the distinction between politics (as a field of power in which interventions by third parties are perceived as diminishing autonomy and enacting influence over local decision making) and economics (as a neutral field shaped by free-market technical considerations) can elide the important ways that Chinese *economic* initiatives have deep implications for the *politics* of sovereignty.[76] This point is certainly not lost on Central American nations, which, as I described in chapter 3 and will further elaborate in the next chapter, know all too well how important PRC markets, investments, and commodities can be to their own national development fates.

The Central American perspectives I have highlighted here interpret the stakes of Chinese infrastructure collaborations in relation to a long history of regional dependency on and exploitation by North American business and state interests through banana-republic extractivism that has left the region a supplier of primary goods rather than a producer of regional development. This history has cemented Central American ideas of sovereignty as control over both territory and resources, as well as active state leadership in the face of external pressures. Therefore, how a refinery, a road, or a canal addresses questions of the ownership of national resources, their use, and the profits derived from them is central to any equation. That PRC policy banks could assume control over vital public resources in the case of a loan default, or that PRC-sponsored firms would use their control of infrastructure to exploit trade and logistics opportunities in the region, is a scenario that represents a serious threat both to the idea of autonomous national development and to local sovereignty. What is more, that a PRC state firm would have exclusive rights to develop a public good—such as an arterial national highway—depriving local firms of not only the income but also the technical knowledge that would accrue to them through the construction process, was another issue that locals read as a threat to sovereignty, for its impact on local capacity to enact national development.

Therefore, the PRC government's representations of noninterference and respect for local sovereignty did not necessarily assuage fears that the Chinese firms' work on crucial infrastructural initiatives might take the region backward rather than forward. In this sense, it's important to see critiques of Chinese infrastructure involvement in the region not as a fundamentally new or different force, but as a continuation of a history of negotiation with hegemonic partners over the terms of development assistance. Indeed, as I analyze further in chapter 6, the way in which the lack of transparency associated with infrastructure initiatives enables or even promotes corruption by local politicians and institutions speaks not only to imperialist pasts but also to some of the fears shaping transpacific futures.

5

TRADE

Brokering Economic Exchange across
Markets and Cultures

Pulling up to Guatemala City's convention center complex for the China-Guatemala Commercial Expo event, one might be forgiven for feeling a bit confused. After all, the massive PRC and Guatemalan national flags flying high over the event locale waved together in harmony, eliding the fact that Guatemala maintains diplomatic relations with Taiwan, not the PRC. Rather than a contradiction, however, the flags exemplified an important dynamic of this current era of transpacific relations: the growing commercial relations between Central America and the PRC. While Central American nations may face difficult choices about which China to recognize as their official political counterpart, there is no such exclusivity when it comes to commercial ties: with or without diplomatic relations, the PRC is open for business. The question, then, is how Central American entrepreneurs and businesses can access the tantalizing Chinese market of 1.3 billion consumers and/or clinch important commercial deals that would allow them to become the local purveyors of Chinese commodities or investment opportunities in Central America.

Despite the sense of promise surrounding this 2018 expo, the fact that these flags were announcing the fifth China-Guatemala Expo was indication enough that the PRC is no newcomer to trade with Central America. If anything, the region's relationship to the PRC has been the cause of alarm as much as excitement since the 1980s. Since 2017, trade between the PRC and Latin America has grown by 18 percent, to total US$257.8 billion, making the PRC the region's second-largest trading partner.[1] However, unlike the larger economies of South

America, for which Chinese trade has represented a massive commodity boom that buoyed regional economies through the 2008 global recession, Central America has not benefited from a similar complementarity in the global division of resources.[2] While Brazil and Argentina could send massive quantities of soy to feed the PRC's pork industry, Venezuela and Ecuador could export petroleum to fuel the Chinese economy, and Bolivia could export zinc, lead, and copper to fortify Chinese manufacturing, Central American nations do not possess the same prized commodities needed to buttress the PRC's industrial development or food security. Instead, Central American exports to Asia have been dominated by sugar, coffee, fruits, wood, and animal byproducts that neither have the same degree of demand nor fetch the same prices as the commodities exported by their South American peers. Up until the 2000s, Central American economies were producing inexpensive shoes, toys, textiles, and plastics that were competing with and eventually losing ground to Chinese goods in local and northern markets. This dynamic has created trade deficits with the PRC, catalyzing debates about how the region might mitigate its commercial losses to China while capitalizing on its opportunities.

For Guatemala, the site of the expo, the PRC now figures as the nation's twenty-seventh export destination, but its second-largest source of imports. As Guatemala's vice minister of commerce, Julio Dougherty, explained to me, the PRC offers attractive access to inexpensive, high-technology equipment for production and the opportunity to enter a large, high-demand market, but "as the official statistics show, Guatemala's dependence on that market is notorious."[3] Therefore the prospect of trade with the PRC provokes a number of questions. What will this current era of transpacific commerce mean for Central America? How can the region change the trade equation to access the benefits of the Chinese market? And perhaps just as importantly, who will forge and negotiate these transpacific commercial relations?

This chapter examines the burgeoning economic relations between the multiple Chinas and Central American nations in order to explore how actors on both sides of the Pacific perceive the challenges and opportunities of business across not just an ocean, but what many perceive to be a major cultural divide. While international relations studies tend to analyze these economic flows through statistics on bilateral trade volume, composition, and deficits, I explore how these exchanges are shaped by both public and private economic calculations and entrepreneurial practices on the ground in Central America. In particular, I build on ethnographic research at the 2018 China-Guatemala Expo, including interviews with vendors, company representatives, expo attendees, and event organizers, to highlight the assumptions driving their efforts and the barriers they perceive. I then situate this and other expos in the larger context of work by chambers of commerce, entrepreneurs, and commercial intermediaries that seek to broker the connections they hope will unlock the panacea of Mainland China's market. By using a transpacific framework, I show how actors and institutions affiliated with the PRC, Taiwan, and the Chinese diaspora, and the various forms of Chineseness they deploy, have created multiple, sometimes competing scales of commercial interaction that alternately support and thwart regional development efforts. Nonetheless, by analyzing the attitudes and efforts of these various, differently situated economic agents, we can interrogate the forms of cultural capital and networks that different actors are deploying to cash in their economic value in the shifting global marketplace.

Exhibiting Transpacific Commerce

Leading up to the 2018 China-Guatemala Commercial Expo, colorful billboards prominently displayed throughout the Guatemala City downtown touted the expo as a major four-day event. These advertisements were embellished by the colorful, iconic images of the PRC national flag, the Forbidden City in Beijing, and a ceremonial Chinese dragon. Radio and television spots added to the buzz, promising a *feria comercial* (commercial fair) lasting all weekend and comprising "80 business representatives and 40 companies." As I would later come to understand from my conversations with both vendors and attendees, this kind of promotional imagery and language created some confusion over the nature of the event and its intended outcomes. Was it a platform for aspiring Guatemalan firms and entrepreneurs to make commercial connections with the Chinese market? Was it a trade show meant to promote PRC-sponsored firms and products and extend their reach in the region? Or was it a political event meant to showcase the wonders of the PRC for Guatemalan citizens and, thus, build diplomatic relations? Ostensibly all of the above, the multivalent event laid bare not just the different expectations that diverse participants brought to the event, but also the different assumptions about and implications of doing business with China that each represented.

Making Guatemalan Business with China

The 2018 China-Guatemala Expo was the product of efforts by the China-Guatemala Chamber of Cooperation and Commerce (CCCCG, or 4CG), a group of private-sector entrepreneurs and industry leaders working together to facilitate the establishment of solid vehicles for promoting "friendship, fraternity, cooperation, commerce, and technology," mainly through the provision of professional services for Guatemalan companies hoping to do business in the PRC.[4] During a 2007 trip to Beijing, members of the 4CG board of directors had met with representatives of the PRC Ministry of Commerce and signed an agreement with the Chinese Council for the Promotion of International Trade (CCPIT). Because of Guatemala's ongoing diplomatic ties with Taipei, the inaugural 2009 expo and each subsequent edition had been developed by 4CG's members and their counterparts in the CCPIT without official Guatemalan governmental representation or the participation of the local Chinese (Taiwan) embassy.

The event was housed within Guatemala City's thirty-three-thousand-square-foot convention hall. Upon entering the hall, guests were corralled through a taped-off path by a small desk at which the young Guatemalan volunteers appeared to be counting the number of attendees but seemed to have no other role (or real information about the event). To the right of the desk, a massive sign offered a map of the convention hall space, showing where different companies were located in rows along the perimeter and in labyrinthine walkways within the hall. Alongside this map was a list of the twenty-five different participating Chinese firms, their products, and their contact information. Past the entryway and into the hall itself, a massive dais with a lighted rose-colored backdrop announced the Commercial Expo of the People's Republic of China in both Spanish and Chinese, framed by a floral border and the Guatemalan and PRC flags. This space was where the inaugural ceremony had taken place, and it invited further photo opportunities of which several guests were taking advantage. The remainder of the hall's floor space had been divided into smaller modules that housed booths for individual firms, both large and small, each identified by an overhead banner and often accompanied by product displays.

Both on that first visit and during the following three days, a wide range of Guatemalans accompanied me into the hall. Thursday's attendees, who arrived in the afternoon as a slow trickle, leaving lots of conspicuous empty floor space in the hall, reflected more of a business crowd, as indicated by the business attire and mostly similar-aged couples or cohorts moving through the space. These visitors tended to spend time at each of the commercial booths, engaging the combination of Chinese and Central American representatives that fronted them, handling the products on display, and/or reading over the print materials provided. By Saturday and Sunday, however, the crowds increased and the mood livened considerably. During these weekend days, the expo demographic grew to include extended families with small children and elderly parents, young couples, and students. Only a small handful of attendees bore visible traces of Chinese heritage, thus giving the impression that the event was not a huge draw for the local Chinese diasporic community or even for visiting Chinese business representatives.[5] Rather than dutifully scrutinizing the commercial products, these

FIGURE 6. The China-Guatemala Commercial Expo in Guatemala City.

weekend attendees tended to cruise the aisles between the booths, haphazardly collecting product brochures or samples without interacting with booth vendors, and spending time taking pictures around the cultural sections of the expo.

Promotional material circulated online by 4CG prior to the event noted that the previous expo in 2014 included "the participation of more than 8,000 Guatemalan and Central American attendees who were able to concretize successful commercial relations," and that Guatemala had witnessed "an important increase in bilateral trade with China [the PRC] over the last years." Nonetheless, this expo was clearly oriented toward exposing Guatemalans to Mainland Chinese products and facilitating new business opportunities. In response to this challenge, PRC-based firms at the expo deployed several strategies to facilitate communication about their product with Guatemalan attendees. Some vendors made an attempt to cater to local culture by fronting their booths with Chinese-heritage Spanish speakers. Other booths were presided over by lanky Latina models in body-contoured dresses, fashion-show makeup and hair, and precariously high heels. Other ventures represented PRC-based companies already doing business in Central America, so their representatives might be hispanized, Spanish-speaking Central Americans from El Salvador or Panama. Still other booths were peopled by Chinese representatives, some of whom spoke Spanish and others who had little to no Spanish, making English, hand gestures, and brochures the functional language of exchange. Indeed, of the twenty-five booths, only four-teen had exclusively Chinese representatives, with another three showcasing a duo of Chinese and local Spanish-speaking representatives.

These communication strategies aside, as I wandered through the exhibits over the four days, both the vendors and the consumers I interviewed expressed confusion about their place within transpacific relations and the role of the expo in relation to them. To begin, it wasn't immediately clear what the goal of each booth was—that is, whether it was selling individual units of a particular prod-uct, looking for local distributors, extending franchises, or just trying to get name recognition in a new market. Confirming that this confusion was not mine alone, by the third day of the expo many vendors had taped computer-printed signs onto their booths, specifying their intentions (for instance, "Seeking Local Dis-tributors"). Nonetheless, some booth representatives attributed this confusion less to the organization of the expo and more to the naiveté of the Guatemalan attendees.

One booth for a PRC-based firm named Mega offered a case in point, as the booth had no products on display and the agricultural scenes on the signs lin-ing its walls did not give a clear sense of what specific goods it was promoting. In response to my query, the Spanish-speaking Guatemalan woman of Chinese heritage who was operating the booth explained that the firm sold "growth enhancers" that improved fertilizer absorption and promoted faster germination of industrial crops—not a product that lent itself to evocative physical exhibits. When I asked how the expo was going in terms of sales, she shook her head in frustration and said, "People don't have any knowledge, they don't know how to do an international transaction. Before, there were a lot of 'fairs' and it was always a fun thing where they gave away a lot of candy, et cetera, so people come to this event imagining it's something like that. They walk by collecting papers and bro-chures just to grab stuff. They don't have any idea as to the products themselves." When I asked her about the proportion of businesspeople among the attendees, she said, "No, these are families and such. The businesspeople know exactly what they want. They research on the web page and they don't need to come to these events. There's generally a lack of sense of how to manage something like this."[6] And to her point, following the inaugural ceremony for the expo, the 4CG board of representatives, prominent Guatemalan business representatives, and PRC industry representatives dined at an exclusive banquet, with details of new deals emerging later in the local news. Clearly the important business was not happen-ing on the expo floor.

This naiveté regarding how to do business with the PRC and its "backstage" deal-making dimensions was not limited to Guatemala, of course, but was something that other interviewees described as characterizing transpacific negotiations throughout Central America. For example, Thomas, an experienced international entrepreneur in Costa Rica who conducted frequent business with PRC firms, told me that he doesn't attend expos but often meets with Chinese business representatives while they are in town for the expos. To elaborate this point, he described an incident a few years back, when several PRC-based businessmen had come to San José for an expo. A prominent local Chinese businessman had organized a banquet at a local restaurant to convene the Chinese visitors and Costa Rican entrepreneurs, and invited Thomas to join them. Over dinner, one of the PRC business representatives showed Thomas a solar briefcase and, when Thomas admired it, offered to give it to him. As Thomas told it, many Central American businesspeople would have simply taken the briefcase at that point as a cool memento from the gathering. He, however, took the briefcase and asked his Chinese counterpart, "What's next?" Thomas suggested purchasing a shipping container of the briefcases if they could set up a local retail business to sell them, and the Chinese vendor happily agreed. Thomas used this story as an example of the kind of negotiation that needed to happen to get Chinese business moving. He laughed at local entrepreneurs who, like the Guatemalans at the 2018 expo, attended the shows but didn't know how to make any use of them, distracting themselves with the products rather than pursuing long-term business opportunities.[7]

Despite these critiques about the utility of the expos for novice Central American entrepreneurs, making a deal was clearly still a primary goal for many at this expo. And while most of the PRC-based businesses were promoting products for Guatemalan firms to buy, tucked into a back corner of the hall was a section devoted to Guatemalan initiatives for "matchmaking." That section included a somewhat random assortment of booths, including a long cupping counter sponsored by Guatemala's massive coffee association, ANACAFÉ, as well as a booth by Agroexport, Guatemala's export industry representative; a shrimp retailer; and a small section featuring the work of a Guatemalan traditional painter. These representatives were clearly supposed to represent some of the major Guatemalan export producers as well as niche products such as local craft traditions. Nonetheless, they did not necessarily have good background on the PRC. For example, the shrimp export company touted its sales to Asia, but the representative was not sure if that meant Taiwan or Mainland China (their brochure later confirmed that it was the former). As I perused this section, it was unclear to me who the intended Chinese interlocutors were that might be seeking to make a match with these Guatemalan businesses; indeed, as noted above, there did not appear to be a significant Chinese population among the attendees at all.[8] What is more, while the PRC-based vendors at the expo sought to attract small-to-mid-size

Guatemalan businesses to buy their products, the Guatemalan firms represented were the largest in their respective industries.[9] When I spoke with the Guatemalan representatives at these booths, all of them said that they got involved because of some connection with someone at 4CG. Therefore, membership in elite business circles clearly mattered just as much as the type of commodity that each sought to sell.

This sense of Central American entrepreneurs' utter lack of understanding of how to do business with their counterparts in the PRC was a constant refrain, both at the expo and throughout my years of research on Chinese presence in Central America. Therefore, despite the matchmaking effort exhibited at the expo, 4CG and the official Guatemalan Chamber of Commerce were all deploying other strategies to connect Guatemalan and Chinese businesses. As I describe below, these efforts included not just organizing expos at home, but guided participation in commercial fairs elsewhere in Latin America and Mainland China. So, while the expo sought to stage the opportunity for business connections, it still took a matchmaker to make a match.

Extending the Reach of Chinese Firms

While this expo and other initiatives (like Nicaragua's proposed grand oceanic canal) would seem to suggest that transpacific economic flows do not know the same borders as political affiliations, they also illuminated where barriers to denser economic relations did exist. Not only did Guatemalans not know how to go about doing business with Chinese firms, but the PRC-based companies as well were still searching for ways to enter the Central American marketplace or to extend their reach to places like Guatemala that did not benefit from diplomatic relations. Expos such as this one became a way for PRC firms to increase their brand recognition and impact.

Scholars of the PRC government's "going global" campaigns have studied PRC efforts to garner not only market share but also global recognition via high-profile brands that create a sense of appeal. The political scientist Joseph Nye has argued that the PRC, despite closing ranks on the United States in terms of its economic growth and global investment portfolio, has lacked the soft power that would make China a persuasive, appealing global power relative to the US.[10] Therefore, it was somewhat ironic that while walking around the expo hall exploring Chinese vendor modules, I was struck as much by what was missing from the exhibition as by what was present there. There was ample representation of everything from cars and vans to manufacturing supplies, from construction materials and fiber optics to jewelry, from curtains to plastics, and from recreational technologies to security cameras and military-grade radio handsets. However, almost none of the big PRC-sponsored firms with strong distribution in Latin American markets, such as Huawei or Great Wall Motors, were present; instead the firms in attendance seemed to be somewhat smaller ones, newer to the market. This observation was striking because it suggested that there were now, in fact, several recognizable, high-profile PRC brands that I and others looked for and expected to see represented there.[11] The PRC's growing visibility and soft power in the region was thus exemplified by the fact that these larger brands were no longer working the expo circuit but had been replaced by newer, smaller firms barely breaking into the international market.

Echoing my observation, many Guatemalan expo attendees I interviewed expressed disappointment at the absence of high-profile PRC brands and products. Indeed, several characterized the event as "sparse" and mentioned that they had come hoping to get a look at specific Chinese brands—most often people mentioned Huawei—or to get a close-up view of the PRC's most famous products in the fields of solar energy, electronics, textile manufacturing inputs, or transportation. One young couple that owned a small food business had come to the expo looking for Chinese ice makers and electric vehicles, hoping to test out the ice makers and purchase one for their enterprise. They had heard that Chinese ice makers were the best and much cheaper than other brands. A middle-aged Guatemalan man who was involved in textile production had come looking specifically for Chinese embroidery machines. These business owners were not naive about Chinese goods but rather had come with designs on scoping out very specific additions to their company's inventory.

Talking to attendees about the products that were on display thus illuminated strong patterns behind Guatemalan consumer perceptions of Chinese products. In justifying their interest in one or another Chinese product, some talked about the cheaper prices and better efficiency of specific Chinese goods relative to other local or international producers. However, a good portion of them qualified their appreciation for Chinese affordability with a disclaimer about the suspect quality of PRC-produced goods. For example, a middle-aged father touring the hall with his teenage sons explained in depth the kinds of calculations that he and others were making to assess the value of Chinese products. "Some [Chinese goods] can represent a twenty-five-to-thirty-percent increase in savings over goods from the US," he began. Then, elaborating further on the value of Chinese products relative to other national brands, he pointed to the PRC-based brand Higer, a manufacturer of buses and vans, and continued. "Trucks that people bring down from the US are cheap, but [being that they're used] they have all sorts of problems that one doesn't know about. Trucks from Japan are great, but they're really expensive. Trucks from China appear to be much more affordable, but you have to check the quality."[12] Given this critical analysis, I asked this father whether he thought increased trade with the PRC would be a good thing. He responded that it would be, "if the presence of more Chinese parts would allow Guatemala to create things. But [the PRC] shouldn't export a lot more finished products, as those would compete with Guatemalan products."[13]

For some PRC firms, the expo represented their first experience in the Central American market and presented them with both a challenging context and a steep learning curve. My interview with a young Chinese representative promoting a logistics firm highlighted this point, in part because he could not speak Spanish and, thus, explained his company's complex product to me in a combination of Mandarin and halting English. He was not pursuing individual buyers at the expo, but rather contacts with firms seeking fiber optics services and supplies for telecommunications at the industrial scale. Therefore, he was one of the many vendors for whom matchmaking with Guatemalan sources at the expo seemed unlikely. And in response to my query, he confirmed that business had indeed been slow.

When I asked how he had gotten involved in the expo, he told me that the PRC government had sent out invitations to various firms to see if they wanted to participate; if they did, the government paid all of their expenses to present at the expo, but they had to commit to presenting at a series of expos within the region. This representative had just come from another expo in Colombia and, after Guatemala, would be heading to Argentina and then El Salvador. His Chinese partner at the booth joined our conversation at this point to add, "It's a bit tiring." When I asked whether diplomatic relations figured into the hosting nations of these expos, he shook his head, saying that since it was business to business, it didn't matter. That said, he added, "I see that they have a 'culture' section here. I think [the PRC government] wants to show people what China is like and help them become familiar with it. That is also political . . . but I don't want to talk about politics."[14] For these Chinese business representatives, political and economic relations with Central American nations occupied separate realms— such that a business representative did not want to go on record as talking about "politics"—but they acknowledged how those two efforts might be conjoined by the public diplomacy aspects of the expo that promoted people-to-people connections, a point to which I will return below.

While PRC-based firms at the expo had varying degrees of market exposure in Central America, many were using the expo to extend that reach and get local distributors and consumers on board. One particularly busy booth was selling jewelry, its countertop lined with displays of pearls and costume jewelry. The Panamanian representatives running the booth told me they had a store in Panama and were set to open a Guatemalan locale in 2019, so they were here showing their wares in hopes of building interest in the brand. To that end, whereas in the Panama store they maintained a $500 minimum purchase, here at the expo, they were selling the products by the strand, a feature that made the booth especially popular among Guatemalan consumers looking for a deal. By contrast, a makeup booth next door was not selling anything but looking for retailers to get their product into the local market. However, on the last day, they sold off the display merchandise, creating a stampede of people rushing to buy mascara and eyeliner at discount rates. At a booth promoting AOC television sets, the representative noted that this brand was already on sale in local stores and the sets were thus not for sale here at the expo; instead the displays were there to provide further brand exposure.

The road to commercial success in Central America, however, was not easy even for the veteran PRC firm representatives. I had met a young Higer sales representative in Costa Rica in 2015 during his first trip outside Mainland China. At that time, he was in the midst of a tour of Latin America during which he and his co-representatives were trying to get Costa Rican auto dealerships to market Higer vans and buses for small-business needs. The work was difficult because although the Chinese vehicles were less expensive than their Japanese or German counterparts, they tended not to have the same safety features. Much to my surprise, I encountered this same sales representative at the 2018 China-Guatemala Expo. At that point, he shared that Higer now had a strong foothold in Costa Rica and a growing presence in Panama but had no market presence in Guatemala. He had been on the road for the last several months, visiting Panama, Costa Rica, and the Dominican Republic to push sales. When I noted that those were all countries with diplomatic relations with the PRC and asked whether that seemed to matter, he said that it did, and that in countries like Guatemala, he was limited to working these expo booths. But he confessed that these expos were not as effective in generating clientele for Higer vehicles or, more importantly, getting them onto local dealers' lots.[15]

Therefore, while Chinese penetration of Latin American markets is seen by many as the trend of the day, the expo revealed the evolving nature of that trans-pacific engagement. In other words, the role of the expo was not simply to sell Chinese products but to give PRC-based firms experience abroad, providing them the opportunity not only to market their products but also to gain sales experience overseas. As younger companies emerge and try to establish a global profile, training a generation of young representatives to go to the Spanish-speaking world to make commercial connections is obviously a priority that the PRC government is willing to subsidize.

Staging Diplomatic Relations

Despite the lack of "official" PRC diplomatic representation, the expo clearly reflected an effort by the PRC government to promote not just economic products but "cultural diplomacy" (*wenhua wiajiao*) that would enhance the PRC's appeal to Guatemalan consumers.[16] Indeed, the expo's interior design had been drawn up by a Beijing-based international exhibition company that travels the globe mounting these kinds of expos for foreign audiences. One of the company's representatives, a bubbly young Chinese woman who introduced herself as Cindy, explained to me that she had just finished shows in Bulgaria and the Czech Republic before coming to Guatemala.

A large, open section at the front of the hall housed what can best be described as the "cultural section" of the expo. It contained two interactive stations featuring a tea ceremony and a calligraphy table, both supervised by young Chinese attendants. Wall-sized, full-color photographic panels of the PRC's impressive urban skylines, natural landscapes, technological feats, ethnic populations, and artisan traditions divided the area into visual narratives about China's richness, beauty, advanced development, and diversity. On another wall, encased silk banners with fancy embroidery showcased artisan traditions, while also communicating important precepts about Chinese civilization, both past and present. For example, one stunning gold-colored silk tapestry, entitled "Belt and Road," depicted concentric circles of laden camels traversing an ancient route of commerce, flanked in the corners by figures of women waving silk scarves. The curation for this piece, written in Chinese and English, read, "The tapestry 'Belt and Road' is hand-woven with natural silk that deeply shows the friendly contacts between peoples and the economic interactions between societies. The silk road 'Belt and Road' brought peace and prosperity to the world."

Reinforcing this cultural diplomacy theme, just around a corner a wall-sized panel depicting the Forbidden City served as the backdrop for an eight-foot-long replica of the PRC's high-speed trains, marked by the logo "CRRC" to denote its having been produced by the PRC's largest rail transit design and engineering company. From the bevy of Guatemalan guests and expo attendees enthusiastically taking pictures next to the train with the Forbidden City behind them, it was clear that this juxtaposition of China's ancient culture and current technological prowess was a compelling projection of the PRC's appeal.[17]

The focus on creating the possibility for cultural as well as business exchange was continued in many of the commercial booths, several of which sported small stands holding miniature replicas of the Guatemalan and PRC flags together. At one of the information booths, young Guatemalan volunteers were plying guests with white balloons emblazoned with the phrase "I love China," in which a heart symbol stood in for the word "love."

These balloons and the brochures and other swag gifted by the various expo representatives became a major focus of attendee interaction with the expo, such that it was not uncommon to see grandmothers and toddlers walking around

FIGURE 7. "I love China" at the China-Guatemala Expo.

toting balloons proclaiming their love for China or holding bags that resembled Halloween trick-or-treat sacks, filled with brochures, stickers, pens, and other branded merchandise for such random Chinese products as Mega's "agricultural enhancement" goods.

While the expo clearly tried to stage the richness of Chinese culture as one way of creating appeal for the PRC government, not every admirer was ready to let aesthetic preferences trump political values. Instead, the PRC's cultural and political differences formed the basis for both positive fetishizations of the exotic Chinese art and culture on display and negative stereotypes about the PRC government or the potentially dubious quality of its goods and companies. When I asked expo attendees what had drawn them to the event, many confessed that it had been their love of Chinese architecture, technology, and art that had brought them. One couple, both thirty-something architects, said they had come to enjoy what they hoped would be examples of Chinese architecture as well as to see products they thought would revolutionize building norms, such as solar energy heating or lighting. A young Guatemalan female art student perusing the hall said that she had come to the expo in the hopes of seeing more Chinese art but was frustrated not to see as much as she had anticipated. After chatting about the beautiful tapestries we were standing in front of, I took advantage of her enthusiasm for Chinese art to ask her whether she hoped to see greater rapprochement between Guatemala and the PRC. Interestingly, she responded, "More cultural exchange, absolutely. More politics? Not so much."[18]

As indicated by Cindy, the Chinese exposition representative who was responsible for staging events of this kind worldwide, the PRC government clearly saw these expos as opportunities for promoting the PRC's soft power, in the sense of creating a positive perception of China abroad. These efforts were not new; indeed, the historian Fredy González describes the 1963 Economic and Commercial Exposition that the PRC sponsored in Mexico City at the height of Cold War tensions. He details how, at that expo, Mexican and PRC flags flew outside the entrance, a Forbidden City facade covered the front of the factory where the event was held, and examples of the PRC's technological feats and trade possibilities filled the building. At that event, the PRC government sought to reconfigure what had been a conversation about the ideological dimensions of diplomatic relations with Taiwan (a democracy) or the PRC (a Communist country) into a showcase for the potential "mutual benefits" of partnership with the PRC.[19] The 2018 Guatemala expo continued that strategy, seeking to exhibit the PRC's cultural, commercial, and technological possibilities in a way that not only elided political differences and the issue of diplomatic relations but also naturalized the idea of PRC-Guatemalan official partnership. After all, with the flags waving together out front, the balloons proclaiming "I love China," and the colorful tourist experience of the Forbidden City simulated through the visual narrative, it was hard to remember that this wasn't the only China in town.

Given this staging of PRC-Guatemalan friendship at the expo, it is also no wonder that the Taiwanese officials at the Chinese embassy in Guatemala regarded the event with ambivalence. When I asked embassy representatives about their relationship to the fair, they stressed that they had none; however, they admitted that they paid close attention to the expo to see what products and firms were represented there and how many people attended. Indeed, they said that the 2018 expo had seemed to be smaller, with fewer PRC firms represented than in previous years. They were also quick to add that Guatemalan exports to Taiwan had increased substantially over the last twelve years of free trade and were much higher than exports to the PRC. When I asked whether they complained at all to their Guatemalan counterparts about the expo's celebration of the PRC-Guatemalan friendship, they insisted they could not prevent economic relations between the PRC and Guatemala, nor would they choose to. Both because of their democratic traditions and also because of their own entanglement with many Mainland Chinese businesses, transpacific commercial connections were something to which they felt all citizens were entitled: economics were separate from politics.[20] Nonetheless, the expo highlighted how political and cultural questions figured prominently in both Chinese and Guatemalan appraisals of the potential benefits of doing business.

In summary, the expo event laid bare several assumptions undergirding local efforts to develop commercial connections with the PRC. First, the PRC has a reputation for culture, innovation, and accessibility that made its products desirable targets of interest not just among larger Guatemalan companies but also among merchants, small-business owners, and regular members of the Guatemalan public. While many of those people attended the expo imagining it to be more of a cultural fair than an economic summit, they found the displays of Chinese commercial and technological prowess impressive. That said, their appreciation was always tinged by the sense that the quality of Chinese products was dubious and had to be checked. As these cases suggest, despite the buzz around increased trade with the PRC—whether one was a retailer of attractive Chinese commodities, an owner of a coveted Chinese product that dramatically lowered business costs and increased competitiveness, or an exporter of lucrative new commodities to the Chinese consumer—the reality of establishing connections with PRC-based vendors or business partners was made difficult by both logistical and cultural barriers. On the one hand, lack of language and knowledge of the Mainland Chinese market required that interested entrepreneurs have personal connections to people at 4CG or enough capital to participate in other ways. On the other hand, fears about the dubious quality of Chinese goods or the motives of potential vendors limited the lengths to which even savvy merchants and investors would go to pursue possible connections. Therefore, the role of elite intermediaries who could curate a trip to Mainland China's markets and preaudit prospective PRC business contacts was essential to this process. As I'll describe in more detail below, Central American governments tended to favor these self-enterprising consultants to broker new commercial connections, thus eliding the deeper cross-cultural knowledge and experience that local ethnic Chinese Central Americans might bring to the table and their parallel efforts to mediate transpacific commercial flows.

Brokering Transpacific Commerce

The biggest barriers to Guatemalan firms doing business with China [PRC] firms are language, distance, and culture; these aspects generate fear among Guatemalans. . . . What they need to advance is to dare to try and to know what they are looking for.

—Diego Ubico, independent international trade consultant

To be clear, Guatemalans had been doing business with China for quite some time. While there had been only five China-Guatemala Expos involving PRC agents, there had been a far more consistent history of business roundtables, or *ruedas de negocio*, that served as matchmaking functions between the Taiwanese and their Guatemalan commercial counterparts. The roundtables enabled face-to-face meetings between entrepreneurs so that they could speak directly about the products they wanted to import into the Guatemalan market. Usually the roundtables would take place the day before the exhibition, and tended to be oriented toward specific sectoral interests where Taiwan had a comparative advantage relative to the local market, such as in the area of tools, automobile parts, or electronics.[21] The Guatemalan Chamber of Commerce also paired these roundtables with trips to the Expo-Comer exhibition in Panama, where Taiwan has historically had a larger presence. However, while its more regular work was focused on collaborating with the Taipei-based embassy to stimulate business connections among Guatemalans and their Taiwanese business counterparts, the chamber of commerce was increasingly facilitating trips to Mainland China to foster commercial connections via the Canton Fair.

Given the burgeoning interest in doing business in Mainland China but the lack of business and cultural skills necessary for it, independent consultants with a strong international trade background stepped in to fill the void as facilitators or "guides" in navigating Central America–PRC relations. These intermediaries were increasingly recruited to help with several challenging dimensions of business in the PRC, including making contacts with Chinese businesses, verifying whether those businesses were legitimate potential collaborators (versus scams), and then negotiating the terms of that collaboration. These brokers represented a veritable niche business that had emerged in Central America around leading tours to the fairs, training Central American professionals in how to work with their Chinese counterparts, and serving as middlemen in business negotiations.

For these scouting trips to Mainland China, the Guatemalan Chamber of Commerce employed the services of an independent consultant, Diego Ubico, with expertise in business administration and international commerce.[22] Ubico's history of facilitating transpacific connections started with his own trip to China in 2007 to procure products for his "social expression" company, which supplied greeting cards, balloons, and related toys to stores like Walmart in Guatemala. Upon his return, he found that his peers and relations were extremely interested in learning how to make connections with firms in the PRC. Therefore in 2012 he began contracting as an intermediary for 4CG and worked with them for one year before seeking a larger clientele with the Guatemalan Chamber of Commerce. Starting in 2013, he began leading trips to Mainland China twice a year for owners of small and medium-sized businesses. The trips included all preparatory logistics work as well as the provision of individual translators and a host of other supports. Ubico reported that although they represented diverse industries, approximately 98 percent of the clients on his trips managed to make successful connections to Chinese suppliers. From those connections, Central American entrepreneurs procured commodities that they would sell within their own brand's catalogue back home in Central America.[23] In addition to taking clients to the Canton Fair, Ubico's service also offered inspections of particular factories with which clients were negotiating the sale of goods, logistics coordination for shipment back to Latin America, and container audit to ensure the integrity of the shipment. The success of this business eventually allowed Ubico to branch out and include participants referred from other regional peers, such as the Salvadoran Chamber of Commerce.

At the expo, other consulting firms like Ubico's were present to help grease the wheels of commercial interactions with the PRC by operating as a referral service for organizations like 4CG. One of these firms was the Asia Investment and Services Group, fronted by a Colombian representative who described the company's work as preauditing PRC-based firms in order to facilitate transpacific connections. He emphasized that people's worst fears were investing a lot of money in something that ended up being only a front and having no guarantee that their investment was safe. Therefore, through his firm's preverification services, Guatemalan buyers could do business with much more security, perhaps without having to take the trip to Mainland China themselves.[24]

This challenge of navigating business in the PRC was not exclusive to Guatemala, but one that all Central American nations were facing as they attempted to forge closer transpacific ties. To that end, the Costa Rican government's Office for the Promotion of Foreign Commerce (PROCOMER) offered training sessions and also led delegations to business fairs in Mainland China. But as PROCOMER's market research manager, Karina López, shared with me, the same kind of cultural confusion that plagued the Guatemalan expo would often similarly thwart these delegations. She described how delegates would return from their trips to the Canton Fair with bags full of cards and samples but no business connection or contract. The next year, they wouldn't want to attend the fair again, because they couldn't see its utility. PROCOMER thus wanted to convey to these entrepreneurs that their presence at the fair was important for giving visibility to Costa Rican firms, but it also stressed to them that making a real connection might take two to three years.[25] Furthermore, she highlighted that the delegations to both the Canton Fair and the Food and Beverage Exhibition in Shanghai were always from the large export companies in Costa Rica, as only they could afford to invest in future trade opportunities at this level. Therefore, what mattered was not simply getting people to China, but teaching them how to make the most of their interactions there in order to enhance the transpacific opportunities.

The need for brokers to help foster PRC–Central America commercial relations spoke to a larger issue than just a lack of business connections in Mainland China; it highlighted the lack of cultural and social capital on the part of Central American entrepreneurs. And this cultural capital deficit was not limited to the realm of economics but in fact also shaped the broader political relations across the Pacific. For example, despite its longer history of negotiations with the PRC, Costa Rica struggled to find people with the appropriate skill sets to fill its diplomatic corps in Beijing. The first Costa Rican ambassador was the former economy minister and business leader Antonio Burgués, who had no diplomatic experience and no specific experience with the PRC. His successor, Marco Vinicio Ruiz Gutiérrez (2010–14), had no such experience either.[26] Perhaps for this reason, the next ambassador, Ricardo Javier León Pérez, was the subject of intense criticism from the outset by both the local Chinese community and the press; they decried the fact that his only credential for the job was a high school diploma and some business experience in Asia. Costa Rican president Guillermo Solís defended his appointee, noting, "He has 40 years experience in Asia. He is a person with entrepreneurial experience in Korea, Japan, Taiwan and China and [is] not only fluent in Mandarin, but also [has] advanced skills in other languages. . . . This is the first time an ambassador of Costa Rica in Beijing speaks fluent Mandarin."[27] Despite these apparently unique qualifications, León Pérez was summarily removed from office in 2017 for a series of "noncompliances" that included failing to produce a single report.[28] He was replaced by Patricia Holkemeyer, a historian of China from the University of Costa Rica—the first person with significant credibility among all communities for her extensive knowledge about and experience with China. Her appointment aside, these staffing challenges for the office of ambassador signal a larger deficit in Central America's stock of potential interlocutors with sufficient cultural capital to engage with the PRC.

Ironically, many members of the local Chinese ethnic communities in Central America had dense commercial relations with agents and firms back in Mainland China as well as the cultural skills necessary to serve as cultural translators for transpacific commercial relations. Indeed, some of the most revered names within the Costa Rican Chinese community are families with large, successful import and manufacturing enterprises that span the Pacific. Nonetheless, the prominent firms in the larger national landscapes have been the Taiwanese manufacturing firms that I described in chapter 3. Therefore, as anthropologists like Adrian Hearn and others have noted, local Chinese firms and entrepreneurs have tended to remain off the radar of transpacific commerce due to the demographics of those involved, the nature of their connections to China, and the scale at which those efforts occurred.[29] These factors situated firms and entrepreneurs with Chinese heritage in a separate realm from the national industrial connections facilitated by the various chambers of commerce.

To bring these other entrepreneurial actors into view, we must first recall that the bulk of Central America's Chinese community is made up of migrants from the Pearl River Valley in Guangdong Province, an area that reflects a history of language, migration, and commerce that is very distinct from that of other parts of Greater China. As I discussed earlier, Henry Yu characterized this network as the "Cantonese Pacific" to reference a long and unique trajectory of movement, trade, and upward mobility among Cantonese-speaking migrants crisscrossing the Pacific.[30] As these migrants have become settled and acquired citizenship or residency in Latin America, mastering Spanish language and becoming more integrated, they have sustained and/or cultivated transnational connections in the Guangdong region and Hong Kong on which many have built their own upward mobility in the Americas. However, in a global context in which the meaning and stakes of Chineseness are increasingly defined by the PRC government in Beijing, ethnic Chinese Central Americans do not necessarily represent the forms of Chineseness currently valued for transpacific relations. A look at Chinese Central American young adults reveals that as the search for legitimate transpacific brokers grows, what it means to be Chinese and how that identity links to shifting global regimes of value have taken on new significance.

Miguel, a twenty-eight-year-old Guatemalan of Chinese descent, embodies one way that these other assemblages of Chinese commerce have evolved alongside but independent of larger national-level initiatives. Miguel's poor, rural-based, largely uneducated parents migrated to Guatemala, where Miguel's uncle had already relocated and gotten established, from the Guangdong region in the late 1980s. He described his parents as "economic refugees given the lack of economic opportunities in China then." Miguel's father began working for his brother before opening his own restaurant, "because that's what Chinese people tell you to do to make a living here," and then eventually started his own copy and print business. Miguel, one of three children in the family, grew up speaking Cantonese at home, attending kung fu classes at the local Salon Chino, and collaborating with the Juventud China (Chinese Youth) group within the Chinese

Association there. He attended Guatemalan schools, eventually receiving a university degree in architecture at the local Francisco Marroquin University. Nonetheless, Miguel stressed how difficult it was to find work as a professional in Guatemala, because "people don't want to pay for the kind of work. Doctors, professors . . . it's the same thing."[31] Therefore, Miguel went to work at his father's copy business and has slowly been taking over as the manager of that enterprise.

Miguel has maintained his close ties to Mainland China through several family trips back to the Guangdong region over the course of his life. However, that connection was transformed through an international youth exchange trip to Guangdong with other members of the Chinese Youth group in 2012. Organized by the Foreign Affairs Office of Guangdong Province, the trip involved approximately thirty students from both Guatemala and Australia and included visits to local tourism and industry sites, as well as a stopover in Foshan and homestays in the rural villages of the Canton region. Miguel recalled how much he enjoyed the trip, in part because of how differently he was treated as part of this group relative to his earlier experiences of being a "Chinese" in China. When I asked what this meant, he explained that when he had traveled on his own or with his family, he was usually treated somewhat rudely by Chinese vendors and officials, who would scold him for asking too low a rate when negotiating prices in the market or for fiddling with a pen while in the immigration line. On the youth trip, by contrast, he was treated like a guest and tourist and indulged at every site.[32]

Now as a small business manager, Miguel was excited to be heading back to Mainland China to the Canton Fair to scout out new opportunities of his own. Rather than attending with one of the official groups led by the Guatemalan Chamber of Commerce or even 4CG, Miguel was traveling alone and meeting up with family friends in Guangdong. He hoped to make connections at the fair to fuel future enterprise possibilities. But rather than having a particular product he was looking to acquire for sale in Guatemala or a particular kind of transnational enterprise that he'd like to forge, he had the sense that the Canton Fair was a place where enterprising Chinese like himself could make connections that would reflect commercial interests on both sides of the Pacific and would have the potential to launch him to the next phase in his family's history of upward mobility. This assumption came as much from his sense of his own cultural capital—including his fluency in Cantonese, his self-admitted embodiment of "old school" values like politeness, hard work, and respect, and his familiarity with the Guangdong region—as from his sense of the PRC. Indeed, while he maligned Guatemala for its lack of opportunities for supporting professional occupations like architecture, he noted that over time he had witnessed significant change in the Guangdong region of Mainland China, such that while his parents had left

China due to a lack of economic possibilities, his family that remained in the PRC now had more opportunities than he did in Guatemala.[33]

In Costa Rica, the story of Zhen offers another telling example of how Chinese Central American young adults with a long history of transnational connections and cultural skills are not only taking advantage of their family histories but retrofitting them to meet ever-changing ideas about what it takes to broker transpacific relations.[34] Zhen's parents left the Guangdong region of Mainland China for Costa Rica in the 1980s. Like Miguel's parents, they followed a standard trajectory for Chinese migrants to the Americas, obtaining restaurant jobs through family connections, working, saving, and progressing. By the time their three children were school-aged, the couple was running their own small restaurant, and their children helped out with the business. Although Zhen's parents learned some Spanish over the years, both continued to socialize with friends within the local Chinese, Cantonese-speaking community. Through hard work and enterprise, they moved out of the service industry into real estate and property development, with a presence in downtown San José.

Zhen grew up speaking Spanish and English but not Cantonese. After completing high school, she enrolled in the National University of Costa Rica, majoring in international relations. Zhen's interest in the subject inspired her to travel and continue her education in Beijing, where she learned Mandarin and then pursued a master's degree in international relations at Tsinghua University—one of the PRC's premier universities. While she initially relied on family financial support, she eventually received a PRC government scholarship to complete her studies. Thus, her family's resources and the PRC government constituted crucial tools for her success.[35] Upon graduation, she gained a post as an assistant to the Costa Rican ambassador in the PRC, a position she held for three years. She assumed responsibility for the embassy's administrative functions, helped Costa Rican businesses establish a foothold in Mainland China, and assisted with PRC leader Xi Jinping's visit to Costa Rica in 2013. Her bicultural background, multilingual skills, and international relations education made her a valuable asset to both PRC and Costa Rican functionaries as they sought to lay the foundation for diplomatic exchanges and development projects. Unfortunately, her post was not an official diplomatic appointment but rather an informal arrangement based on convenience; therefore, she returned to Costa Rica in 2014.

Upon her return to Central America, Zhen took advantage of her Beijing degrees, Mandarin-language skills, and local knowledge to pursue various private consulting opportunities—assuming the role of translator for groups of visiting Mainland Chinese tourists, participating in training sessions on medical goods produced in a local free trade zone, accompanying Costa Rican entrepreneurs to the PRC, and sometimes curating PRC businesses' scouting tours of

Costa Rica. She was invited by the PRC government to participate in a trip to Mainland China for "eminent young overseas professionals" from the Chinese diaspora; like Miguel, she showed me photos of the many amazing friends and business connections she'd made with Chinese diasporic young adults in Vietnam, Australia, and elsewhere around the world. Lately she worked with a local high school in the Guangdong region to set up cultural exchanges between PRC and Costa Rican schools so as to feed a growing interest, on both sides of the Pacific, for increased cultural knowledge and commercial opportunity.

Unlike Miguel, who drew on his family's heritage and transnational connections to forge new business opportunities that reproduced a history of personal networks firmly located in Guangdong and Central America, Zhen's experience speaks to a generation of young Chinese Central Americans—in her case, self-titled Chino Ticos—born to Cantonese-speaking parents but raised and educated in Spanish in the Americas, who have "retooled" their Chinese cultural repertoire in order to embody contemporary and strategic forms of Chineseness that enable them to play a role in transpacific relations. Zhen did not go to Mainland China to acquire ethnic "authenticity" for validation within local communities in Costa Rica, but to acquire strategic elements of a global China in hopes of developing a transnational status. In other words, the forms of Chineseness she aspired to are not found locally or in an ancestral Chinese village; they are produced through transnational connections to the center of the PRC government's capitalist development. Indeed, her retooled Chinese identity includes Mandarin-language skills and cultural capital accruing from academic degrees and professional experience in Beijing, as well as professional self-enterprise, rather than family enterprise in Costa Rica.

One might read Miguel's and Zhen's professional trajectories in terms of a traditional ethnic entrepreneur, as they build on their ethnic Chinese identity to lay claim to the PRC's rising value by positioning themselves as transpacific brokers. However, the configurations of Chineseness that they mobilize reflect complex, strategic assemblages of diverse cultural traits and social connections that they have actively acquired, rather than simply embodied. These diverse elements come from different sources than those of their parents' generation and hold different meanings. Both Miguel's and Zhen's trajectories highlight the growing impact of PRC government cultural diplomacy efforts, including scholarships for study at Mainland Chinese universities and programs for younger Chinese diaspora, rather than the pathways created by transnational ethnic networks. Their experiences as participants in exchanges and as "eminent young overseas professionals" gave them a dramatically different picture of Mainland China than the negative memory held by their parents, positioning the PRC as a place of cosmopolitanism and entrepreneurial opportunity, rather than the site of a regressive Communist past or a nostalgic homeland. Therefore, while their elders represented a long history of transpacific commercial relations, these Chinese Central Americans embodied distinct forms of Chineseness that ratified their value in the global marketplace in a way that was precluded for older generations of Chinese diasporic community entrepreneurs.

This focus on the entrepreneurial future shaped Chinese Central American young adults' sense of their own exceptionalism and unique capacity to broker transpacific relations in a way that non-Chinese business elites could not. Another Chino Tico, Marcos, who received an engineering degree in Costa Rica and augmented it with a year of language study in Beijing before returning to Costa Rica to work for IBM, certainly saw himself in this light. He acknowledged that he occupied a unique position from which to facilitate investments and transpacific exchange. "We have the local knowledge," he said. "We know how the market works here. We know Tico tastes and preferences . . . and we can offer this knowledge through our own language, the language of the investors."[36] Miguel, Zhen, and Marcos, then, embodied the unique combination of cultural and social capital necessary to do business across the Pacific, facilitating new connections among their non-Chinese compatriots and commercial opportunities with their PRC counterparts. Whether they chose to deploy these skills for their own economic upward mobility (as Miguel did) or serve as brokers for larger private and public interests (as Zhen and Marcos did), it was not a static or essential sense of their Chineseness that made them well suited for facilitating transpacific flows; despite their dense commercial connections to Greater China, it was their newly acquired experience with a global China and their privileged relation to it that distinguished them.

Nonetheless, when I asked members of ACG or the official chambers of commerce in Guatemala and Costa Rica about collaborations with members of the local Chinese community, none of them drew on the skills or "services" of these Chinese Central Americans to promote their own transpacific endeavors. Indeed, they often seemed somewhat taken aback by the question and the suggestion that they might look to that community to satisfy the needs of international commerce. "They operate separately; we don't have any real connections to them," was the usual refrain. Instead, the two worlds—that of the national economic elite and the Chinese diaspora—seemed to crisscross each other, working across different registers. How do we account for this bifurcation between official public relations with the PRC government and the ongoing, deeply rooted but also shifting private connections maintained by the Chinese community?

One explanation is politics. In recounting for me their biographies, many of these Chinese Central Americans emphasized how their families had discouraged them from participating in anything that smacked of politics. Given that many of their parents had left Mainland China in the late 1980s and early 1990s in response to political repression there, their experience with politics in the PRC had certainly been negative. On the other side of the Pacific, the history of discrimination and persecution of Chinese communities in the Americas through the twentieth century (see chapter 2) served as a powerful disincentive for making oneself visible within Central American politics as well. Therefore, facilitating individual and private-sector connections between Central America and the PRC felt palatable to some of these young adults in a way that serving as a high-profile independent consultant working for, say, the local chamber of commerce would not. One route seemed to represent private economic interests, while the other public and, therefore, necessarily political interests. Nonetheless, as these individuals begin to test their own abilities and understand them in relation to changing national contexts in which they see a dearth of qualified business and political representatives to serve as intermediaries of PRC–Central American relations, many may find that their value as brokers cannot be denied.

The Guatemalan expo highlights the burgeoning PRC–Central American relations that are forming with or without diplomatic relations. And even though the PRC is not a new economic partner in Central America, this contemporary moment of commercial exchange is structured in such a way as to challenge or privilege particular kinds of connections. Guatemalan and many other everyday Central American entrepreneurs perceived Mainland China as a place of unlimited possibilities, either because of the consumers they could reach or because of the inexpensive commodities or services they could bring back home to Central America. Nonetheless, identifying and successfully navigating these business relations with unknown firms across what felt to many to be a vast cultural border entailed assuming many potential risks. Firms based in and/or sponsored by the PRC, meanwhile, also struggled with how to gain experience in Central American markets and how to expand their reach once established in the region.

The 2018 China-Guatemala Commercial Expo illuminated many of these challenges and opportunities, while emphasizing the entangled nature of economic, cultural, and political goals. The expo was as much a public diplomacy effort by the PRC government as it was an opportunity for establishing economic partnerships; by promoting familiarization with a particular picture of the PRC and Chinese culture, the event sought to cultivate appreciation for the country's many riches and its potential. Given Guatemala's lack of diplomatic relations with the PRC, these cultural and economic narratives must be read as part of a political project to highlight the benefits of collaboration not with Taiwan, but with the PRC in particular. This strategy appealed to some expo attendees who marveled at the cultural richness and the technological prowess evident in the displays, but it also triggered ongoing worries about the suspect quality of Chinese products and PRC government politics. Where expo attendees could embrace the idea of more trade, many were quick to qualify what kind and to what end, rather than welcome it unconditionally.

The promise of new transpacific opportunities increases the need for brokers who can mediate transpacific commercial relations. And yet Central American countries generally find themselves lacking in personnel who can play this important role. The emergence of private consultants who can fill this void has been useful for facilitating relations among the top industry representatives in their respective countries and curating access to PRC commercial activities; however, operating at a different register are a new generation of Chinese Central Americans versed in shifting forms of both Chineseness and Central American culture, who are ideally positioned to serve as transpacific brokers. This constituency was not present at the expo, nor has it sought out the role of high-profile consultant for national firms looking to establish connections in the PRC, because its agents are mediating flows that crisscross and run parallel to these national efforts. Recognizing the value of local Chinese communities to processes of local economic development, and connecting these multiple, up to now distinct, layers of commercial flows, will be crucial to the future of transpacific developments.

6

CORRUPTION

Hunting Tigers and Chopping Chorizo across the Pacific

Bribery, graft, kickbacks, money laundering. Front-page scandals involving high-ranking officials, police, and business elites from China to Latin America have underscored corruption as a contemporary problem of governance on both sides of the Pacific. In 2012, Chinese president Xi Jinping launched a crusade to punish and prevent corruption among PRC bureaucrats and state agencies. His campaign to "hunt high-level tigers" and "low-level flies" had led to the punishment of 750,000 cadres by 2016. Highlighting the breadth of the definition of corruption and its perceived pernicious effects on governance, these measures include the "eight rules and six prohibitions" banning bureaucrats not only from taking gifts and bribes, but also from visiting expensive restaurants, hotels, or private clubs, playing golf, or using government funds for personal travel, among others.

In Costa Rica, a landslide popular vote in 2014 elected President Guillermo Solís, who ran on the slogan "No más chorizo!"—literally, "No more sausage!"—an evocative euphemism for the "fat" or "pork" grafted off of public projects. Costa Rica was not unique in confronting a long history of corrupt governmental practices; indeed, that campaign slogan could have been applied to just about any country in Latin America during that time period. In Guatemala, following on the heels of the 2015 resignation and indictment of President Otto Pérez Molina and his vice president, Roxana Baldetti Elías, on charges of customs fraud, money laundering, and corruption, newly elected president Jimmy Morales came to office on the platform of "Ni corrupto, ni un ladrón"

(Neither corrupt nor a thief). Four years later, however, as he was leaving office, Morales himself came under investigation for allegations of fraud and corruption within his own family.

Farther south, scandals in Brazil further highlighted not only the scale of corruption but also its imbrication in systems of power that stretch across the region. Investigations of the state oil company Petrobras exposed Lavo Jato, or Operation Car Wash, in which company officials solicited kickbacks in exchange for contracts and politicians used Petrobras funds to bankroll their political campaigns. The ensuing Odebrecht scandal, which exposed bribes made by the Brazilian construction company for infrastructure project contracts all over Latin America, accentuated the scope of corruption in Brazil, resulting in millions of dollars in penalties for Odebrecht and landing former president Lula da Silva in jail for his alleged part in the corruption networks. The Odebrecht scandal forcefully demonstrated how local corruption practices were often deeply entangled with transnational development processes.

Although corruption has long figured as a central theme in Latin American politics, both the public mobilization against it and the resulting indictments from these recent high-profile corruption cases seem to reflect an increased attention to and policing of corruption. Indeed, since the 2010s, grassroots mobilizations from Rio de Janeiro to Guatemala City have swelled as citizens have taken to the streets to protest the abuse of public power that had until this time been the order of the day. Scholars such as Muir and Gupta have argued that it is corruption's capacious meaning and diverse contextual applications that have made it a compelling means of confronting questions of inequality and rights across such diverse political and cultural landscapes.[1]

These local-level mobilizations have been framed and validated by the work of multilateral institutions that have positioned corruption as a global phenomenon, albeit one located primarily in the Global South. Multilateral institutions and individual governments have increasingly produced regional anticorruption agreements to fight corruption across borders, as well as developed indices to track perceptions of corruption and rank governments accordingly. One reason why the Guatemalan and Brazilian cases were able to produce criminal charges and jail time for the elite officials involved was that local protests converged with multilateral efforts to monitor and reduce corruption worldwide.[2]

With the inauguration of the current wave of transpacific relations in the early 2000s, scholars and policy analysts have expressed particular concern about the role that corruption might play in contemporary China–Latin America relations. This concern stems from the assertion that, as Ariel Armony puts it, "people in China, as in most of Latin America, move in a deep sea of informality, in which unwritten rules, bribery and/or personal connections are the gatekeepers to resources controlled by individuals in positions of power."[3] Despite acknowledgment that these dynamics operate on both sides of the Pacific, the PRC, in particular, has been perceived as the bigger worry, due to what Ariel Armony and Julia Strauss describe as its "profound imbrication of political power and economic advantage" that stems from "vague norms" and nonexistent "enforcement of separation of party, state and enterprise."[4] Xi Jinping initiated the PRC government's most ambitious anticorruption campaign to date in 2012 as part of the Central Party's efforts to consolidate power and sustain China's economic restructuring. Nonetheless, given the perceived high level of corruption in PRC state-run enterprises and overseas development aid, some Latin Americanists have worried about the possibility of China "exporting corruption" to Latin America.[5]

In the previous chapters of this book, the ubiquity of corruption, or at least allegations of it, are present in all domains of transpacific developments—bilateral treaties, infrastructure projects, commercial connections, and even diplomatic relations. We can recall Costa Rican critiques that the Moín refinery and Route 32 were constructed on inflated cost estimates, partisan project evaluations, lack of transparent and public bidding, and elevated employee salaries and perks. In Nicaragua, we can recall the canal treaty between Ortega and Wang Jing as one that was ratified through accelerated congressional review and involved terms that were shrouded in opacity, and one whose agent, Wang Jing, occupied the ambiguous position of both private Hong Kong entrepreneur and potential PRC government agent. All of these projects represented important public works—be they refineries, roads, or canals—whose involvement with different kinds of Chinese firms or affiliates seemed to threaten that public good.

Rather than probing these cases to assess whether China is an ethical actor or one that promotes corruption, I examine corruption as what Dieter Haller and Chris Shore call "an idiom through which people try to make sense of the *political* world they inhabit," as well as the actual practices and policies that idiom produces and reflects.[6] In this sense, I draw on anthropology's ability to provide "contextual mediation" of the meaning and function of corruption as a defining feature of transpacific relations.[7] Specifically, what kinds of scandals are understood in terms of corruption and who is implicated in those critiques? What does the prevalence of anticorruption discourse produce in terms of specific politics and practices at different levels of action? And how do these politics and practices matter for the future of transpacific developments?

To answer those questions, this chapter explores the discourse and policies surrounding corruption as an essential feature of transpacific relations, and analyzes how corruption has become the central frame through which Central Americans talk about and imagine the significance of transpacific relations. Building on my argument about the multiple Chinas in Central America, I show how local corruption perceptions conflate PRC, Taiwanese, and Chinese diasporic actors and processes to make sense of Chinese economic and political aims today. I then ask how those claims of corruption have produced new political and economic practices aimed at thwarting corruption allegations from different scales of engagement. Finally, I examine the implications of these perceptions of corruption and their correspondent anticorruption policies for the future of transpacific relations.

In this exploration, I draw on official project documents and sources, case materials, and media coverage, as well as public lore or gossip about the projects as articulated within specific communities. Although unsubstantiated, local rumors about corruption tell us just as much about the public lives of the projects in question as do the official documents; they highlight how these projects are imagined and experienced by citizens in ways that go far beyond their official intent or sponsorship. Therefore, I invoke local testimonies not to indicate their "truthiness" as much as to index the particular logics, evidence, and interpretations mobilized by everyday people as they experience and make sense of these projects in the moment.[8] In each case, I do my best to maintain the anonymity of particular subjects so as not to expose them for the particular knowledge that they disclose, some of which might be confidential; however, I do identify the type of community in which these interlocutors are located as a way of better situating their context and their relationship to the projects at hand. At the end of this chapter, I note what these public perceptions produce, regardless of their veracity, and why they are so important to the future of transpacific developments.

China's Place within Global Anticorruption Efforts

Corruption is an age-old practice, and yet it has taken on heightened salience in the contemporary moment. Many trace the current understanding of corruption to the 1990s when countries in Latin America and Africa were undergoing transitions to democracy, thus situating the problem of corruption as endemic to the Global South. Framed by World Bank president James Wolfensohn's evocative 1996 description of corruption as a "cancer" driving poverty in the developing world, a "convergence of interests" from international organizations, national governments, transnational companies, and local movements helped to create a new global governance regime that many have termed the "anticorruption industry."[9] The anticorruption industry's emergence was marked by the desire to know, measure, and fight corruption as a universally important problem and one with real material consequence for both individual nations and global development policy worldwide.[10] International organization offshoots from the World Bank, such as Transparency International, have created indexes that measure and rank perceptions of corruption globally.

Over the two decades following Wolfensohn's remarks, preventative and punitive means of dealing with corruption have been written into international accords, donor conditions, national laws, and business contracts. For example, in 1996, the Organization of American States adopted the Inter-American Convention against Corruption, signed by twenty-four states across the Western Hemisphere and setting forth a series of measures to "facilitate and regulate cooperation" among signees around standards of conduct, enforcement mechanisms, and financial oversight, among other things.[11] In 2004, the United Nations General Assembly approved the United Nations Convention against Corruption to serve as an "effective international legal instrument against corruption."[12] In these agreements, corruption has become not only a primary area of concern but also a concrete domain of intervention and reform. Therefore, international anticorruption policies have proliferated new regulations, audits, and reductions in bloated bureaucracies—policies that seek to enhance efficiency and transparency not just of individual state employees, but of the state itself. For example, Peter Meyer explains how the US government's Central American Regional Security Initiative places conditions on funds to Central American nations, promising to withhold 75 percent of assistance "until the Secretary of State certifies that the governments are 'taking effective steps' to combat corruption; however, the same initiative couples the anti-corruption fight with a mandate to increase revenues, improve border security and address human rights concerns, among other issues."[13] For this reason, some critics have described this anticorruption industry as part of a post-Washington consensus, in which evidence of progress in instituting transparency and good governance domestically has increasingly become a condition for Western aid.[14]

The PRC has represented something of an anomaly within this global anticorruption movement and thus has been notably absent from scholarship on the global anticorruption campaign often associated with the West. To be clear, the PRC government has been repeatedly maligned by the West for its trenchant "no strings attached" philosophy toward lending, a policy that critics claim makes China a "rogue donor" propping up corrupt states.[15] Nonetheless, the PRC's staunch policing of national sovereignty and lack of dependence on international financial institutions have meant that it has not been the specific target of the hegemonic international anticorruption campaign. Moreover, the PRC's perceived high levels of corruption, accompanied as they are by simultaneously high levels of growth, have contradicted the World Bank's argument that corruption stifles economic development.[16] Therefore, despite the PRC government's anti-corruption efforts, which include more anticorruption reforms than any other country in the world, its corruption has tended to be studied as a political and ethical problem attributed to the PRC's exceptionalist domestic politics, rather than as part of an economic project linked to a larger global regime.[17]

One reason for this exceptionalist approach is the PRC's nonliberal state structure. The all-encompassing role of the Communist Party in the nation's political and economic system means that corruption cannot be mapped on the same public-private divides that serve as the point of departure for corruption discourse that posits an essential difference between "public office" and "private gain."[18] In the PRC, those lines have been blurred by postreform Chinese economic policy that privileges state-organized and state-financed enterprises as well as the entrepreneurialization of local government, thus making the effort to distinguish between individual and collective, private and public interests especially fraught.[19]

In response to this reality, Xi's calls to promote traditional ideas of "honor to frugality and shame to extravagance" among all party members represent what Macabe Keliher and Hsinchao Wu have described as an effort to "transform the people who make up the state, rather than the structure of the state itself.[20] In part, this view reflects PRC government efforts to "consolidate power within the party" in response to varying challenges to Central Party authority since the initiation of economic reforms in 1979 and especially after the political turmoil of 1989.[21] These market-driven economic reforms provided increased opportunities for corruption, both in volume and in type, highlighting an increase in large-scale and collective corruption cases.[22] Therefore, in lieu of transformations in the political system—such as the institution of an independent judiciary or democratic reform—Xi's anticorruption policies seek to construct what Janine Wedel and her coauthors call an "ideal type of what a 'normal' citizen should be."[23]

While state politics may be one reason for the PRC's exceptional relationship to corruption, culture is another. China boasts a long tradition of social relations that operate through alternative normative frameworks marked by social networks and patronage relations.[24] For example, Smart and Hsu have highlighted how the boundaries between corruption and the Chinese concept of *guanxi*—a practice understood as "personal relations or networks"—are highly ambiguous, perceived as building trust and thus morally positive while also easily sliding into corruption and perceived as negative.[25] Therefore, even though *guanxi* is a dynamic, historically and situationally contingent practice relative to corruption, its practice as an "integral part of doing business" in reform China has continued and grown even as "public awareness of (and disgust at) corruption was raised to new heights."[26]

The practices the PRC government has used to tackle corruption thus index the particularities of a state-controlled economy as well as the highly moralistic formulation of the problem. In the latest wave of anticorruption efforts, the PRC government has sought to strengthen the role of its Central Commission for Discipline Inspection, the main agency in charge of overseeing anticorruption cases, and to make visible criminal prosecution of big-name culprits. It has also set up hotlines for citizens to report cases of corruption and encouraged bureaucrats to come forward and confess their own sins, so as to emphasize the individual, ethical requirements of each citizen in the fight against corruption.

Of importance for Central America in particular, Chinese anticorruption policies have also been applied to the operation of PRC-affiliated businesses investing overseas as part of the state's "going out" policy. A 2011 amendment to the PRC government's criminal law extended anticorruption laws to the bribing of foreign government officials or international organizations, with violators facing mandatory imprisonment and fines, thus raising the extraterritorial stakes of Chinese corruption. Indeed, investigations found that in 2013, PRC stated-owned companies spent $1.1 billion on overseas travel, public vehicles, and hospitality.[27] As a result, Xi slashed budgets for spending by state employees, both at home and in state development projects abroad, hoping to promote more mixed ownership and efficiency within state-owned companies. In this way, state efforts to both preventatively and punitively reduce graft and also diminish the possibility of corruption have effectively sought to restructure the way that business is done by PRC government-supported firms abroad.

In Central America, the PRC government's anticorruption policies have affected what kinds of businesses could persist, which were no longer tenable, and what new strategies were required of Chinese economic agents in order for their economic endeavors to be viable. The shuttering of luxury Chinese restaurants where expensive banquet-style business deals had previously been made represents one example of anticorruption's impact on the Central American economic landscape. Shifts in PRC government employee entrepreneurial practices to maximize state resources on smaller budgets represent another. As I have argued elsewhere, these shifts required actors associated with Chinese economic initiatives to experiment and pursue new strategies that sought to assume the appropriate mix of public-private enterprise, which has become emblematic of the PRC's postreform governance.[28] However, they did not necessarily lessen local perceptions of corruption as a central feature of transpacific relations.

Despite PRC government efforts to diminish corruption among its firms working overseas, Central Americans often perceived Chinese development practices to be ethically fraught. In making their assessments, they cared less about PRC government or business regulations and more about well-entrenched stereotypes about Chineseness. As I explain in the next section, Central American views were shaped by a powerful assemblage of historical, ethnoracial, and economic dynamics that have tended to reaffirm rather than reduce local perceptions of Chinese corruption.

Orientalizing Corruption on the Ground in Central America

While contemporary media and policy conversations about corruption tend to focus on Mainland China, I have argued throughout this book that Central America has been home to at least three different forms of China that have shaped regional development—Chinese diaspora communities, Taiwanese officials and private businesses, and PRC state officials, banks, and firms. And while Central Americans do make important distinctions between these Chinese actors—for instance, perceiving a Taiwanese road as supporting sovereignty while scrutinizing a PRC-built road for potential exploitation—what is striking within corruption discourses is how these various forms of China are conflated to confirm a single story about the values underlying what is presumed to be a universal Chineseness. These dubious values are not synonymous with corruption, but they tend to authorize suspicions about Chinese projects, allowing Central Americans to read potential threat into the initiatives. It is, therefore, important to consider how the presence of these multiple Chinas and forms of Chineseness has impacted conversations about and perceptions of Chinese corruption in Central America.

To locate the source of these enduring ideas about Chineseness, it's instructive to return to Central America's history to see how past discourses and relations have shaped ideas in the present. As I described earlier, nineteenth-century Central American residents originally admired the industriousness of the Chinese workers contracted to construct railroads in Panama, Guatemala, and Costa Rica. Nonetheless, as these migrant laborers settled into local communities and began to pursue commercial activity, locals often maligned them for their alleged "pernicious" habits and monopolizing tendencies. Local citizens not of Chinese descent accused Chinese petty merchants of exploiting the communities in which they operated, representing a foreign Other set apart from hispanized society and functioning like an "octopus that consumes and consumes, nothing more."[29] This stereotype of the Chinese as willing to go to any length to make a profit, even subjugating their own kin as family enterprise employees, created a lasting sense of the Chinese as defined by unethical commercial and communal relations. The historian Erika Lee identifies these "racialized understandings of Chinese as economic, social and cultural threats" as reflective of a "hemispheric

Orientalism" that "traveled across borders and commonly defined the Chinese as a threatening invasion."[30]

These Orientalist stereotypes have persisted. Even today, locals I spoke to were quick to stigmatize local Chinese businesses based on the perception that their owners were engaged in nefarious commerce, including pirated commodities or even trafficked employees. The lore that Chinese restaurateurs would pack their soups with rat or dog meat invoked the most corrupt image of Chinese businesses trying to maximize profit at the expense of their customers. In those discourses, rather than people representing corruption as the misappropriation of public goods for private gain, they invoked it to make an ethical commentary about an essentialized Chinese abuse of public trust for private gain.

Evidence of the persistence of these Orientalist formulations and their consequences was visible in San José's Chinatown in 2017. As I walked down the pedestrian walkway to track the fate of the original retailers on the strip and the presence of new Chinese businesses, I encountered two different Chinese import stores that had been shut down. The heavy metal pull-down gate closed over the facade of one of the stores was plastered with bumper-sticker-sized notices announcing that it had been "Closed by the Department of Health." A few bottles of unopened Chinese oyster sauce stood haphazardly abandoned in front of the store door as another indicator of the raid. When I asked members of the local Chinese community about the closures, they complained about the unfair treatment that Chinese businesses received relative to other enterprises in the area. They described how, in the last year, at least three different businesses within the Chinatown district had been shut down by government agencies for minor infractions of their business license, including such trivial offenses as selling foods past their expiration dates. Residents alleged that the Department of Health would disproportionately target Chinese businesses and close them down for inconsequential violations to punish them for their perceived success at the expense of other local businesses, and they complained that the government was hypervigilant of Chinese businesses while turning a blind eye to other businesses. For example, they recounted how consumers had registered multiple complaints against a nearby Nicaraguan diner for its many blatant code violations but received no government response. Chinese residents understood these practices as a clear case of profiling, and one that followed a long tradition of unfairly targeting Chinese businesses.[31]

Taiwanese officials and employers in Central America during the late twentieth century tended not to participate in the petty commerce, restaurant, and small family business sectors to the same degree as their Cantonese forerunners, but they were also subject to these ongoing stereotypes about Chineseness. Despite their generally more middle-to-upper-class status and positions as state representatives or large business owners, their efforts to facilitate commerce and political friendship between Taiwan and the Central American nations unwittingly reproduced those stereotypes, with a twist. Taiwanese politicians and diplomats produced this effect through their patronage of local politicians and checkbook diplomacy. To woo political friends, Taiwanese officials normalized a system of public diplomacy that pivoted on the use of discretionary funds to curry political favor. Individual Central American politicians privately benefited from Taiwanese officials' no-strings-attached "Taiwan funds" or chartered fancy familiarization tours to Taipei; meanwhile, local constituents often wondered whether these perks were taking away from the original projects for which Taiwanese funds were allocated. Therefore, at least until 2008, Taiwanese official aid was often distributed and perceived socially as part of a "wink, wink, nod, nod" system of influence peddling. In the worst cases, however, these Taiwanese practices rose to the level of illicit contributions to elected officials' political campaigns.[32]

Wealthy Taiwanese businessmen who brought their enterprises overseas to set up shop in Central America were similarly perceived as benefiting from and sustaining a system of state corruption, albeit this time on the part of the Central American governments. As described earlier, both Guatemalan and Costa Rican regimes awarded these entrepreneurs Central American passports in exchange for relocating to the region and, many have argued, gave them carte blanche in terms of the operation of their factories in order to ensure profitability. Therefore, in contrast to their small-business Cantonese counterparts, corruption lore surrounding Taiwanese businesses pivoted on their apparent immunity from state surveillance, rather than their profiling. Nonetheless, many locals recounted how Taiwanese employers' reputation for sweatshop factory conditions and union busting affirmed their stereotype of the unyielding Chinese boss who sacrificed labor regulations to turn a profit. The Taiwanese employers as well as their Central American state sponsors, then, were seen as embroiled in a reciprocal relationship of privilege and exploitation. Even though Taiwan was perceived as a transparent, democratic counterpart to the PRC, the practices of its public and private representatives reinforced perceptions of all Chinese as necessarily suspect.

Finally, as noted above, locals criticized more recent PRC government initiatives for their lack of transparency and the impression they created of seeking favorable conditions at the expense of local governments or their citizens. When Costa Rica established diplomatic relations with the PRC, that switch was the result of a year of covert negotiations pursued by then president Oscar Arias Sánchez.[33] The new agreement between the PRC government and Costa Rica included a nondisclosure clause. All of this secrecy left many locals with the impression that the PRC government was trying to close a shady deal with its Costa Rican counterpart. It took a lawsuit by a local newspaper to force the Costa Rican government to publish the terms of that agreement. Therefore, while the PRC framed its relationship with Central American nations in terms of mutual benefit and a win-win association, locals perceived it as a chess match to which the PRC government ultimately had a winner-take-all approach.

For many Costa Ricans, the ill-fated Moín petroleum refinery (or *refinería china*) project that I described in chapter 4 became proof of this concept of corruption. The refinery initiative was originally designed as a joint venture between the PRC state oil company SINOPEC and the Costa Rican energy company RECOPE. As suspicions about the validity of the feasibility study were exposed, Costa Ricans that I talked to quickly read those developments as a sign that PRC agents had sought to make the deal look better than it was by hiring a subsidiary firm to do the project evaluation. Even after the evaluation was redone by a North American firm, questions about inflated employee salaries, expensive trips to Mainland China, and other project anomalies convinced people that the entire project was set up to benefit the Chinese, hence the derogative tone they lent to the term *refinería china*. Several people rehearsed to me the same logic of dubious Chinese behavior fueling the project from the beginning, saying, "This is payback for the stadium!" or "Now China [the PRC] is collecting the debt from the stadium it gave us. With them, nothing is free!" For these critics, the PRC's gift of the national stadium was always perceived as something of a Trojan horse, one that from the outside impressed due to its size, engineering prowess, and apparent benevolence, but inside bore intentions of conquest. Therefore, corrupt practices on the part of Chinese SINOPEC employees could be interpreted as embodying the intentions of a necessarily unscrupulous PRC government.

As noted above, part of what made the secrecy behind PRC-sponsored project negotiations feel like corruption to most Central American observers was the fact that the PRC government's single-party, authoritarian status confounded the public-private distinction so crucial in definitions of corruption. In other words, it felt safe to assume that Chinese firms were ultimately negotiating in a way that was in alignment with and would benefit the PRC government, whereas negotiations with state officials were seen as creating favorable terms for its companies. The inability to distinguish between public and private actors—as we saw in the case of Wang Jing in Nicaragua—thus tainted all Chinese initiatives as potentially dubious, conflating both national and private interests.

PRC-sponsored initiatives in the region were thus often regarded with skepticism, and controversies were automatically perceived as evidence of corruption. For example, when the PRC state firm Anhui Foreign Economic Construction

Company (AFECC) constructed Costa Rica's national stadium, it brought over six hundred Mainland Chinese workers to do the construction. Housed in a labor camp just off-site, they remained essentially quarantined from Costa Rican society and the rest of San José. In July 2010, when media photographs showed Mainland Chinese stadium workers and equipment operating across the street from the stadium at a private condominium construction site, the Costa Rican Chamber of Construction not only echoed the public outcry but filed an official complaint. Chinafecc, the local AFECC subsidiary, had petitioned Costa Rican immigration officials for forty visas to use Chinese workers from the stadium in the condominium project. However, the Ministry of Labor ruled against the visa extensions and noted that in the original agreement, all of the visas were for the twenty-three-month stadium construction project only. That said, the company was not barred from requesting the transfer of workers from the stadium to private projects after the fact.[34]

Explaining how this ambiguity had arisen, an engineer involved with the project attributed the roots of the conflict to the original deal made by Oscar Arias Sánchez in his negotiations with the PRC government representatives. According to this engineer, when Arias signed an agreement authorizing the PRC-based

FIGURE 8.   Condominium project across from the Costa Rican national stadium.

construction firm to build the stadium, he had given permission for one hundred workers to stay beyond that project in order to complete the construction of a high-rise condominium development across the street from the stadium, which was owned by a diasporic Chinese entrepreneur. This interpretation not only potentially implicated Arias in the condominium scandal but also highlighted how conflated notions of Chineseness—of PRC-sponsored firms versus local diasporic developers—might have informed Arias's sense that the two structures could fall within the purview of Chinese construction efforts.

After incidents like the condominium scandal, PRC representatives' efforts to conduct normal business came under additional scrutiny. In San José, most foreign embassies are located within a particular part of town called Rohrmoser, near the Sabana Park. After 2007, the "new" PRC embassy was located in a building there; however, diplomatic staff expressed a desire to move to a space outside the busy city center. They worked with a business owner in the local Chinese community to find a property about one hour outside of San José in a much more bucolic, removed setting. According to local gossip within the Chinese community, PRC government representatives purchased the property for $18 million, a figure that, in the locals' estimations, was significantly higher than the actual property value. The difference between the sale price and the property value, according to one community member who was close to the source, represented the exorbitant "commission" that the local contact had hoped to procure from making the deal. However, the deal quickly went south for a number of reasons. For starters, newly initiated anticorruption measures from Beijing made the PRC government negotiators leery of the high price tag and even more suspicious of the Costa Rican intermediary who had set up the arrangement. Furthermore, PRC embassy representatives heard from others that having the embassy so far out of town would make it appear as if China had secrets to protect. Therefore the plan was scrapped, and the PRC embassy remained in its original location within the bustling embassy district.

The PRC government also purportedly sought to mitigate allegations of corruption against it by being much more selective about the development collaborations it undertook. For example, many in the Costa Rican business communities that I talked to read the PRC government's lack of new development initiatives in Costa Rica as a reflection of Beijing's frustration with Costa Rican corruption and bureaucracy. They pointed to projects like the Chinatown as having raised Beijing's ire over the graft taking place under cover of its projects. As the PRC government sought to rein in corruption within its own borders, it certainly could not tolerate abuse of its investments overseas.

Thomas, a businessman with extensive commercial relations with Chinese firms, elaborated this view in one of our interviews, explaining why new

PRC-sponsored infrastructure projects in Costa Rica had slowed. "Every time Costa Rican officials would sit down with Chinese [PRC] representatives to discuss a project," he said, "the Ticos would be looking for where to get a cut. The Chinese got tired of the Ticos looking for chorizo [sausage] at every turn."[35] As he relayed his critique, Thomas ran one forefinger over the other, simulating the act of slicing or shaving meat off a sausage, a colloquial gesture to signify trying to get a "cut" or some "pork" from the transaction. By his analysis, all Costa Rican projects tried to build in a certain amount of excess fat, which could be pocketed by Costa Rican collaborators as part of their piece of the pie (to mix metaphors). The trade-off, however, was that the need to build in this cut increased the total expense of any project, making it difficult both for the PRC representatives to swallow and for the Costa Rican legislature to approve. Therefore, widespread corruption on the part of Costa Rican state officials made the PRC government and its agents wary of collaborations because they would involve extensive negotiations over how to finance the projects in such a way as to enable sufficient kickback for these officials.

As these various cases suggest, tales about Chinese corruption were deployed even when the incidents they referred to did not reflect corruption in the sense of the misuse of public funds for private purposes. Instead they highlighted the cumulative effect of centuries of racialized stereotypes about Chinese culture, combined with various subsequent Taiwanese and Mainland agents and practices that together reified Chineseness as essentially defined by its dubious commercial, cultural, and political practices, designed ultimately to deceive and exploit opportunities. Therefore, the same "wily" and "pernicious" qualities attributed to nineteenth-century immigrants were projected onto the PRC state representatives, Taiwanese officials, and local diasporic businesses to justify local distrust of their motives and practices. Whether these efforts actually took the form of corruption per se varied, but the purportedly primordial tendency toward profit-seeking, monopolizing, exploitative behavior on the part of Chinese agents made all transpacific initiatives subject to allegations of corruption.

Anticorruption Arrangements in Central America

Central American critiques of the Chinese were not, however, the only way that corruption discourses were articulated in this current era of transpacific developments; Central American governments themselves were also the objects of similar critiques. In other words, many of my interlocutors viewed joint PRC–Central American projects as instances of corruption not only because of suspicions about Chinese intent, but also for the opportunities these initiatives afforded *local* politicians to line their own pockets. Therefore, their critiques of transpacific collaborations echoed scholarly concerns about both China and Latin America being defined by their norms of bribery, personal connections, and corruption. But rather than those norms being something that China "exported" to Central America, they lamented how contemporary relations exacerbated this already existing tendency within local government.

Take the Chinatown initiative in San José described in chapter 2. The enterprising San José mayor, Johnny Araya, negotiated that million-dollar collaboration with his counterpart in Beijing to include construction of a Tang Dynasty arch at the Chinatown entrance, as well as the import of traditional lampposts to be installed along the five-block pedestrian walkway. What had been a busy traffic artery and bus route would be transformed into a quaint aesthetic reproduction of millennial Chinese culture. Part of the construction work, therefore, included tearing up the asphalt and sidewalks in order to lay a cobblestone surface along the length of the main strip and installing decorative lighting accents along the way.

Both during and after the project construction, local residents read that landscape as a primer for lessons on corruption. First, three months past the district's inauguration celebration, residents pointed to the fact that the traditional lampposts were far fewer in number than was listed in the project budget, with some already removed. They read this deficiency as a sign that sufficient lamps had not been purchased with the funding provided and that even those that were installed were later taken down for resale and additional profit. Second, rumors that Mayor Araya's family owned a brick and cobblestone manufacturing company led many observers to speculate that the main goal of the massive renovation was simply to provide an expensive contract for Araya's family business.[36] When the district experienced massive sewage issues and traffic problems due to the dome-shaped speed bumps placed in each intersection, those critiques of the district's most basic functionality only heightened the sense of the project's having been driven by private profit-seeking interests rather than solid engineering sense or a concern for the public good.

Rather than assessing whether or not these allegations are true, or even how effective Central American anticorruption efforts have been, I suggest that we examine the new forms of governance and entrepreneurism that anticorruption has generated. To that end, in what follows I analyze three Central American contexts to pinpoint specific strategies that a diverse range of state and nonstate actors have mobilized in response to the question of corruption. I draw on anonymous accounts offered by politicians, activists, and businesspeople involved in these operations to highlight their generative impact and implications. Far from constraining the practices of individuals, businesses, and governments, these anticorruption efforts have produced political and economic responses that will indelibly shape the future of transpacific relations.

Guatemala

Given its history of armed conflict, genocide, and state-level impunity, Guatemala represents one extreme of the anticorruption movement, where the stakes for citizens appear especially high. With the resolution of the thirty-year armed conflict in 1996, Guatemalan state and civil society representatives reached out to the United Nations for help in combating the increasingly pervasive presence of criminal organizations and corruption throughout the country. The UN assembled and sponsored the International Commission against Impunity in Guatemala (CICIG) to function as an independent body to help investigate cases of organized crime and illicit processes that had "infiltrated the state." The commission's mandate allowed it "to carry out independent investigations, to act as a complementary prosecutor and to recommend public policies to help fight the criminal groups that are the subject of its investigations."[37] Between 2008 and 2019, the organization brought 120 cases to trial, in which 400 of the defendants were sentenced, a remarkable feat in a country where corruption and impunity have run rampant.[38] CICIG's success in bringing cases against high-level politicians involved in complex transnational corruption scandals has been especially remarkable. And while the PRC has not been involved in most of these scandals, its visibility in select cases illustrates how conceptions of Chineseness continue to fuel the image of corruption within transpacific relations.

Jaguar Energy's 2010 hiring of a Chinese company to construct an electric plant in Masagua, Guatemala, provides a case in point. Jaguar, a subsidiary of the US energy firm Ashmore Energy International Ltd., originally employed the Chinese Machine New Energy Corporation (CMNC) to take over construction of the plant and provide $200 million in financing. By 2012, however, major disagreements between the CMNC and Jaguar erupted over the terms of their contract. Originally, the Guatemalan government had approved the CMNC's petition to contract specialized (read imported Mainland Chinese) labor for periods of three months to two years until the plant was up and running and could employ Guatemalan labor. Over the following years, the CMNC apparently solicited as many as eight hundred visas for both professional and manual laborers to work on the project, and provided residence for those employees in an encampment on the periphery of the energy plant. However, according to one Jaguar employee I spoke with, Jaguar was moved to fire the PRC-based firm for failure to complete the plant construction on time and up to code, making the plant nonfunctional.[39] Jaguar replaced the CMNC with a North American firm to finish the job. The CMNC, however, wouldn't vacate the construction site, leading Guatemalan immigration officials to raid the plant and call for the passports of the Mainland Chinese employees. The CMNC was not able to produce these in the allotted time, so seventy-eight of the employees were taken to an immigration detention center in Guatemala City, where they were sequestered in inhumane conditions. When PRC government officials came from the embassy in Costa Rica to meet with their compatriots, Guatemalan officials impeded the visit, ostensibly at the request of Jaguar representatives.[40] In the meantime, CMNC representatives attempted to breach the plant premises to demand compensation. In response, Jaguar private security and Guatemalan National Police occupied the site and, in the ensuing violent clash with CMNC employees, left fifteen Chinese employees injured.[41]

CICIG's subsequent investigation of this case revealed that the problem extended far beyond the disagreement between Jaguar and the CMNC, to implicate the highest offices of the Guatemalan government in influence peddling and corruption. Indeed, while the labor and contract disagreement between the Chinese firm and Jaguar seemed at first to be the main site of impropriety, it was only the tip of an iceberg that included a ring of illicit relations, including the Guatemalan customs and taxes office. The Jaguar misdeeds thus became one of several pieces of evidence used in indictments against former vice president Roxana Baldetti Elías, former president Otto Pérez Molina, and twenty-eight accomplices who were charged with customs fraud, illicit association, and corruption as a result of their role in what became known as the "La Linea" scandal.[42] When news of the fraud broke, Guatemalan citizens came out into the streets in droves to demand the resignation and impeachment of Baldetti and Pérez Molina. The resulting "Basta Ya!" (Enough!) movement, composed of social-media-connected youth as well as other social actors, used these corruption scandals to manifest their hope for *una Guatemala distinta* (a different kind of Guatemala). The scandal thus reiterated the fact that corruption was part and parcel of Guatemalan government protocol, enriching officials who used these contracts to negotiate private benefits. The indictment of so many high-ranking Guatemalan officials made it clear that although Chinese firms weren't exporting corruption, they might be enabling local sources of it. Therefore, the work of independent, third-party investigators like CICIG, alongside widespread mobilization by civil society groups, proved crucial to breaking through the layers of cronyism and norms of graft that saturated Guatemalan politics and getting to the truth.

CICIG's success in challenging the well-entrenched norms of corruption in the highest branches of the Guatemalan government created overwhelming support for the body's work, with a 2019 poll showing that 72 percent of the Guatemalan population approved of CICIG's efforts.[43] What's more, during my fieldwork, I repeatedly saw the impact of its efforts firsthand as it restored citizens' faith in their ability to confront and dismantle corruption and also convinced elites of the need to preemptively shield themselves from allegations of corruption. For example, there were signs that companies with a long history of obtaining contracts to do infrastructure work, such as the road reconstruction I detail in chapter 4, were racing to find ways to mitigate appearances of corruption. Indeed, I heard several reports that one renowned local firm known for regularly acquiring road projects was actively seeking new philanthropic opportunities as a way of highlighting its altruistic impulses over its profit-seeking motives. Therefore, at least for a time, CICIG's success had begun to provoke a cultural shift in local ideas about corruption and impunity.

Of course, any entity that seeks to trouble such deeply held norms and systems of elite benefits and patronage runs the risk of falling prey to it. In 2019, President Jimmy Morales revoked the visa of CICIG director Iván Velásquez, barring him from returning to Guatemala and thus essentially shutting down CICIG's operations. Despite protests from both civil society and United Nations representatives, Morales terminated CICIG's commission before the organization's agreement came up for renewal.

In summary, Guatemalan citizens perceived the entire field of work on infrastructure, especially projects that included collaboration with Chinese, as sites of corruption. To root out the deeply entrenched, systemic roots of this problem, anticorruption efforts in Guatemala produced an international, independent commission—CICIG—to combat impunity. The efficacy of CICIG's work not only produced unheard-of indictments in terms of both the volume and the scope of those judgments, but also promulgated a sense of empowerment among citizens, suggesting that anticorruption work could enact real accountability and transformation in the local political landscape. CICIG's work brought down elites, but also pushed companies to demonstrate their morality in other ways so as to avoid suspicion. The overall impact of these efforts remains to be seen, given that they were not enough to keep Morales from banishing CICIG once it began to investigate corruption claims against him. Nonetheless, the Guatemalan story suggests that the combination of civil society mobilization and international intervention can produce results.

Costa Rica

In Costa Rica, a lack of armed civil conflict, a strong history of democratic process, and well-established institutions have meant that while corruption is acknowledged as a norm of governance, Costa Ricans have turned to domestic resources to address the problem. Despite increasing worries about impunity within the local press, scholars of Costa Rican politics have argued that acts of corruption that may have previously gone unnoticed (or at least unproven) are now increasingly exposed by more aggressive media and prosecuted by new and/or stronger state anticorruption agencies and laws.[44] Therefore, what has increased is not so much the incidence of corruption in Costa Rica as the visibility of these acts in the public imaginary. Rather than drawing on externally constituted third parties such as CICIG, the country has doubled down on its own democratic institutions to purge corruption and ensure transparency. Nonetheless, the association between transpacific exchanges and corruption remains a central focus of local corruption discourse.

Costa Rica's 2017 "Cementazo" ("Big Cement," or, as many called it, "Chinese Cement") scandal offers an important case in point. The controversy emerged as part of a media investigation that revealed collusion between a local building developer and a Costa Rican Central Bank deputy. The developer sought to import cement from Mainland China to undercut two multinational firms with a stranglehold on the local Costa Rican market, but irregularities surrounding his business loan from the Costa Rican National Bank generated concern.[45] The developer set up a company, Sinocem, to import the Chinese cement, but he apparently also pursued negotiations with congressional leaders to get permission to import the foreign brand, thus engaging in influence peddling and potentially customs fraud. The ensuing investigations by a legislative commission implicated former president Guillermo Solís, a Supreme Court judge, the attorney general, and members of Congress.[46] In response, the new attorney general proposed the creation of a special unit to train and employ prosecutors to fight corruption.[47] This effort sought to draw on the country's strong civil service class and court system to build its own prosecutorial force.

The Cementazo case was remarkable for several reasons. First, it again highlighted how relations with the PRC or its affiliates have tainted and exposed local cases of impunity. Like "Chinese Refinery scandal" before it, "Chinese Cement scandal" became a moniker for an act of local corruption that did not, in fact, involve wrongdoing by the Mainland Chinese, in this case the Chinese cement producers from which the Costa Rican developer was sourcing his imports. Nonetheless, it painted the PRC as the source of cheaper goods that were being brought in to undercut local markets and catalyzed conversations about the quality of Chinese cement. Even though the reason that Chinese cement imports were prohibited was strict regulations about cement expiration dates, the popular conversations about the scandal that ensued built on longstanding suspicions of the quality of Chinese goods as a reflection of the lack of regulation and quality control in the PRC. Therefore, while the scandal was really about irregularities in the loan the developer received and how local politicians had been recruited to enable the loan and/or change regulations about cement imports, the specter of Chinese cement eventually overwhelmed the case, reinforcing the stigma attached to Chinese products.

This high-profile case also demonstrated the generative nature of anticorruption efforts, suggesting how PRC-affiliated firms might adjust their business practices to avoid the taint of corruption. If we look back to the refinery scandal, for example, that incident taught PRC government-supported firms that their preference for nondisclosure agreements and project evaluation by their own subsidiary firms could not persist. Instead those scandals solidified the understanding that to avoid delays and imbroglios, Chinese firms would have to preemptively seek out independent third-party assessments on prospective projects. It is worth noting that when work on Route 32 began, the China Harbor Engineering Company immediately procured an independent feasibility study to avoid any allegations that the contract sought to favor particular outcomes. In this sense, there were signs that anticorruption efforts and regulations within Costa Rica were changing the way that the PRC-sponsored firms were doing business in the region.

The specter of corruption also influenced with whom PRC-based firms sought to do business. Several Central American business representatives I consulted with suggested that PRC state banks and investors were moving away from collaboration with public-sector agents in favor of seeking out private-sector partnerships for future projects. While this kind of public-private partnership had been identified by the PRC government in 2016 as one of its strategies for collaboration in the region, locals characterized this shift as a reflection of both local corruption and the instability of Central American political regimes, which could not be counted on the way that private business could to bring a project to expeditious and profitable completion.[48] Up until 2016, PRC policy banks had tended to negotiate contracts directly with local government representatives. However, locals claimed that the Chinese were growing tired of these state-to-state initiatives and were instead increasingly seeking out public-private or private-sector partnerships to more effectively advance their projects. By hiring a private management group, especially one with both local business savvy and ties to Mainland China, the banks could be assured of more efficient coordination of projects. This perception that Costa Rican corruption had been so bad as to stymie project opportunities, and thus drive Chinese banks to turn to private-sector expertise to make investments more efficient and reliable, was a telling indictment of local politics. The turn to public-private collaborations, therefore, seemed to represent an important shift in PRC–Central American development collaborations to date.

Local private businesses also embraced the profit potential of emergent public-private arrangements given that the large infrastructure projects pursued by the PRC-sponsored firms offered the possibility of annuities. As one local entrepreneur told me, "Once the original loan amount gets paid back, the Chinese [the PRC] pull out, leaving the private side with amazing annuity that the government can't touch. These projects are jackpots." According to this individual, it behooved the PRC policy banks to invest in a $700 million public-private partnership on a road project, as the PRC government "could fly the Belt and Road flag on it." Private partners, he added, also had another incentive to participate, as the use of tolls would allow the construction loan to be paid off in twelve years, with remaining annuities producing profit.[49]

To reiterate, these views on the direction of Chinese business in Costa Rica reflect local perceptions of and lore about corruption within the business community, rather than substantiated claims. However, they offer provocative indicators of the way that people on the ground are thinking about the PRC's economic activity in Central America and the impact of anticorruption efforts on these processes. In particular, they highlight efforts by both Chinese and Costa Rican representatives to enact new business and governance practices to avoid allegations of corruption. These shifts promised important new patterns of Chinese development collaboration in the region that sought to enhance project efficiency and investment returns, even as they raise the question of how enhanced oversight of corruption in the public sector will be able to deal with increasing Chinese presence in the private sector.

Nicaragua

In Nicaragua, corruption has served as a central frame not only for criticisms of the Sandinista regime in general—in 2020, Transparency International's Corruption Index ranked Nicaragua number 159 on a list of 180 countries—but also for characterizing the canal project and its aftermath, in particular.[50] In chapter 4, I outlined how Nicaraguan president Daniel Ortega's negotiation of the massive canal concession with Wang Jing had been condemned by activists for the way the secretive deal favored Ortega's personal and political profits at the expense of the nation's sovereignty and the status of environmental and citizen rights within it. Nicaraguan citizens especially worried about how the canal concession might be misused for illicit speculation, thus intensifying the impunity with which third parties could exploit local resources at the country's and its citizens' expense. As in other cases explored in this chapter, despite the lack of official PRC participation in or even endorsement of the project, "China" figured prominently in local condemnations of the project's ethics.

As you will recall, the canal authorized the development of the 173-mile canal zone territory, even in the absence of the realization of the canal itself. It also ceded control of the zone for fifty to one hundred years, and waived all potential indemnity related to environmental impacts.[51] As the activist Mónica López Baltodano noted, these conditions amounted to the "surrender of the nation's sovereignty to a private company."[52] By her account, this abdication of sovereignty could open the door to the establishment of enterprises accountable to neither the state nor the Nicaraguan people, thus exacerbating the probability of corruption and illicit speculation across a major swath of national territory. Therefore, residents of the zone facing property expropriation, environmentalists interested in preserving Central America's largest freshwater lake (Lake Nicaragua), and communities facing dramatic transformation of their landscape to accommodate the forecast airports, free trade zones, and intraregional transport systems feared that this initiative not only was born of corruption but would serve as a platform for reproducing and even proliferating it.

Given that the canal concession was negotiated with a Hong Kong–based private entrepreneur, what role did the politics of China and Chineseness play in this story of corruption? Many Nicaraguans that I spoke to painted the Chinese more as enablers of the problematic concession than as protagonists per se. Nonetheless, activists feared that the enormous scope of the canal concession might distract people from the installation of smaller Chinese extractive projects in the zone, opening the door to new mining or petroleum ventures that would normally be met with stiff public opposition. Furthermore, the fact that there was so little clarity on the terms of the agreement or even the nature of the Chinese firm, HKND, made fighting the concession quite difficult legally and politically. The lack of transparency about and accountability for the concession's developments, therefore, looked and felt a lot like the practice associated with PRC-sponsored projects elsewhere in the region and stoked fears of dubious Chinese intentions.

Whereas in Guatemala and Costa Rica, the governments have sought to mitigate allegations of corruption, through suprastate or state-level initiatives, in Nicaragua, President Daniel Ortega has gone the other way and embraced even tighter, more brutal authoritarian tactics against the Nicaraguan people. Rather than fighting corruption, he has sought to shut down its critics and, in the process, inflicted state violence and massive displacement that have provoked international anticorruption efforts against his regime. While I examined the infrastructural dimensions of the canal earlier, here let me return to their relationship to corruption in particular.

Although critics have maligned Ortega for the canal concession from the beginning, not all Nicaraguans were against the initiative at the outset. Nonetheless when Ortega's forces lashed out against protesters in April 2018, that act brought to the fore questions about the legitimacy of the Sandinista regime, how it was doing business on behalf of the nation, and how it was waging a politics against its own people. Ortega responded to this public opposition by attempting to suppress and criminalize dissent through the persecution of protesters and the use of extrajudicial violence that left over three hundred dead and two thousand injured.[53] By July 2018, these efforts included Ortega's expansion of antiterror laws so as to legitimize his incarceration and punishment of political opponents.[54] By arguing that protesters reflected the interests of organized crime and terrorism, he was, in effect, subverting their claims to embody legitimate dissent and repositioning them as corrupting influences within the system. Indeed, Nicaraguan nongovernmental organizations providing legal counsel to detainees reported that 477 people were prosecuted in connection with the protests. Among these were 136 people accused of terrorism-related offenses.[55]

On the international front, critics decried both the violence and the corruption of Ortega's government and, through anticorruption efforts, sought to isolate Nicaragua as a pariah state. Specifically, in June of 2018, the United States meted out sanctions against Nicaragua, freezing Ortega family accounts and prohibiting the Ortegas' travel to the United States. Treasury Secretary Steven Mnuchin declared, "This [i.e., the Trump] administration is committed to holding the Ortega regime accountable for the violent protests and widespread corruption that have led to the deaths of hundreds of innocent Nicaraguans and destroyed their economy."[56] On the one hand, these international efforts answered calls to address the violent repression that Nicaraguan activists were facing at home, thus demonstrating again the powerful nexus between the global anticorruption regime and civil society protests. In this sense, the international sanctions represented an effort to delegitimize Ortega internationally so as to provoke good governance and transparency at home. On the other hand, US sanctions can also be read as an instrumental effort on the part of the United States to thwart further Chinese incursion into the region and, especially, the construction of a second canal. Regardless of their true intentions, to date, none of these efforts seem to have had the desired effect of pushing Ortega toward early elections and thus ending the deadlock.

On the domestic front, however, anticorruption efforts have fortified new forms of activism that will ultimately be crucial not only to unseating Ortega and enabling substantive regime change, but also to mobilizing against the kind of illicit business practices potentially enabled by the canal concession. In response to these threats and the added insult of Ortega's attacks against civil society, activists like Mónica López Baltodano have fought to restore the rule of law through the mobilization of a cross-sectoral political constituency of activists that encompasses peasants, students, workers, and urban residents of all kinds. Not relying on a single strategy, they have appealed to local courts, international judicial bodies, international solidarity groups, and Nicaraguan citizens to denounce Ortega's corruption and violence. In doing so, they have begun to seed a strong grassroots counterforce to state corruption that is also developing significant international solidarity connections. Indeed, López Baltodano framed this movement as a revindication of the rural, campesino identity as a counterpoint to corrupt, urban modern national identity, as well as a transcendental political force through which Nicaraguans in general might mobilize against a variety of exploitative forces, including extractive industries, oil concessions, and Ortega's dictatorship.[57]

To summarize, in Nicaragua the canal concession dramatically escalated the stakes of Ortega's cronyism and corruption, bringing a huge swath of the national territory under private, unregulated, and long-term control. Although Chinese agents (here in the form of the private Hong Kong entrepreneur at the outset and then as unidentified Chinese agents on the ground) were implicated in the concession, the secrecy and expediency with which canal negotiations had been pursued cannot be read as simply a reflection of PRC business practices, but rather centrally implicate Ortega and his Sandinista regime. Nonetheless, Chinese involvement and the audacity of the project's territorial aspirations and financial cost made the project ripe for allegations of corruption in the extreme. In response to those allegations, Ortega sought to quash dissent rather than challenge the critiques of civil society and international actors. In doing so, however, he helped to catalyze the ire of the international anticorruption regime, as well as a new social movement that, ultimately, hopes to undo not only the concession but the very dictator who signed it into existence.

Looking to the future, the presence and conflation of multiple forms of China and Chineseness in Central America—encompassing Orientalist stereotypes about "wily and pernicious" Chinese migrants in the nineteenth century, swindling Taiwanese state officials and exploitative Taiwanese factory owners, and the ambiguous agents and practices of Mainland Chinese firms—suggest that no matter what practices PRC-affiliated firms utilize (i.e., whether they recruit independent third-party feasibility studies or work with the private sector more than the public sector), Chinese initiatives will continue to be read with a particular skepticism born of centuries of stereotypes of Chinese otherness. Central American responses to them will have to navigate the complex terrain of grassroots, state, and international interests and authorities to assert control over the direction of national development. This raises the question of whether the new era of transpacific relations will incite policies and practices that can transcend the taint of corruption, or whether that dynamic will continue to serve as the essential infrastructure on which the regions' multiple actors and interests collaboratively build.

LOCATING DEVELOPMENT FUTURES

At the end of the twentieth century, critical development theorists argued that development was a concept that should be laid to rest. By extending Western modernity and its attendant miseries and inequalities on a global scale, it had done more harm than good. These critics looked to Eastern philosophy or to the margins of global capital for other sources of inspiration to reenvision and restructure our world.[1] Not all actors in the Global South, however, were anxious to give up the promise of development. Despite its potentially ruinous effects, many clamored for a chance to access the credit, the infrastructure, the industry, the trade connections, and the consumption possibilities savored by those who had gone before them. Therefore, the political and economic ascendance of actors from the Global South and their collaboration in institutions that might supersede the Western establishments that have defined global development goals, tactics, and terms since the end of World War II seemed to augur the prospect of a refigured global landscape.

It is no wonder, then, that the PRC's emergence as both a development success story and an increasingly powerful donor has created significant debate about the shape of the future of development. Because China has embraced global capitalism with a fervor equal to that of its Western counterparts, its "rise" has certainly not suggested the end of capitalist development. Indeed, if anything, the PRC's success at restructuring global production chains and capturing global markets has simply shifted our sense of the possible means to that end. The PRC's promotion of centralized planning, state-owned enterprises, and state finance seems to point to qualitative differences in how to pursue poverty reduction and economic growth. Its one-party political system, rejection of democratic reform, and insistence on a policy of noninterference in its partners' domestic affairs suggest shifts in the liberal principles on which Western-dominated development was founded. Therefore, the contemporary context bodes important challenges to the status quo, even as it promotes certain continuities with it.

Western pundits have tended to respond to this shifting landscape by positing a new standoff between superpowers with competing development models—one good, one bad—thus interpreting the PRC's significance through a familiar zero-sum frame. During Secretary of State Mike Pompeo's April 2019 tour of Latin America, for example, he issued an ominous warning to the governments of the region about the danger of China relative to the United States: "China, Russia, they're showing up at the doorstep, but once they enter the house, we know they will use debt traps, they will disregard rules, and they will spread disorder in your home. . . . On this continent, the United States is showing up as never before, reminding our friends of how much we have in common, of how much our interests align, and how much we love you."[2]

Not one to skirt hyperbole, Pompeo left no doubt about the spatial and affective assumptions that have structured the United States' hegemony over Latin America. Through intimate terms like "home," "friends," "love"—the idea of "our backyard" is notable here for its absence—he paints the contours of a new era of geopolitics in which the cozy domestic relations between regional neighbors have come under threat by a dangerous new kid on the block.[3] Suffice it to say, most Latin Americans would not recognize the shifting regional politics in those terms.[4]

Therefore, to read the global development landscape and China's place within it in this mutually exclusive way misses the point. For one, this reductivist framing compresses the multiple forms of China and Chineseness that shape the nature and stakes of Chinese development both in Central America and more broadly. Furthermore, it also erases the durability and even fertility of development as a potent imaginary and field of action. More than just a scoreboard for tallying hegemony, for many people around the world development continues to serve as a crucial organizing principle for defining who we are and what kind of a world we want to live in. Development gives shape to our aspirations for a good life and also lays bare the vast inequalities that preclude them. And so, instead of asking whether China is transforming the world, we should ponder what new worlds are being conjured through the shifting infrastructure of global development.

The Infrastructure of Emergent Worlds

This book opened with a portrait of Chinese development under construction in the Costa Rican national stadium. That portrait draws our attention not only to the multiple Chinas present on the local landscape—the local Chinese diaspora, Taiwan, and the PRC—but also to the multivalent nature of infrastructure as an index of development. By invoking ideas of a "First-World stadium," or a "Costa Rican Nest," local narratives affirmed that the stadium represented more than just a gift from benevolent Chinese donors; it also showcased the tensions and aspirations of current development relations and future possibilities. It simultaneously marked the arrival of modernity and the promise of global visibility, as well as signaled the possibility of increasing dependency on and vulnerability to China. What other possibilities might it portend?

In assessing those possibilities, Costa Ricans, like their Central American counterparts more broadly, were drawing on a legacy of infrastructure building in the Americas that reflected their position and aspirations within shifting global power relations. Remember, for instance, the nineteenth-century railways built by Minor Keith to expand the United Fruit Company's export enclave and regional monopoly. As they laid the tracks for national development, those rail lines both institutionalized and symbolized Central America's status as a region of exploited banana republics relative to a hegemonic United States. They also affirmed how racial hierarchies were built into processes of nation building and forms of regional modernity through the use of Chinese and Afro-descendant construction workers.

If infrastructure has the power to materialize inequality, however, it also proposes the scaffolding on which to build new futures. The Nicaraguan historian Frances Kinloch describes nineteenth-century early modernizers' desire to build an interoceanic canal through Nicaragua as "a symbol of progress and the dream of [becoming] a 'cosmopolitan nation.'"[5] Jacobo Arbenz Guzmán's road-building efforts in Guatemala in 1951 similarly aspired to construct new routes to regional autonomy and economic self-determination. In these cases, infrastructure offered a means of conjuring ideas about the future and one's place in alternative global imaginaries.

At our particular historical juncture, the PRC government has increasingly appeared to function as both architect and general contractor for the infrastructure of the development landscape, determining where and how the center of global activity will be located and how others might be connected to it. Nonetheless, what exactly the infrastructure of transpacific developments is constructing is far from clear.

Take, for example, the most ambitious of the PRC's global projects, the Belt and Road Initiative. Rather than reading this initiative as a blueprint for Beijing's global aspirations, a focus on multiple Chinas points us in different directions. The geographers Thomas Narins and John Agnew have highlighted the irony that no one official BRI map authorized by Beijing exists; they interpret this "useful fuzziness" as helping China navigate questions of sovereignty.[6] If we think of this cartographic fuzziness from the perspective of transpacific relations, we can also see how the diverse possibilities of directionality, points of connection, types of infrastructure, and ownership arrangements suggested by multiple maps have made the BRI attractive and relevant to Central American actors a long way from the original silk road that inspired it. Indeed, it is the project's very open-endedness that has permitted Central Americans to imagine an attractive place for themselves within it.[7] In this sense, rather than simply fitting itself into an already established grid of international relations, the BRI allows for proliferating maps that, as Anna Lowenhaupt Tsing puts it, "make us imagine globality in order to see how it might succeed."[8] And for some of the Central Americans I've described in this book, the visions of the global that result may very well exceed the terms of their construction, at least as far as they concern China.

Therefore, while it may be tempting to assess Chinese development in Central America as a proxy war between US and Chinese global hegemony, a transpacific analytic suggests that we ask, rather than assume, what these projects show us about the future worlds they are underwriting. In the narratives I've presented here, we see Central Americans building on Chinese infrastructure projects to reenvision the region's peripheral location, refiguring it as a global intersection for exchange and circulation. Their visions look to the promise of canals, ports, and high-speed railways to restructure east-west and north-south axes of connection in a way that promises new visibility and value. In this sense, they imagine a map in which transpacific relations are centered and Central America is central. These readings of infrastructure are not naive about the power relations that structure them; indeed, throughout the narratives we see as much skepticism about Chinese interests as we do enthusiasm for their potential material outcomes. Even when the capital and labor come from the PRC, they do not necessarily produce greater appreciation for China or Chineseness. As a result, there is no guarantee that all development roads lead to Beijing. Instead, locals perceive the prospective infrastructure possibilities as enabling greater transpacific connections not only with the PRC but with other economic partners, such as Taiwan, Korea, and Hong Kong. Far from locking them into dominion under a hegemonic Beijing, infrastructure offers the promise of a refigured global landscape defined by connections to multiple Chinas and forms of Chineseness.

Here we might recall my Costa Rican friend Ricardo and his read on the San José Chinatown. Ricardo's own history of ongoing circulation between Macao, Canada, Shanghai, and Costa Rica informed his proposal for an alternative Chinatown that would reflect the modern aesthetic of a cosmopolitan Shanghai or an upscale, suburban Los Angeles–style mall. Rather than a testament to some millennial, essential Chinese culture or a history of Chinese diasporic ghettoization in the Americas, he envisioned the Chinatown as a space that would bring together various forms of Chineseness and modernity forged through transpacific exchanges. For him, this urban district would index not only shifting future worlds oriented toward the Pacific, but also the potential centrality that Central America and brokers like himself might acquire with them. And while these worlds might not be as attractive to working-class Central Americans who could not afford this type of cosmopolitan luxury, Ricardo's vision cues us to the different assemblages of race, place, and identity that are reflected in and enabled by development infrastructure and the future worlds they bring into view.

Rescaling Sovereignty

And yet, the worlds being conjured through transpacific exchanges are not only about expansiveness and possibility; they also highlight the centrality of sovereignty as a concept that structures and differentiates people and places within the global development landscape. My transpacific analytic highlights how sovereignty remains a crucial concept for distinguishing among the multiple Chinas and evaluating their impact. It also serves as the terrain on which rescaled ideas of future worlds are emerging.

Within the development landscape, sovereignty has been an important principle deployed by both Taiwan and the PRC to distinguish their identities and policies. The PRC has promoted its One China policy specifically to reinforce its national sovereignty and to diminish Taiwan's claims to representing an autonomous state entity within the international system. What is more, it has promoted the idea of sovereignty and noninterference in partner nations' domestic politics as a fundamental philosophy undergirding its development policies. This stance seeks to distinguish the PRC from actors like the United States that have a long history of tying aid and finance to requirements for particular political and economic outcomes within recipient nations. Taiwan, meanwhile, has clamored to protect its sovereignty and affirm its legitimacy as an autonomous political entity through its development partnerships with countries in Central America and beyond. As we saw in the case of the road-building project Taiwan sponsored in Guatemala, Taiwan has also framed its development investments as explicitly promoting greater sovereignty in recipient nations. Therefore, the relationship between development and sovereignty figures centrally in the politics of these multiple Chinas, seeking to position each as a legitimate but also distinctive international actor.

A long history of movement and exchange through Central America has also contributed to defining both the meaning of Chineseness there and efforts by states to establish sovereignty through it. Think here of Chinese diaspora who came to the Americas to help construct the incipient nations or of Taiwanese manufacture tycoons who sought visas to move to Central America so as to eventually access the United States. Their histories highlight how people evade and move through sovereign borders, building on translocal connections that transcend national boundaries and affiliations. In doing so, these actors' circulation across the Pacific and the Americas engendered and reproduced distinct forms of Chineseness. The xenophobic policies and legal restrictions enacted by Central American states to regulate, end, or even stimulate that movement defined local formulations of national identity and sovereignty in opposition to Chineseness. As such, they accentuate the importance of sovereignty even as they demonstrate the different scales of action in which it is constituted and challenged. When we look to the future worlds emerging from contemporary transpacific relations, then, we have to ask how the question of sovereignty is being rescaled.

Costa Rica offers us an example of how sovereignty might be rescaled within this development landscape. There, debates about projects like the petroleum refinery or highway collaborations with the PRC government are not simply about China's global strength or checks on it, or even about Costa Rica's relative dependency or autonomy. Instead they project Costa Rica's dream of becoming a green nation, a goal that has been reinforced by and given new form through its experience with China. Despite the fact that Costa Rica is a small country of only four million and still ranks as a developing country, experiences like the refinery renovation have inspired its efforts to conjure a green world in which Costa Rica figures as a global leader. As evidence of that move, Costa Rica has pledged to make the country carbon neutral by 2021, an ambitious effort that would place it far ahead of wealthier and larger nations. Former president Guillermo Solís identified this goal as part of the "constitutional right of the people to enjoy a clean environment."[9] Even though this dream holds on to the idea of national space and constitutional rights as a crucial starting place for action, it conjures a future in which global and national climate concerns are one, in which local ecologies and global landscapes are seen as intertwined. Furthermore, it imagines a world in which Costa Rica is not simply responsive to the conditions or actions of global powers like China—that is, acting as a banana republic at the mercy of foreign actors—but rather a protagonist in shaping the terms of its own development. These projects thus induce debates about what kinds of trade-offs citizens are willing to make to achieve the future worlds that transpacific developments help them to imagine. What role Chinese development might play in constructing this future is still to be determined; however, by questioning, rather than just assuming, the scale and impact of development projects, we can see how they might be building something other than just Chinese hegemony.[10]

Recent challenges have underscored the vulnerabilities that come with living in a highly globalized world. Plummeting global energy markets and the devastating effects of climate change showcase the limits of national efforts to control phenomena that circulate freely, even if unevenly, across multiple levels of social and political life. Nations cannot buffer themselves from warming sea temperatures, increasingly devastating hurricane seasons, or air pollution. Global public health threats like the coronavirus pandemic have driven this point home even more forcefully. While individual states have tried to shield themselves from the ravages of highly mobile viruses, we've seen that shutting down borders cannot ensure control over a nation's health. In this context, sovereignty has functioned as much as a mandate of local government as the property of the state, sometimes even putting the two at odds. Therefore, protecting national interests has required working in concert with actors operating at different scales of action, within and across borders, who nonetheless imagine themselves as enjoined in a common project that may or may not correspond to the nation.

These reflections thus ask us to consider which values and forms of political community should shape emergent worlds and how they can be territorialized in a way that is not dependent on the sovereignty debates of the past. They push us to recognize solidarities that crisscross and transcend the nation and to develop tools of engagement that do not necessarily rely solely on constitutional politics. In Nicaragua, for example, opposition to the proposed canal and the corrupt politics it represented brought into being dreams of a cross-sectoral, coalitional, new social force, led by peasants. Like the Zapatista movement in Chiapas, Mexico, and its mantra "Another world is possible," these social formations both reflect and bring to life new imaginaries for human existence built on translocal connections, forming different and sometimes unexpected alliances. Furthermore, they seek to build new institutions and forms of interrelation to materialize their vision. Rather than assuming we already know who the good guys and bad guys are in processes of social change, redefining questions of sovereignty can realign the kinds of social solidarities that we mobilize to claim rights and future possibilities.

Identifying Racialized Exceptions

As my analysis of transpacific developments has made clear, the world conjuring enabled by development remains situated within deeply unequal relations, defined and reproduced in large part through the prism of identity and race. Even when the PRC might be read as a rising political economic power, the specter of race allows it to be quarantined within an Orientalist worldview that alternately marginalizes China and centers it as the source of global strife, but always positions it as exception and Other. A transpacific analytic thus highlights how the future worlds being conjured build on and reconstitute particular assemblages of race, identity, place, and development that have been formative to Western modernity.

The Central American development projects I've explored illustrate how hemispheric Orientalisms forged in the nineteenth century have served as the frame through which contemporary worlds are being conjured and interpreted. Central American ideas of Chineseness gleaned from a history of hemispheric transmigration, formulations of race, and exclusionary legal systems have worked together to shape local understandings of the nature and motivations of a wide range of Chinese actors, not limited to the PRC government. They have sustained stereotypes about Chinese inscrutability, industriousness, exploitative tendencies, and difference that inflect contemporary efforts to establish commercial relations with individual Chinese firms across the Pacific, to interpret the motivations of PRC government projects, and to decide who is qualified to broker relations with Chinese officials.

We can see traces of this dynamic in Guatemalan narratives about doing business with China. On the one hand, attendees at the 2018 expo extolled the cultural virtues of millennial China, admiring its exotic textiles, calligraphy, and architecture. They also valued the technological innovation of Chinese high-speed trains, solar panels, and cars, and their inexpensive price tags. This appreciation for Chinese cultural and economic production, however, was coupled with a strong sense of suspicion and lack of trust of the quality of Chinese goods and the potentially dubious intentions of PRC-based firms. What's more, it did not promote a desire for political rapprochement with the PRC. Instead, in the realm of economics and politics, Orientalist renderings of the potential Chinese threat served to mitigate Beijing's hopes of extending its reach in the regional market. Critiques of Chinese politics and potentially insidious business practices reinscribed the PRC as a radically different development partner that must be approached with caution rather than celebration. Even for those entrepreneurs who sought out Chinese economic connections through visits to the Canton Fair, distrust of Chinese enterprise at all levels—the legitimacy of the firm, the quality of the products, and the solidity of the contract—required the use of local guides who claimed to know the Chinese cultural and business landscape and could thus ensure the integrity of their transactions.

These racialized formulations also reflect how transpacific exchanges are situated within global development hierarchies. You may recall how, for instance, when describing Chinese development, several of my Costa Rican interlocutors complained about the PRC conflating Costa Rica and Africa as similarly underdeveloped spaces. They said Taiwan, on the other hand, knew that Costa Rica was different from Africa. Implicit in those statements was not simply a critique of the PRC but also an indication of the ongoing racialization of global development relations more broadly. Remember that Costa Rica had quarantined black Afro-descendant and Asian migrants on its Caribbean coast well into the twentieth century so as to avoid the contamination of its white national identity by these racial Others. In their current objections to being "lumped in" with Africa, a place they identified as being farthest from the kind of Western modernity to which they aspired and which they felt they embodied, my Central American interlocutors were rehearsing historical assemblages of race, identity, place, and development. Within them, Costa Rica was positioned as representing Western whiteness in a way that merited appreciation for both its cosmopolitanism and its regional exceptionalism. Africa, on the other hand, figured at the bottom of the pyramid, representing quintessential ideas of underdevelopment. China and Chineseness took on variable meanings, embodying both wealthy development donor and Third-World labor. Taiwan's association with democratic, capitalist principles mitigated its difference and allowed for some degree of affinity; however, even the PRC's bigger checkbook could not completely erase its negative associations with otherness.

These examples highlight how hemispheric Orientalisms and the larger racial formations of which they are a part continue to shape present and future development worlds. The PRC's economic prowess and growing political influence are revered for the kinds of development possibilities they can offer, but the PRC is still not trusted in Central America as "one of us." As I've argued here, that is not because Central Americans are unfamiliar with China or Chineseness, which have been formative in regional nation building and forms of modernity. Instead, just as the multiple Chinas operating here have shaped contemporary expectations for what Chinese development should mean and accomplish, race continues to form a crucial lens through which transpacific developments are perceived, assessed, and negotiated. In part, this means that Western fears about a Chinese invasion of Latin America or even of a new era of Chinese global hegemony must be tempered by an acknowledgment of how race continues to structure and legitimate certain actors and practices within the global landscape. It also means that we must begin to look to different kinds of circulations, exchanges, identities, and forms of Chineseness not delimited by Beijing to understand the contours and politics of the future worlds conjured by transpacific developments.

Notes

INTRODUCTION

1. By the development industry, I mean academics, state policy practitioners, and international financial institutions. See Escobar 1995 for a discussion of the growth of this industry after 1949.

2. The World Bank Poverty and Equity Data Portal estimates that the amount of Chinese citizens earning below the international poverty rate of $1.90 per day had dropped to 0.7 percent of the population by 2015.

3. Gallagher, Irwin, and Koleski 2012; Gallagher and Myers 2019.

4. Gallagher and Myers 2019.

5. Ramo 2004.

6. See Ferchen 2013 on convergences between the China Model and the Washington Consensus.

7. See for example, John Mearsheimer's (2006, 2019) argument about the impossibility of China's "peaceful rise" and his theory that China's increasing efforts to establish hegemony will provoke increasing competition and conflict on the global stage.

8. See for example, Jenkins 2019 on the impact of Chinese development policies in Africa and Latin America. Indeed, while China did give preferential lending to countries like Venezuela and Bolivia, with self-proclaimed leftist leaders, it also pursued economic relations with Brazil and Argentina, as well as strategic trade partnerships with Costa Rica, Peru, and Chile.

9. The combination of China's state banks and its participation in the AIIB and the BRICS bank makes its global lending potential even more formidable.

10. Gallagher and Myers 2021.

11. Gallagher, Irwin, and Koleski 2012.

12. Since the 1949 defeat and exile of the Chinese Nationalist government, there have been two political entities that have claimed the title of China—the socialist People's Republic of China (PRC) in Mainland China and the democratic Republic of China in Taiwan. The One China policy stipulates that the PRC represents the sole Chinese sovereign state, thus barring other countries from maintaining official diplomatic relations with Taiwan. The "One Country, Two Systems" policy refers to the PRC's constitutional designation of Hong Kong and Macao as "Special Administrative Districts," which allows them local forms of government, economic relations, and legal systems, even as Beijing maintains control over their foreign affairs. This status was negotiated for these territories as part of their reunification with Mainland China in 1997 and 1999, respectively, and is currently being tested by Beijing's 2020 passage of a security law that enables the PRC to enforce antisedition and extradition policies in Hong Kong, thus placing in question Hong Kong's political autonomy. For more on the PRC government's outreach to diasporic communities, see Thunø 2002.

13. This critical view of public policy and recommendations for "studying through" policy are articulated by Wedel et al. 2005.

14. See for example Huntington 1996 on the clash of civilizations and, even earlier, Weber 1968 on the Protestant ethic in the West and Confucianism in China.

15. I elaborate on my usage of the term "assemblage" in chapter 1. Here, let me note that I am building off of critical geography and anthropological formulations that have themselves built on the work of DeLanda 2006 and Deleuze and Guattari 1981.

16. See for example Cumings 2009, 427–29; Dirlik 1998, 8–9; and McCord 1993.

17. Matsuda 2012, 5.

18. Lin and Yeoh 2014, 53–54.

19. Xiang 2014, 102.

20. See Lee 2005 and Chang 2019 on hemispheric and comparative Orientalisms in the Americas. Traditional area studies has historically been a powerful way of producing knowledge about specific regions, insisting on close linguistic competence, a specific disciplinary lens, and a holistic interdisciplinary understanding to "know" a place. See Sakai 2019, Walker 2019, and Walker and Sakai 2019 for analyses of what area studies presumes and how it divides and separates.

21. Efforts to do so have helped to reconsider transpacific pasts, including Chinese-Mexican relations in the late twentieth century and generations of Cantonese remigrations throughout Asia and the Americas. For China-Mexico, see González 2017; for Cantonese Pacific, see Yu 2018; and for transpacific futures, see Anderson, Johnson, and Brookes 2018.

22. This quote is attributed to the famous anthropologist Alfred Kroeber and then later again to the anthropologist Eric Wolf from his 1964 text, *Anthropology*.

1. TRANSPACIFIC ASSEMBLAGES

1. On newness, see, for example, Armony and Strauss 2012, 1.

2. Boelhower 2008, 86. For more on transatlantic studies, also see Boelhower 2019.

3. Hoskins and Nguyen 2014, 4.

4. Anthropologists and geographers have variously drawn on the work of Bruno Latour 1993, as well as Michel Foucault and Deleuze and Guattari 1981 to articulate different definitions of assemblages. See, for example, Ong and Collier's (2004) formulation of "global assemblages," or Escobar's (2008) idea of *redes* as assemblage. For critical geography, see McFarlane 2011; and Dittmer 2013.

5. McFarlane and Anderson 2011, 125; Anderson and McFarlane 2011, 162.

6. Deleuze and Guattari 1981, 272.

7. Anderson and McFarlane 2011, 163; McFarlane and Anderson 2011, 125.

8. I return to this question of scale and the construction of new worlds through transpacific developments in the conclusion.

9. See Slack 2010 and Hu-DeHart 1995 for more on these early forms of transpacific encounter and exchange.

10. An example of this phenomenon was the 2008 scandal surrounding contaminated milk and baby formula produced in China. The poisonous melamine added to Chinese milk supplies to boost protein levels caused the death of six infants and created lasting distrust of Chinese food suppliers, despite the application of severe penalties for the milk producers and heightened regulation of the industry (Bloomberg News 2019).

11. See Avendaño and Dayton-Johnson 2015; and Dussel Peters 2018.

12. People's Republic of China 2008.

13. People's Republic of China 2016.

14. See Wise 2020 for more on the impact of these strategic trade partnerships.

15. Xinuanet English News 2019.

16. Chinese Ministry of Foreign Affairs, Department of Latin America and Caribbean Affairs 2016.

17. Ellis 2018a. See also Ferchen 2011 for an analysis of the boom-or-bust issue in relation to the region's commodity boom.

18. Again, see Avendaño and Dayton-Johnson 2015.

19. Oftentimes the list of Central American countries is limited to Spanish-speaking countries, which excludes Belize, a former British colony.

20. World Bank 2021.

21. Avendaño and Dayton-Johnson 2015; Dussel Peters 2018.

22. See Ray et al. 2017, as well as Garzon 2017. See also Casey and Krauss 2018.

23. See especially Ray et al. 2017 for a more thorough analysis of the environmental impact of Chinese development in Latin America. However, more recent analyses, such as Jenkins 2019 have challenged some of that negative reputation through a more comprehensive study of the economic impacts of Chinese development efforts in Africa and Latin America.

24. I provide a much more comprehensive and in-depth look at elements of this history in subsequent chapters.

25. Torres Rivas 1993, 33–34.

26. Torres Rivas 1993, 34–39; Colby 2013, 14.

27. Dosal 1995, 38.

28. See Schlesinger and Kinzer 1983, 106.

29. See Smith and Adams 2011, 2–3.

30. For an excellent history of the canal and its infrastructural and environmental implications, see Carse 2014.

31. See, for example, Ellis 2018b.

32. See Grandin 2004, 188–90; and LaFeber 1984, 311. For more on US support for authoritarian regimes in the region, see LaFeber 1984; Joseph, LeGrand, and Salvatore 1998; and Rosenberg and Solis 2007. The list of other Cold War "friendly dictators" supported by the US includes Roberto Suazo Córdova in Honduras, General Manuel Noriega in Panama, Rafael Trujillo in the Dominican Republic, and Augusto Pinochet in Chile, to name just a few examples.

33. Aguilera Peralta 2010.

34. DeHart 2010, 9–10.

35. For more on US Cold War development strategies in Central America, see Grandin 2004.

36. For critical analysis of this shift in development, see Cooper and Packard 1997; and Escobar 1995.

2. CHINESE DIASPORIC COMMUNITIES

1. Song 2013, 2.

2. Some of the ethnographic work presented in this chapter has appeared earlier in DeHart 2015. In that piece, I examine the Chinatown project more for what it tells us about global city-building projects and the role of ethnic Chinatown spaces within them.

3. Araya Monge 2012.

4. See DeHart 2015 for more on how this project engaged and reflected global city-building strategies and sought to use the ethnic Chinatown space as an opportunity for global tourist consumption opportunities.

5. See Hearn 2013 and Lausent-Herrera 2011 for more on Latin American Chinatowns. See also Lin 1998; Ling 2012; and Shah 2001 for more general conversations about Chinatown formations and the processes of discrimination and ethnic solidarity that forged them.

6. Personal interview, San José, Costa Rica, August 1, 2012.

7. Araya Monge 2012.

8. Levitt 2012.

9. Obregón Valverde 2012.

10. The Paseo de los Estudiantes (the Students' Walk) is an iconic space of Costa Rican national identity because this two-block stretch of Ninth Street was the site of a 1919 uprising against the dictator Federico Tinoco staged by students from the prestigious nearby high school, Liceo de Costa Rica.

11. See Loría Chaves and Rodríguez Chaves 2001, 160; Chen Apuy 1992; Leon Azofeifa 1988; and Putnam 2013 for Central American experiences of discrimination.

12. Matsuda 2012, 5.

13. It lasted from 1823 to 1841.

14. Criollos were those Spanish subjects born in the Americas. Their subordination to Spanish subjects born in Spain was one of the principal causes of the wars of independence that put an end to Spanish colonialism.

15. This was not the case in Costa Rica, which, because it was farther from the vice-royalty administrative centers and not heavily populated by indigenous people, tended to be characterized by more medium-sized agricultural plots during this period.

16. For more on the history of Central America, see Torres Rivas 1993; and Bethell 1991.

17. For excellent analyses of the relationship between Chinese labor and migration flows to the Americas and their relationship to the Qing Dynasty, see González 2017; Young 2014; and Yun 2008.

18. Chang-Rodríguez 1958, 380.

19. See Cohen 1971, 314; Hu-DeHart 1989, 107–8; and Young 2014, 31.

20. See León Azofeifa 1988, 72–73; Yun 2008, xv–xvi; and Young 2014, 46–48.

21. Cohen 1971, 311; and Robinson 2010, 105.

22. Cohen 1971, 311.

23. Cohen 1971, 316.

24. Chou 2001, 80; and Cohen 1971, 317.

25. Barreno Anleu 2004, 17.

26. Huesmann 1991, 717.

27. Huesmann 1991, 715; Loría Chaves and Rodríguez Chaves 2001, 180; and Putnam 2002, 40.

28. The Chinese government negotiated a treaty with Peru in 1874, and in 1877 a convention between China and Spain discontinued contract labor and declared Chinese in Cuba and elsewhere free (Chang-Rodríguez 1958, 383).

29. Putnam 2002, 84.

30. Hu-DeHart 1998, 263–64; Hearn, Smart, and Hernández Hernández 2011, 144.

31. Young 2014, 131–52.

32. Putnam 2013, 101.

33. Yu 2018. For different reasons, Hu-DeHart (1998, 253) has defined the coolie labor migration period in terms of a "Latin American Pacific."

34. Yu 2018, 178, 200.

35. See Lee 2005.

36. Scientific racism and the idea of whitening were central to most Latin American nations' development at this time.

37. See Chang 2019; Hu-DeHart 2010; González 2017, 24–42; and Young 2014, 129, regarding anti-Chinese movements in Mexico and Peru.

38. See Soto Quirós 2009 and Huesmann 1991 for the specifics of Central American Chinese. See also Chang 2019 for a discussion of the "comparative Orientalism" that we can trace across the region.

39. See Huesmann 1991; Loría Chaves and Rodríguez Chaves 2001; and Soto Quirós 2009.

40. Loría Chaves and Rodríguez Chaves 2000, 211, citing *Tipografía Nacional* 1906, December 29, Art. 16, Decreto 27. See additional examples in Soto Quirós 2009.

41. Loría Chaves and Rodríguez Chaves 2001, 179.

42. See Conniff 1983, 11–12; Mon 2013, 46; and Siu 2005, 115–16. See also Loría Chaves and Rodríguez Chaves 2001 and Soto Quirós 2005.

43. Chen Mok 2013, 5 (citing Bartels Villanueva 2012); and Chen Apuy 1992.

44. See Loría Chaves and Rodríguez Chaves 2000, 19.

45. Lau Sandino 2016, 27; Robinson 2010, 110; and Chen Apuy 1992.

46. Lau Sandino 2016, 14; Siu 2005, 160–61.

47. Instituto Nacional de Estadística y Censos, Costa Rica 2011.

48. See DeHart 2017a for further analysis of how these diverse backgrounds shaped the ways in which local community members understood their own Chinese and Central American identities, especially among youth.

49. Research on the Punta Arenas Chinese Association in Costa Rica is currently being undertaken by Dorcas Tang. That association was the first Chinese Association in Costa Rica and maintains a strong constituency.

50. Those association efforts have encountered obstacles with the diplomatic changes between their respective national governments, as the Beijing-based embassies have tended to prohibit their local Chinese Associations from participating in congresses that take place in Central American countries that still recognize Taiwan.

51. Compare this portrait with Ma and Cartier 2003, or with Mazza 2016, which provides a longitudinal overview that attempts to consolidate estimates from various sources. These two studies highlight the radically different numbers produced by different analyses.

52. In Havana, Cuba, and Lima, Peru, the Chinatowns are historical districts that dominate several streets, boast massive Chinese arches, and host a thriving and growing Chinese community.

53. Personal interview, San José, Costa Rica, July 26, 2012.

54. Personal interview, San José, Costa Rica, July 25, 2012.

55. Personal interview, San José, Costa Rica, July 25, 2012.

56. Personal interview, San José, Costa Rica, July 27, 2012.

57. See Shah 2001; Ling 2012; and Lin 1998.

58. See Hoffman 2006; and Hubbert 2014.

59. Li 1997. On ethnoburbs more generally, see also Fong 1994.

60. Murillo 2013.

61. By 2017 the pedestrian street had been rebranded as a "gastronomic district" set to host occasional food truck events and festivals.

3. TAIWAN

1. Personal interview, San José, Costa Rica, July 16, 2012.

2. Cheng and Córdoba 2009; Córdoba 2005; Von Feigenblatt 2009.

3. Dwyer 2017; and Gao 2018.

4. Other Central American nations maintain official relations with Taiwan, despite increasing business collaborations with the PRC.

5. BBC Mundo 2017.

6. Esteban Rodríguez 2008; and Cheng and Córdoba 2009.

7. ICDF 2019, 3.

8. ICDF 2019, 7.

9. ICDF 2019, 16, 23.

10. ICDF 2019, 16.

11. Personal interviews, San José, Costa Rica, July 6, 2013.

12. MOFA 2009.

13. Lee and Hetherington 2018.

14. Indeed, the only critique I ever heard of Taiwan was its involvement in corruption, a point to which I'll return in chapter 6.

15. Personal interview, San José, Costa Rica, July 27, 2012. In addition to comparing the different Chinas and their respective development policies, I also read this comment and others like it as an index of the ongoing importance of racial hierarchies in defining the global development landscape. To this interviewee, the association with Africa was as much about being treated as a generic "developing country" as it was about being lumped in with Africa, which was presumed to occupy the lowest rung of development relative to white Western modernity.

16. See Alexander 2014, 65–66; Cheng and Córdoba 2009; and Esteban Rodríguez 2013.

17. Nye 2004.

18. Personal interview, San José, Costa Rica, July 27, 2011.

19. In January 2017, Tsai Ing-wen embarked on a tour of Central America that included meetings with heads of state and visits to local projects. During that time, Guatemala conferred on her the prestigious Order of the Quetzal as a gesture of its appreciation for the two nations' long history of friendship in a region characterized by shifting relations. After all, just six months later, Panama left Taiwan to establish relations with the PRC.

20. Personal interview, Managua, Nicaragua, June 21, 2017.

21. López and Lee 2019.

22. López and Lee 2019.

23. Erikson and Chen 2007, 79.

24. Personal interview, Guatemala City, October 2, 2018.

25. Personal interview, Guatemala City, October 2, 2018.

26. Efe News 2019.

27. For analyses of Chinese soft power more broadly, see Kurlantzick 2007; Halper 2010; and Jacques 2009. For empirical analyses that take up the question of Chinese development and economic impacts in Africa in particular, see Brautigam 2009; and Jenkins 2019.

28. Gereffi and Pan 1994.

29. Van Wunnik 2011; and Petersen 1992.

30. Gereffi and Pan 1994, 129–30.

31. Clark 1997.

32. Lau Sandino 2016, 52.

33. Van Wunnik 2011, 267.

34. Ruiz 1992, 1.

35. Jenkins, Esquivel, and Larraín B. 1998, 35.

36. Lau Sandino 2016, 30.

37. Personal interview, Guatemala City, July 24, 2017.

38. Anner 2003; Frundt 2002.

39. Personal interview, San José, Costa Rica, June 21, 2013.

40. Personal interview, Guatemala City, July 22, 2017.

41. Lau Sandino 2016, 13.

42. Lau Sandino 2016, 12.

43. Personal interview, Guatemala City, July 22, 2017.

44. Chang 2017, 51.

45. Lau Sandino 2007, 6.

46. Personal interview, San José, Costa Rica, June 21, 2013.

47. Personal interview, Managua, Nicaragua, July 3, 2017.

48. Personal interview, San José, Costa Rica, June 18, 2013.

49. I suspect the experiences of this generation of Chino Ticos are similar to those that I describe, albeit oriented toward Taipei; however, without more data, I cannot generalize.

50. Personal interview, San José, Costa Rica, July 21, 2013.

51. Personal interview, San José, Costa Rica, July 27, 2012.

52. While smaller, regional ethnic or mutual-support organizations emerged within the coastal Chinese communities of Central America in the early twentieth century, the founding dates of the national associations include Guatemala 1922, Nicaragua 1942, El Salvador 1943, Honduras 1943, Panama 1943, and Costa Rica 1960 (Lau Sandino 2016). Lau Sandino attributes the associations' founding dates to the Chinese communities' responses to the discriminatory contexts and anti-immigration legislation they experienced in Central America during this period.

53. See Siu 2005, 54–85, on these Chinese beauty pageants.

54. Siu 2005, 183.

55. Personal interview, San José, Costa Rica, July 26, 2012.

56. Siu 2005, 189.

57. Calix Ng 2017, 3.

58. Personal interview, San José, Costa Rica, July 27, 2012.

59. Personal interview, San José, Costa Rica, July 24, 2015.

60. Personal interview, San José, Costa Rica, July 27, 2012.

61. Siu 2005, 189.

62. Personal interview, San José, Costa Rica, July 6, 2013.

63. Personal interview, Guatemala City, July 21, 2017, and July 22, 2017.

64. See Siu 2005, 66–67.

65. Personal interview, San José, Costa Rica, August 4, 2015.

66. Increased interest in Mandarin-language study after 2007 was reflected in the dramatic increase in the number of Chinese-language classes and schools in Costa Rica (DeHart 2017b, Levin 2011). Non-Chinese and Chinese students frequently cited the desire to do business in China as a main motivation for their language choice.

4. INFRASTRUCTURE

1. See Anand, Gupta, and Appel 2018; Gupta 2015; and Harvey and Knox 2015 for further discussion of how infrastructure, especially roads, constructs temporality and social relations.

2. Council on Foreign Relations 2019.

3. World Bank 2018.

4. Koop 2019; and Desheng 2019.

5. Myers and Gallagher 2019, 2. See also Inter-American Dialogue 2018.

6. Hemeroteca PL 2017.

7. Silva 2017.

8. For phase one, the plan was to expand eleven kilometers of the highway at an estimated cost of $17.3 million over the course of eighteen months. Phase two, initiated in 2013, took on the widening of the highway stretch from kilometer twenty-seven to fifty-seven, with the addition of two new bridges. Phase three of the project, stretching from Sanarate to El Rancho, began in 2015 after a limited international bidding process in which Taiwan offered to donate $50 million and lend another $50 million at 1 percent interest, to be repaid over the course of twenty years, to continue the work of widening the highway, at a cost estimated at $119 million. This time the Guatemalan government

agreed to pay the $19 million residual, but president Otto Pérez Molina tied the agreement to a commitment for Taiwan to provide technology transfers around solar and wind power to the Institute of National Electrification and the Ministry of Energy and Mines. Pérez Molina began asking Taiwan to take on phase four of the project, extending the highway amplification to Puerto Barrios, in 2016, and president Jimmy Morales continued that lobby during Tsai Ing-wen's visit to Guatemala in 2017. For this phase of the construction, Taiwan was to donate $250 million and lend $350 million (at 1.5 percent interest), with Taiwan's Overseas Engineering and Construction Corporation undertaking construction of the project. In 2019, President Jimmy Morales continued to negotiate financing for the final and shortest phase of the project with Taiwan's president, Tsai Ing-wen. In 2020, Guatemalan president Alejandro Giammattei announced that he would divert the remaining Taiwanese funds away from the road project to renovate and expand regional hospitals; however, work was to continue on the highway amplification project, hopefully through the help of Inter-american Development Bank funds (Espina 2020).

9. Personal interview, Guatemala City, October 2, 2018.

10. Personal interview, Guatemala City, July 22, 2017.

11. Personal interview, Guatemala City, October 2, 2018.

12. Personal interview, Guatemala City, October 2, 2018. Taiwanese officials confirmed that the project included five hundred workers, the vast majority of whom were Guatemalan, and two dozen consultants from Taiwan.

13. Personal interview, Guatemala City, October 2, 2018.

14. For an overview of US policy, see Tarnoff and Lawson 2009; on the status of US policy relative to other donors, see Berthélemy 2006.

15. Hernández Mayen 2017.

16. Personal interview, Guatemala City, October 2, 2018.

17. The port renovation was undertaken by the Dutch firm APM Terminals after bids by Chinese firms were rejected, some say on the basis of sovereignty concerns.

18. CONAVI 2016, 7–8; Pisu and Villalobos 2016, 19.

19. CONAVI 2016, 7. Infrastructure in the region is not solely the business of state ventures. As I described elsewhere, the growing private enterprises associated with the PRC are also significant agents in this space, even if they are often conflated with state agencies.

20. See DeHart 2012 for more on local views of imported Chinese labor on local projects.

21. La prenda libre 2017.

22. The consortium was called Grupo Consenso (Consensus Group). CentralAmericaData 2014.

23. World Bank 2011; and CentralAmericaData 2013.

24. Fornaguera 2014.

25. See Zhang 2002 and Solinger 2002 for more on Chinese labor camps. For information about labor for the construction of Costa Rica's national stadium, see DeHart 2012 and *La nación* 2011.

26. Ruíz 2015.

27. SETENA 2016.

28. CRHoy 2016.

29. Personal interview, San José, Costa Rica, October 8, 2018.

30. The 2017 figure comes from Grajales Navarrete 2016. The 2019 figure was reported as part of a personal interview, San José, Costa Rica, October 8, 2018.

31. Personal interview, San José, Costa Rica, October 8, 2018.

32. Córdoba González 2019.

33. Personal interview, San José, Costa Rica, October 8, 2018.

34. See for example Watkins, Lai, and Bradsher 2018 for an overview of these critiques and the place of specific infrastructure projects within them. For more on Central America in particular, see Arias Retana 2018.

35. The *Financial Times* has featured a series of stories dealing with this issue. See for example Weinland 2019 and Hornby 2019.

36. See for example Ellis 2020, 6.

37. At the CELAC China-LAC summit in April 2014, Xi Jinping announced that China would offer Latin America a financing package of $35 billion, including preferential loans ($10 billion), a special loan for infrastructure projects ($20 billion), and a China-LAC cooperation fund ($5 billion). The China Development Bank is in charge of the infrastructure loan, which can finance energy, road, transportation, port logistics, electricity, mining, and agricultural initiatives in Latin America in conjunction with Chinese businesses (Chinese Ministry of Foreign Affairs 2016, 39, 41).

38. MOFA 2007.

39. IADB 2012.

40. China Aid Data 2011.

41. Bermúdez Vivez 2012; and Villalobos Clare 2013.

42. Dyer 2013; and RECOPE 2012, 6.

43. Bermúdez Vives 2012.

44. RECOPE 2012, 5.

45. RECOPE 2012, 5.

46. Fernando Lara 2016.

47. Dyer 2013.

48. Solís 2013, 38A.

49. This despite the fact that the Guatemalan reformer Jacobo Arbenz Guzmán's efforts to nationalize land belonging to United Fruit was viewed by the US not as a defense of sovereignty but rather as an attack against US interests, thus legitimizing CIA support for the 1954 coup that unseated Arbenz and put an end to an era of democratic reform (see Schlesinger and Kinzer 2005, 100–105; Smith and Adams 2011, 2–3).

50. Mata 2013, 5A.

51. Araya 2013.

52. DeHart 2018a.

53. US Department of State and US & Foreign Commercial Service 2016.

54. Personal interview, San José, Costa Rica, July 27, 2011.

55. As the anthropologist Fernando Coronil (1997) originally argued in his analysis of the Venezuelan petro-state, it was precisely the state's ability to claim control over territory and act as a mediator over its riches with foreign companies that allowed it to assert dominion over Venezuelan society.

56. Personal interview, Managua, Nicaragua, July 28, 2012.

57. UNICEF 2016.

58. Daley 2016; McCall and Taylor 2018.

59. Cui 2018, 152.

60. Environmental Resource Management, *Estudio de impacto ambiental*, 2015, cited in López Baltodano 2017, 13.

61. Environmental Resource Management, *Estudio de impacto ambiental*, 2015, cited in López Baltodano 2017, 13.

62. Also as part of the concession, Wang Jing agreed to establish important telecommunications services within the country via the firm Xinwei, thus extending cell service across the patchily connected nation.

63. McCall and Taylor 2018, 199.

64. Regarding the canal, Panamanian general Omar Torrijos was quoted as saying, "What nation of the world can withstand the humiliation of a foreign flag piercing its own heart?" US conservatives opposed to the treaties characterized them as appeasement and an example of American decline (Grogin 2001, 297). Among those in opposition to the treaty were prominent politicians like ex-governor and presidential hopeful Ronald Reagan, who characterized the agreement as surrendering US interests in the region.

65. Personal interview, Managua, Nicaragua, July 3, 2017.

66. A chronicle of updates on the canal's progress can be tracked through the monitoring organization Dredging Today. The last update for the project was posted on May 10, 2016.

67. Casting further doubts on the economics of the project, the local political commentator Enrique Sáenz highlighted how, if one actually calculated the remuneration necessary for the canal to be viable, it was clear that the global shipping industry would not have the volume, and thus the demand, for the combination of the enhanced Panama Canal and this additional canal to move the project forward. Furthermore, he pointed to the fact that since neither Costa Rica (Nicaragua's neighbor) nor the US was complaining despite the concession's obvious economic and political ramifications for them, it was pretty clear that there was no real prospect of a canal. Personal interview, Managua, Nicaragua, July 3, 2017.

68. Personal interview, Managua, Nicaragua, July 3, 2017.

69. Personal interview, Managua, Nicaragua, June 21, 2017.

70. *Global Construction Review* 2018.

71. Personal interview, Managua, Nicaragua, June 21, 2017.

72. López Baltodano 2017, 459–60.

73. Personal interview, Managua, Nicaragua, July 13, 2017.

74. Inter-American Commission on Human Rights 2019.

75. Personal interview, Guatemala City, October 8, 2018.

76. González 2015.

5. TRADE

1. Xinhuanet English News 2018. See also Dussel Peters 2018 and 2019 for more on Central American commerce with China; and Myers and Wise 2017 for China–Latin America relations more broadly.

2. See Avendaño and Dayton-Johnson 2015.

3. Email interview, May 1, 2019.

4. Cámara de Cooperación y Comercio China-Guatemala (4CG), http://camarachi naguatemala.org/. These services included assisting entrepreneurs in the procurement of travel visas to China, guiding participation in the Canton Fair, and verifying prospective Chinese trade partners.

5. While I interviewed attendees, I did not ask them about their ethnic background. Where folks identified different national identities, I did record this; however, as I note below, the fact that the expo ostensibly represented a hispanized, non-Chinese demographic suggested that local Chinese entrepreneurs with dense commercial ties to Mainland China were not forging their connections here, nor were visiting PRC businessmen scouting new Guatemalan import opportunities here.

6. Personal interview, Guatemala City, September 8, 2018.

7. Personal interview, San José, Costa Rica, October 11, 2018.

8. It was unclear how these Guatemalan firms would distinguish themselves from the Costa Rican, Salvadoran, and Nicaraguan firms similarly trying to market their coffee, sugar, seafood, and other agricultural products to China.

9. As I learned later, they were also the same firms that tended to participate in the Taiwanese roundtables and the Canton Fair trips, as they could afford to participate.

10. According to Nye (2004), soft power is a country's ability to persuade others and get what it wants through appeal. One of the central distinctions that Nye makes about the US versus countries like China is the ubiquity of US brands around the world, which generates both recognition and attraction. China, he argues, lacks that visibility and appeal. In a revised article in 2005, Nye acknowledges China's gains in soft power as a result of its economic aid and multilateralism but insists that China still falls far behind the US in cultural industries and educational status.

11. Scholars of global China have emphasized this fact (in particular Gill and Huang 2006; Wuthnow 2008; Hunter 2009; Li 2006; and Shambaugh 2013), while journalist sources have also reproduced and challenged this concept (Kurlantzick 2007).

12. Personal interview, Guatemala City, September 9, 2018.

13. Personal interview, Guatemala City, October 2, 2018. Confirming this gentleman's astute assessment, Guatemalan Chamber of Commerce representatives noted that the local perception that Taiwanese products offer both lower prices and higher quality was one of the distinguishing factors between Chinese and Taiwanese commodities.

14. Personal interview, Guatemala City, September 8, 2018.

15. Personal interview, Guatemala City, September 8, 2018.

16. For analyses of China's cultural diplomacy efforts, see Wuthnow 2008; Gill and Huang 2006; and Hubbert 2019.

17. For more on Chinese public diplomacy through expos, see Hubbert 2017, 2019, 75.

18. Personal interview, Guatemala City, September 9, 2018.

19. González 2017, 121–24.

20. As one embassy representative explained to me, "Guatemala has the right to cultivate commercial relations with any country. Even where there's not diplomatic relations, we promote economic relations." Personal interview, Guatemala City, October 2, 2018.

21. Personal interview, chamber of commerce, Guatemala City, October 2, 2018.

22. Ubico's educational experience included a BA in business administration and an MA in international commerce, as well as certificates from the Ministry of National Defense and the Superior Education Command of the Guatemalan Army. In 2019, he was appointed the first secretary and consul to the Guatemalan embassy in Japan.

23. FaceTime interview, August 9, 2019. Entrepreneurs looking to export goods to the Chinese market did not participate in these trips, and there were few clients who participated simply to get a look at the market.

24. Personal interview, Guatemala City, September 8, 2018.

25. Personal interview, San José, Costa Rica, October 9, 2018.

26. Although Ruiz Gutiérrez did not speak Mandarin or have extensive experience, his office was aided by the presence of a young Costa Rican woman of Chinese descent who had just finished her master's degree at Tsinghua University. I speak more about Zhen below.

27. Rico 2015.

28. Solano 2017.

29. Hearn (2016) speaks to this dynamic in Mexico and Cuba in particular. See also McKeown 2008 and Ong and Nonini 1997, which address this dynamic in relation to other Chinese diasporic populations in the Americas.

30. Yu 2018.

31. Personal interview, Guatemala City, September 26, 2018.

32. Personal interview, Guatemala City, September 26, 2018.

33. Personal interview, Guatemala City, September 26, 2018.

34. See DeHart 2017a for a fuller analysis of how both Zhen's class background and PRC government diplomacy helped to support the particular formulation of Chineseness that she cultivated.

35. For more on the role of class status and Chinese public diplomacy in the forging of these diasporic entrepreneurs, see DeHart 2017a.

36. Personal interview, San José, Costa Rica, October 15, 2018.

6. CORRUPTION

1. Muir and Gupta 2018.

2. Importantly, in the case of Brazil, the clampdown on state corruption was also the product of important reforms in the judicial system enacted by the Workers' Party (Ruales 2018). Clearly, Lula da Silva and other Workers' Party representatives never imagined that these same measures would later be used against them.

3. Armony 2012, 104.

4. Armony and Strauss 2012, 15.

5. Armony 2012.

6. Haller and Shore 2005, 21 (emphasis mine). See also Gupta 1995.

7. Muir and Gupta 2018, S13.

8. For example, Coombe (1997, 252) notes that rumor, due to its lack of "identifiable source . . . makes it accessible to insurgency, while its transitivity makes it a powerful tactic," whereas Scheper-Hughes (2002, 36) speaks to the "ontological insecurity" that people living in the marginal spaces of the global economy experience.

9. Gephart 2009.

10. Ivanov 2007.

11. OAS 1996.

12. UNODC 2004, 1.

13. Meyer 2016, 10.

14. See for example Molenaers, Dellepiane, and Faust 2015; and Rose-Ackerman 2012.

15. Condon 2012; and Gallagher, Irwin, and Koleski 2012.

16. Huang 2015. Of course, China might be even more developed were it to reduce corruption; nonetheless, its growth has been sustained in part by the powerful coexistence of institutions promoting resource extraction and productive investment goals (Wise 2020).

17. Manion 2009, 85.

18. Armony and Strauss 2012.

19. Manion 2009, 106–7.

20. For PRC corruption discourse, see *China Daily* 2013; for its political intent, see Keliher and Wu 2015.

21. Li 2016, 450; Chow 2015; and Yuen 2014.

22. He 2000; and Gong 2002. For instance, Wedeman (2004) has documented the "intensification" of corruption—that is, the increase in high-level, big-stakes transactions—in China during the 1990s despite multiple anticorruption campaigns. Manion (2009, 24) corroborates this claim and details the prevalence of "economic offences" such as bureaucratic commerce, predatory exactions, and corrupt exchanges as constituting the majority of prosecuted corruption cases.

23. Wedel et al. 2005, 37–38.

24. Ivanov 2007, 35.

25. Smart and Hsu 2013, 167.

26. Smart and Hsu 2013, 177.

27. Marro 2014.
28. DeHart 2018b.
29. Loría Chaves and Rodríguez Chaves 2000, 211, citing *Tipografía Nacional* 1906, December 29, Art. 16, Decreto 27. See additional examples in Soto Quirós 2009.
30. Lee 2005, 238.
31. See, for example, Young 2014, 218–33, and Chang 2017, 124–60, for cases of Chinese businesses that were not only targeted by government officials for raids but also subject to prejudicial laws that sought to put them out of business.
32. See chapter 2; also see Erikson and Chen 2007, 79.
33. Personal interview, San José, Costa Rica, July 28, 2011. While Arias has justified these covert conversations by noting that there was much for the PRC and Costa Rica to work out before Taiwan became aware of the conversation, it may also be true that he kept negotiations with the PRC quiet to avoid the wrath of the United States, which critiqued the diplomatic switch. In that vein, he justified his decision to embrace Beijing by holding up his copy of the book *On China* by Henry Kissinger, saying that the US, too, had put economic interests above politics.
34. *La nación* 2010.
35. Personal interview, San José, Costa Rica, October 15, 2018.
36. The power of this claim, unsubstantiated as far as I could tell, was significant, as many years later I found Facebook postings still alluding to the allegation by supporters of Araya. Clearly that particular rumor had spread far and wide enough to be taken seriously by people well beyond my direct interlocutors.
37. United Nations, Political and Peacebuilding Affairs 2019.
38. CICIG 2019b, 50–51.
39. For example, the CMNC had apparently built the plant according to Chinese construction norms, not Guatemalan protocol, such that they installed on essential machinery red buttons to indicate "On" and green to indicate "Off." Personal interview, Guatemala City, July 24, 2017.
40. Marroquín 2015.
41. For coverage of the many aspects of the scandal, including the Chinese company, see *Prensa libre* 2015; Diario la hora 2015; Marroquín 2015; and Palacios 2015.
42. La Linea constituted a customs fraud scheme in which containers of imported merchandise were undervalued in exchange for kickbacks to customs officials and their leaders in the executive branch (CICIG 2015).
43. CICIG 2019a.
44. Wilson 2014b. Wilson (2014a, 4) also claims that Costa Ricans' understanding of and experience with corruption is focused less on paying bribes to public officials (with which they have little personal experience) and more on the corrupt acts of politicians and public officials who are exposed in the media for using their public office for personal gain.
45. Russell 2019.
46. Freedom House 2018.
47. Freedom House 2018.
48. People's Republic of China 2016.
49. Personal interview, San José, Costa Rica, October 15, 2018.
50. Transparency International 2018.
51. Environmental Resource Management, *Estudio de impacto ambiental*, 2015, cited in López Baltodano 2017, 13.
52. Personal interview, Managua, Nicaragua, July 16, 2017.
53. Human Rights Watch 2019.
54. Kinosian and Pérez Osorio 2018.

55. Human Rights Watch 2019.

56. Talley and Whelan 2018.

57. Personal interview, Managua, Nicaragua, July 6, 2017.

CONCLUSION

1. See Escobar 1995; and Rahnema and Bawtree 1997.

2. Gehrke 2019.

3. Although he mentions Russia along with China, only China appears here as the "new" actor. Given the United States' longstanding worries of Communist interference in Latin America via the Soviet Union, Russia seems like a fairly familiar threat, even if its current heft doesn't approximate its perceived presence during the Cold War.

4. Not only would many debate the "love" between the nations, given the history of US intervention in regional politics, but they would also challenge the idea of the United States "showing up as never before," given waning US attention since the 2010s. Indeed, President Donald Trump's withdrawal of aid to Central American governments in 2019 in retribution for their failure to staunch the flow of northbound migration is just one example of the increasingly chilly relation between "neighbors."

5. Kinloch 2015, 342.

6. Narins and Agnew 2019, 809.

7. See Inter-American Dialogue 2018 on Chinese infrastructure transport in Latin America. The maps provided offer a provocative portrait of how the region might be envisioned and reconfigured through those initiatives.

8. Tsing 2005, 57.

9. Climate Action 2017.

10. See for example recent reports about China's efforts to make the BRI green and sustainable (Goh and Cadell 2019).

Works Cited

Aguilera Peralta, Gabriel. 2010. "Central America between Two Dragons: Relations with the Two Chinas." In *Latin America Facing China: South-South Relations beyond the Washington Consensus*, edited by Alex E. Fernández Jilberto and Barbara Hogenboom, 167–80. New York: Berghahn Books.

Alexander, Colin. 2014. *China and Taiwan in Central America: Engaging Foreign Publics in Diplomacy*. Palgrave MacMillan Series in Global Public Diplomacy. New York: Palgrave MacMillan.

Anand, Nikhil, Akhil Gupta, and Hannah Appel, eds. 2018. *The Promise of Infrastructure*. Durham, NC: Duke University Press.

Anderson, Ben, and Colin McFarlane. 2011. "Assemblage and Geography." *Area* 43 (2): 162–64.

Anderson, Warwick, Miranda Johnson, and Barbara Brookes, eds. 2018. *Pacific Futures: Past and Present*. Honolulu: University of Hawai'i Press.

Anner, Mark. 2003. "Defending Labor Rights across Borders: Central America's Export Processing Zones." In *Struggles for Social Rights in Latin America*, edited by Susan Eva Eckstein and Timothy P. Wickham-Crowley, 147–66. New York: Routledge.

Araya, Mónica. 2013. "Costa Rica, China y el clima: Un momento decisivo." *La nación*, June 7, 2013.

Araya Monge, Johnny. 2012. "Chinos y Costarricenses en el barrio Chino." *La nación*, March 16, 2012. http://www.nacion.com/opinion/foros/Chinos-costarricenses-barrio Chino_0_1256674357.html.

Arias Retana, Gustavo. 2018. "Seduced by China, Central America Overlooks Risks." *Dialogo*, September 12, 2018. https://dialogo-americas.com/articles/seduced-by-china-central-america-overlooks-risks/.

Armony, Ariel. 2012. "Exporting Corruption." *Americas Quarterly* 6 (1): 104–7.

Armony, Ariel, and Julia Strauss. 2012. "Going Out (zou chuqu) and Arriving In (desembarco)." *China Quarterly* 209 (March): 1–17.

Avendaño, Rolando, and Jeff Dayton-Johnson. 2015. "Central America, China, and the US: What Prospects for Development?" *Public Affairs* 88 (4): 813–47.

Barreno Anleu, Silvia. 2004. "La Huella del Dragón: Inmigrantes chinos en Guatemala, 1871–1944." Master's thesis, Centro de Investigaciones y Estudios Superiores en Antropología Social.

Bartels Villanueva, Jorge. 2012. "Los inmigrantes chinos en la ciudad de Puntarenas (1850–1927): Un acercamiento comparativo desde las regiones de Costa Rica." Presentation at the International Symposium of China Studies, University of Costa Rica, Pacific Campus, Puntarenas, June 18–19, 2012.

BBC Mundo. 2017. "Por que panamá rompió su vinculo histórico con Taiwán y estableció relaciones diplomáticas con China." June 13, 2017. https://www.bbc.com/mundo/noticias-america-latina-40256859.

Bermúdez Vives, Mario. 2012. "Ampliar la refinería de Moin dejaría rentabilidad de 19%." *El financiero*, October 4, 2012. http://www.elfinancierocr.com/economia-y-politica/Refineria-Recope-Soresco_0_166183391.html.

Berthélemy, Jean-Claude. 2006. "Bilateral Donors' Interest vs. Recipients' Development Motives in Aid Allocation: Do All Donors Behave the Same?" *Review of Development Economics* 10 (2): 179–94.

Bethell, Leslie, ed. 1991. *Central America since Independence.* Cambridge: Cambridge University Press.

Bloomberg News. 2019. "China's Lethal Milk Scandal Reverberates a Decade Later." January 21, 2019. https://www.bloomberg.com/news/articles/2019-01-21/china-s-lethal-milk-scandal-reverberates-a-decade-later.

Boelhower, William. 2008. "The Rise of the New Atlantic Studies Matrix." *American Literary History* 20 (1–2): 75–100.

Boelhower, William. 2019. *Atlantic Studies: Prospects and Challenges.* Baton Rouge: Louisiana State University Press.

Brautigam, Deborah. 2009. *The Dragon's Gift: The Real Story of China in Africa.* Oxford: Oxford University Press.

Calix Ng, Carlos. 2017. "Saludo del presidente de la junta directiva de la asociación de beneficiencia de la colonia china en Guatemala." Convention program, 45th Convention of the Central American Federation of Chinese Associations, Guatemala City, August 17–19, 2017, 3.

Carse, Ashley. 2014. *Beyond the Big Ditch: Politics, Ecology, and Infrastructure at the Panama Canal.* Cambridge, MA: MIT Press.

Casey, Nicholas, and Clifford Krauss. 2018. "It Doesn't Matter If Ecuador Can Afford This Dam: China Still Gets Paid." *New York Times,* December 24, 2018. https://www.nytimes.com/2018/12/24/world/americas/ecuador-china-dam.html.

CentralAmericaData. 2013. "Costa Rica: Questions over the Chinese Company That Will Build the Highway." November 26, 2013. https://en.centralamericadata.com/en/article/home/Costa_Rica_Questions_Over_The_Chinese_Company_That_Will_Build_Highway.

CentralAmericaData. 2014. "Costa Rica: Resistencia de empresarios a Proyecto vial." February 24, 2014. http://centralamericadata.com/es/article/home/Costa_Rica_Resistencia_de_empresarios_a_proyecto_vial.

Chaguan. 2018. "Think of China as a Giant Sub-prime Lender in Latin America" *Economist,* November 3, 2018. https://www.economist.com/china/2018/11/03/think-of-china-as-a-giant-sub-prime-lender-in-latin-america.

Chang, Augusto. 2017. "La situación y vida de la comunidad China en Guatemala." Convention program, 45th Convention of the Central American Federation of Chinese Associations, Guatemala City, August 17–19, 2017, 51.

Chang, Jason Oliver. 2019. "Comparative Orientalism in Latin American Revolutions: Antichinismo of Mexico and El Salvador." *Latin American Research Review* 54 (4): 992–1006.

Chang-Rodríguez, Eugenio. 1958. "Chinese Labor Migration into Latin America in the Nineteenth Century." *Revista de historia de América* 46: 375–97.

Chen Apuy, Hilda. 1992. "La minoría China en Costa Rica." *Revista reflexiones* 1 (5). http://revistas.ucr.ac.cr/index.php/reflexiones/article/view/10551.

Chen Mok, Susan. 2013. "Radiografía de una inmigración China en Puntarenas, Costa Rica." *Revista estudios,* Universidad de Costas Rica, no. 26. http://revistas.ucr.ac.cr/index.php/estudios/article/view/8842/8324.

Cheng, Joseph and Córdoba, Thaís. 2009. "The Establishment of Diplomatic Relations with China: A Study of Costa Rica's Rationale." *Journal of Comparative Asian Development* 8 (2): 333–64.

China Aid Data. 2011. "China Development Bank Provides $900 Million USD Loan for Oil Refinery Expansion, Project ID 37285." http://china.aiddata.org/projects/37313?iframe=y.

China Daily. 2013. "Xi's Appeal to Curb Waste Gets Warm Response." January 30, 2013. https://cpcchina.chinadaily.com.cn/2013-01/30/content_16186955.htm.

Chinese Ministry of Foreign Affairs, Department of Latin America and Caribbean Affairs. 2016. "Basic Information about China-CELAC Forum." April 2016. http://www.chinacelacforum.org/eng/ltjj_1/P020161207421177845816.pdf.

Chong Ruiz, Eustorgio. 1992. *Los chinos en la sociedad Panameña.* Panama City: Editorial Arosemena del Instituto Nacional de Cultura.

Chou, Diego. 2001. *Los chinos en Hispano América.* San José, Costa Rica: FLACSO, Sede Academico.

Chow, Daniel. 2015. "How China's Crackdown on Corruption Has Led to Less Transparency in the Enforcement of China's Anti-Bribery Laws." *UC Davis Law Review* 49 (2): 685–701. https://lawreview.law.ucdavis.edu/issues/49/2/Symposium/49-2_Chow.pdf.

CICIG (International Commission against Impunity in Guatemala). 2015. "A prisión preventiva ex presidente Pérez Molina." September 8, 2015. https://www.cicig.org/casos/a-prision-preventiva-ex-presidente-otto-perez-molina/.

CICIG (International Commission against Impunity in Guatemala). 2019a. "Encuesta Prodatos: 72% de la población guatemalteca apoya labor de la CICIG." April 5, 2019. https://www.cicig.org/apoyo-ciudadano/poblacion-guatemalteca-apoya-labor-de-la-cicig/.

CICIG (International Commission against Impunity in Guatemala). 2019b. "El legado de la justiciar en Guatemala: Informe de final." https://www.cicig.org/wp-content/uploads/2019/08/InformeLegadoJusticia_SI.pdf.

Clark, Mary. 1997. "Transnational Alliances and Development Policy in Latin America: Non-traditional Export Promotion in Costa Rica." *Latin American Research Review* 32 (2): 71–97.

Climate Action. 2017. "Costa Rica Pledges Carbon Neutrality by 2021." January 20, 2017. http://www.climateaction.org/news/costa_rica_pledges_carbon_neutrality_by_2021.

Cohen, Lucy. 1971. "The Chinese of the Panama Railroad: Preliminary Notes on the Migrants of 1854 Who 'Failed.'" *Ethnohistory* 18 (4): 309–20.

Colby, Jason. 2013. *The Business of Empire: United Fruit, Race, and U.S. Expansion in Central America.* Reprint ed. Ithaca, NY: Cornell University Press.

CONAVI (Consejo Nacional de Vialidad). 2016. "Acuerdo de Contrato y a las Adendas 1, 2, 3, y 4 del 'Proyecto del diseño, rehabilitación y ampliación de la ruta nacional n 32 carretera, Braulio Carillo, sección intersección ruta nacional n 4, Limón.'" April 26, 2016. https://cgrfiles.cgr.go.cr/publico/docsweb/documentos/sala-prensa/boletines/2016/refrendo-boletin-contrato-ruta-32.pdf.

Condon, Madison. 2012. "China in Africa: What the Policy of Nonintervention Adds to the Development Dilemma." *Praxis: The Fletcher Journal of Human Security* 27. https://papers.ssrn.com/sol3/papers.cfm?abstract_id=2693220.

Conniff, Michael. 1983. *Black Labor on a White Canal: West Indians in Panama, 1904–1980.* Research Paper Series No. 11, May 1983. Albuquerque: University of New Mexico Press. https://digitalrepository.unm.edu/laii_research/17.

Coombe, Rosemary. 1997. "The Demonic Place of the 'Not There': Trademark Rumors in the Postindustrial Imaginary." In *Culture, Power, Place: Explorations in*

Critical Anthropology, edited by Akhil Gupta and James Ferguson, 249–76. Durham, NC: Duke University Press.

Cooper, Frederick, and Randall Packard. 1997. *International Development and the Social Sciences: Essays on the History and Politics of Knowledge.* Berkeley: University of California Press.

Córdoba, Thaís. 2005. *The Significance of Costa Rica in Taiwan's Diplomacy and the Competition from Beijing.* San José: Génesis de la Lima.

Córdoba González, Juan Diego. 2019. "Gobierno admite que ampliación de la ruta de limón tomará más tiempo de lo previsto." *La nación*, February 16, 2019. https://www.nacion.com/el-pais/infraestructura/gobierno-admite-que-ampliacion-de-la-ruta-a-limon/GNBQIRHJEFA4RMMJPTS5NJWRII/story/.

Coronil, Fernando. 1997. *The Magical State: Nature, Money, and Modernity in Venezuela.* Chicago: University of Chicago Press.

Council on Foreign Relations. 2019. "China's Massive Belt and Road Initiative." May 21, 2019. https://www.cfr.org/backgrounder/chinas-massive-belt-and-road-initiative.

CRHoy. 2016. "Setena otorga viabilidad ambiental para ampliar ruta 32." December 2, 2016. http://www.crhoy.com/nacionales/setena-otorgo-viabilidad-ambiental-para-ampliar-ruta-32/.

Cui, Shoujun. 2018. "The Chinese-Backed Nicaraguan Canal: Domestic Rationale, Multiple Risks, and Geopolitical Implications." In *Building Development for a New Era: China's Infrastructure Projects in Latin America and the Caribbean*, edited by Enrique Dussel Peters, Ariel C. Armony, and Shoujun Cui, 144–63. Pittsburgh: Asian Studies Center, Center for International Studies, University of Pittsburgh; Red Académica de América Latina y el Caribe sobre China.

Cumings, Bruce. 2009. *Dominion from Sea to Sea: Pacific Ascendancy and American Power.* New Haven, CT: Yale University Press.

Daley, Suzanne. 2016. "Lost in Nicaragua, a Chinese Tycoon's Canal Project." *New York Times*, April 3, 2016. https://www.nytimes.com/2016/04/04/world/americas/nicaragua-canal-chinese-tycoon.html.

DeHart, Monica. 2010. *Ethnic Entrepreneurs: Identity and Development Politics in Latin America.* Stanford, CA: Stanford University Press.

DeHart, Monica. 2012. "Remodeling the Global Development Landscape: The China Model and South–South Cooperation in Latin America." *Third World Quarterly* 33 (7): 1359–75.

DeHart, Monica. 2015. "Costa Rica's Chinatown: The Art of Being Global in the Age of China." *City & Society* 27 (2): 183–207.

DeHart, Monica. 2017a. "Chino Tico Routes and Repertoires: Cultivating Chineseness and Entrepreneurism for a New Era of Transpacific Relations" *Journal of Latin American and Caribbean Anthropology* 23 (1): 74–93.

DeHart, Monica. 2017b. "Who Speaks for China? Translating Geopolitics through Language Institutes in Costa Rica." *Journal of Chinese Overseas* 13: 181–205.

DeHart, Monica. 2018a. "China-Costa Rica Infrastructure Projects: Laying the Groundwork for Development?" In *Building Development for a New Era: China's Infrastructure Projects in Latin America and the Caribbean*, edited by Enrique Dussel Peters, Ariel C. Armony, and Shoujun Cui, 3–23. Pittsburgh: Asian Studies Center, Center for International Studies, University of Pittsburgh; Red Académica de América Latina y el Caribe sobre China.

DeHart, Monica. 2018b. "The Impact of Chinese Anti-corruption Policies in Costa Rica: Emerging Entrepreneurialisms." *Journal of Latin American Geography* 17 (2): 167–90.

DeLanda, Manuel. 2006. *A New Philosophy of Society: Assemblage Theory and Social Complexity*. New York: Continuum.

Deleuze, Gilles, and Felix Guattari. 1981. *A Thousand Plateaus: Capitalism and Schizophrenia*. Minneapolis: University of Minnesota Press.

Desheng, Cao. 2019. "Latin American Countries Envision BRI Teamwork." *China Daily*, May 24, 2019. http://www.chinadaily.com.cn/a/201905/24/WS5ce727e8a3104842260bd786.html.

Diario la hora. 2015. "Caso Redes: MP realiza señalamientos en una trama de trafico de influencias." July 14, 2015. https://web.archive.org/web/20150714225001/http:/lahora.gt/caso-redes-mp-realiza-senalamientos-en-una-trama-de-trafico-de-influencias/.

Dirlik, Arif, ed. 1998. *What Is in a Rim? Critical Perspectives on the Pacific Region Idea*. 2nd ed. New York: Rowman and Littlefield.

Dirlik, Arif. 2006. "Beijing Consensus: Beijing 'Gongshi'; Who Recognizes Whom and to What End?" Globalization and Autonomy Online Compendium, January 17, 2006. http://www.chinaelections.org/uploadfile/200909/20090918025246335.pdf.

Dittmer, Jason. 2013. "Geopolitical Assemblages and Complexity." *Progress in Human Geography* 38 (3): 385–401.

Dosal, Paul. 1995. *Doing Business with the Dictators: A Political History of United Fruit in Guatemala, 1899–1944*. Reprint. Lanham, MD: Rowman and Littlefield.

Dredging Today. 2016. "HKND Group Meets with Nicaraguan Chamber of Construction." May 10, 2016. https://www.dredgingtoday.com/2016/05/10/hknd-group-meets-with-nicaraguan-chamber-of-construction/.

Dussel Peters, Enrique. 2018. "Comercio e inversiones: La relación de Centroamérica y China, ¿hacia una relación estratégica en el largo plazo?" Comisión Económica para América Latina y el Caribe, Sede Subregional en México. https://dusselpeters.com/132.pdf.

Dussel Peters, Enrique. 2019. "China´s Recent Engagement in Latin America and the Caribbean: Current Conditions and Challenges." Carter Center, Atlanta, GA. https://dusselpeters.com/145.pdf.

Dwyer, Colin. 2017. "In Transit, Taiwan President Set to Stop in US, Much to China's Displeasure." National Public Radio, January 7, 2017. https://www.npr.org/sections/thetwo-way/2017/01/07/508688074/in-transit-taiwan-president-set-to-make-a-stop-in-u-s-to-chinas-displeasure.

Dyer, Zach. 2013. "Resignation the Latest Chapter in Troubled Refinery Project." Tico Times, June 11, 2013. https://ticotimes.net/2013/06/21/resignation-the-latest-chapter-in-a-troubled-refinery-project.

Efe News. 2019. "Guatemalan President Reiterates Support for Taiwan during Official Visit." April 30, 2019. https://www.efe.com/efe/english/varios/guatemala-president-reiterates-support-for-taiwan-during-official-visit/50000269-3964431.

Ellis, Evan, R. 2014. *China on the Ground in Latin America: Challenges for the Chinese and Impacts in the Region*. New York: Palgrave Macmillan.

Ellis, Evan R. 2018a. *The Future of Latin America and the Caribbean in the Context of the Rise of China*. Center for Strategic and International Studies Report. https://www.csis.org/analysis/future-latin-america-and-caribbean-context-rise-china.

Ellis, Evan R. 2018b. "La evolución de las relaciones Panamá-China de desarrollo económico y sus implicaciones estratégicas para los Estados Unidos y la región."

Legislación y economía, September 2018. http://edicion.revistalegislacionyeco
nomia.com/Septiembre2018/Revista/index.html#p=34.

Ellis, Evan R. 2020. "Chinese Engagement in Latin America in the Context of Strategic Competition with the United States." Testimony before the US-China Economic and Security Review Commission, June 24. 2020. https://www.uscc.gov/sites/default/files/2020-06/Ellis_Testimony.pdf.

Erikson, Daniel, and Janice Chen. 2007. "China, Taiwan, and the Battle for Central America." *Fletcher Forum for World Affairs* 31 (2): 69–89.

Escobar, Arturo. 1995. *Encountering Development: The Making and Unmaking of the Third World*. Princeton, NJ: Princeton University Press.

Escobar, Arturo. 2008. *Territories of Difference: Place, Movements, Life, Redes*. Durham, NC: Duke University Press.

Espina, Cindy. 2020. "Giammattei busca cambiar el destino de préstamos de Taiwán." *El periódico*, February 1, 2020. https://elperiodico.com.gt/nacionales/2020/02/01/giammattei-busca-cambiar-el-destino-de-prestamos-de-taiwan/.

Esteban Rodríguez, Mario. 2008. "The Diplomatic Battle between Beijing and Taipei in Latin America and the Caribbean." *Chinese Yearbook of International Laws and Affairs* 25 (1): 65–88.

Esteban Rodríguez, Mario. 2013. "¿China o Taiwán? Las paradojas de Costa Rica y Nicaragua (2006–2008)." *Revista de ciencia política* 33 (2): 513–32.

Fallows, James. 2013. "Today's China Notes: Dreams, Obstacles." *The Atlantic*, May 3, 2013. https://www.theatlantic.com/china/archive/2013/05/todays-china-notes-dreams-obstacles/275544/.

Ferchen, Matt. 2011. "China–Latin America Relations: Long-Term Boon or Short-Term Boom?" *Chinese Journal of International Politics* 4: 55–86.

Ferchen, Matt. 2013. "Whose China Model Is It Anyway?" *Review of International Political Economy* 20 (2): 390–420.

Ferguson, James, and Akhil Gupta. 2008. "Spatializing States: Toward an Ethnography of Neoliberal Governmentality." *American Ethnologist* 29 (4): 981–1002.

Fernando Lara, Juan. 2016. "Anulación de refinería quedo varada." *La nación*, July 4, 2016. http://www.nacion.com/nacional/servicios-publicos/Anulacion-refineria-quedo-varada_0_1570842924.html.

Fish, Issac. 2013. "Thomas Friedman: I Only Deserve Partial Credit for Coining the 'Chinese Dream.'" *Foreign Policy*, May 3, 2013. https://foreignpolicy.com/2013/05/03/thomas-friedman-i-only-deserve-partial-credit-for-coining-the-chinese-dream/.

Focus Taiwan. 2018. "Taiwan Provides Tailor-Made Development Aid." May 30, 2018. http://focustaiwan.tw/news/aipl/201805300014.aspx.

Fong, Timothy P. 1994. *The First Suburban Chinatown: The Remaking of Monterey Park, California*. Philadelphia: Temple University Press.

Fornaguera, Iraela. 2014. "Cinco empresas nacionales proponen ampliar la nueva ruta a Limón." *La nación*, March 14, 2014. http://www.nacion.com/nacional/infrae structura/empresas-nacionales-proponen-ampliar-Limon_0_1402259929.html.

Freedom House. 2018. "Freedom in the World 2018: Costa Rica." https://freedom-house.org/country/costa-rica/freedom-world/2018.

Frundt, Henry. 2002. "Central American Unions in the Era of Globalization." *Latin American Research Review* 37 (3): 7–53.

Gallagher, Kevin, Amos Irwin, and Katherine Koleski. 2012. *The New Banks in Town: Chinese Finance in Latin America*. Washington, DC: Inter-American Dialogue. https://www.thedialogue.org/resources/the-new-banks-in-town-chinese-finance-in-latin-america/.

Gallagher, Kevin, and Margaret Myers. 2021. China–Latin America Finance Database. Washington, DC: Inter-American Dialogue. https://www.thedialogue.org/map_list/.

Gao, Charlotte. 2018. "Tsai Ing-wen Made a Rare, High-Profile Stopover in the US." *The Diplomat*, August 14, 2018. https://thediplomat.com/2018/08/tsai-ing-wen-made-a-rare-high-profile-stopover-in-the-us/.

Garzon, Paulina. 2017. *China's Grip on Ecuador's Energy Matrix*. Washington, DC: Wilson Center. https://www.wilsoncenter.org/sites/default/files/media/docu ments/event/v2_pg_china_grip_on_equador_energy_mix_updated_version. pdf.

Gehrke, Joel. 2019. "Pompeo to Latin America: 'We Love You, China Doesn't." *Washington Examiner*, April 12, 2019. https://www.washingtonexaminer.com/policy/defense-national-security/pompeo-to-latin-america-we-love-you-china-doesnt.

Gephart, Malte. 2009. "Contextualizing Conceptions of Corruption: Challenges for the International Anti-corruption Campaign." GIGA Research Programme: Power, Norms and Governance in International Relations. GIGA Working Paper No. 115, December 11, 2009. https://papers.ssrn.com/sol3/papers. cfm?abstract_id=1534589.

Gereffi, Gary, and Mei-Lin Pan. 1994. "The Globalization of Taiwan's Garment Industry." In *Global Production: The Apparel Industry in the Pacific Rim*, edited by Edna Bonacich, Lucie Cheng., Norma Chinchilla, Nora Hamilton, and Paul Ong, 126–46. Philadelphia: Temple University Press.

Gill, Bates, and Yanzhong Huang. 2006. "Sources and Limits of Chinese 'Soft Power.'" *Survival* 48 (2): 17–35.

Global Construction Review. 2018. "Nicaragua Canal Builder Vacates Swanky Hong Kong Office." April 27, 2018. https://www.globalconstructionreview.com/news/nicaragua-canal-builder-vacates-swanky-hong-kong-o/.

Goh, Brenda, and Cate Cadell. 2019. "China's Xi Says Belt and Road Must Be Green, Sustainable." Reuters, April 24, 2019. https://www.reuters.com/article/us-china-silkroad/chinas-xi-says-belt-and-road-must-be-green-sustainable-idUSKCN1S104I.

Gong, Ting. 2002. "Dangerous Collusion: Corruption as a Collective Venture in Contemporary China." *Communist and Post-Communist Studies* 35: 85–103.

González, Fredy. 2017. *Paisanos Chinos: Transpacific Politics among Chinese Immigrants in Mexico*. Berkeley: University of California Press.

González, Vicente. 2015. "The Limits to China's Non-interference Foreign Policy: Pro-state Interventionism and the Rescaling of Economic Governance." *Australian Journal of International Affairs* 69 (2): 205–23.

Grajales Navarrete, Irina. 2016. "Construcción de la nueva ruta 32 empezaría en julio de 2017." *El Mundo*, August 30, 2016. http://www.elmundo/.cr/nueva-ruta-ew-empearia-julio-2017.

Grandin, Greg. 2004. *The Last Colonial Massacre: Latin America in the Cold War*. Chicago: University of Chicago Press.

Grandin, Greg. 2006. *Empire's Workshop: Latin America, the United States, and the Rise of the New Imperialism*. New York: Holt.

Grogin, Robert. 2001. *Natural Enemies: The United States and the Soviet Union in the Cold War, 1917–1991*. Lanham, MD: Lexington Books.

Gupta, Akhil. 1995. "Blurred Boundaries: The Discourses of Corruption, the Culture of Politics, and the Imagined State." *American Ethnologist* 22 (2): 375–402.

Gupta, Akhil. 2012. *Red Tape: Bureaucracy, Structural Violence, and Poverty in India*. Durham, NC: Duke University Press.

Gupta, Akhil. 2015. "'Suspension' Fieldsights—Theorizing the Contemporary." Cultural Anthropology Online, September 24, 2015. https://culanth.org/fieldsights/suspension.

Haller, Dieter, and Chris Shore. 2005. "Introduction: Sharp Practice." In *Corruption: Anthropological Perspectives*, edited by Chris Shore and Dieter Haller, 1–28. London: Pluto.

Halper, Stefan. 2010. *The Beijing Consensus: Legitimizing Authoritarianism in Our Time*. New York: Basic Books.

Harvey, Penny, and Hannah Knox. 2015. *Roads: An Anthropology of Infrastructure and Expertise*. Ithaca, NY: Cornell University Press.

He, Zengke. 2000. "Corruption and Anti-corruption in Reform China." *Communist and Post-Communist Studies* 33: 243–70.

Hearn, Adrian. 2013. "Chinatown Havana: One Hundred and Sixty Years below the Surface." In *Chinatowns around the World: Gilded Ghetto, Ethnopolis, and Cultural Diaspora*, edited by Bernard P. Wong and Tan Chee-Beng, 163–86. Leiden: Koninklijke Brill.

Hearn, Adrian. 2016. *Diaspora and Trust: Cuba, Mexico, and the Rise of China*. Durham, NC: Duke University Press.

Hearn, Adrian, Alan Smart, and Roberto Hernández Hernández. 2011. "China and Mexico: Trade, Migration, and Guanxi." In *China Engages Latin America: Tracing the Trajectory*, edited by Adrian Hearn and José Luis León-Manríquez, 139–57. Boulder, CO: Lynne Rienner.

Hemeroteca PL. 2017. "1959: Inauguración de la carretera al Atlántico." *Prensa libre*, November 28, 2017. https://www.prensalibre.com/hemeroteca/inaugurada-la-carretera-al-atlantico.

Hernández Mayen, Manuel. 2017. "En riesgo trabajos en ruta al Atlántico." *Prensa libre*, April 11, 2017. https://www.prensalibre.com/guatemala/politica/en-riesgo-trabajos-en-ruta-al-atlantico/.

Hoffman, Lisa. 2006. "Urban Transformation and Professionalization: Translocality and Rationalities of Enterprise in Post-Mao China." In *Translocal China: Linkages, Identities and the Reimagining of Space*, edited by Tim Oakes and Louisa Schein, 109–37. New York: Routledge.

Hornby, Lucy. 2019. "Beijing Pledges to Address Debt Worries over Belt and Road." *Financial Times*, April 24, 2019. https://www.ft.com/content/f7442058-66f9-11e9-9adc-98bf1d35a056.

Hoskins, Janet, and Viet Thanh Nguyen, eds. 2014. *Transpacific Studies: Framing an Emerging Field*. Honolulu: University of Hawai'i Press.

Huang, Yukon. 2015. "The Truth about Chinese Corruption." *The Diplomat*, May 29, 2015. http://thediplomat.com/2015/05/the-truth-about-chinese-corruption/.

Hubbert, Jennifer. 2014. "'We're Not THAT Kind of Developing Country': Environmental Awareness in Contemporary China." In *Sustainability in the Global City: Myth and Practice*, edited by Cindy Isenhour, Gary McDonogh, and Melissa Checker, 29–53. Cambridge: Cambridge University Press.

Hubbert, Jennifer. 2017. "Back to the Future: The Politics of Culture at the Shanghai Expo." *International Journal of Cultural Studies* 20 (1): 48–64.

Hubbert, Jennifer. 2019. *China in the World: An Anthropology of Confucius Institutes, Soft Power, and Globalization*. Honolulu: University of Hawai'i Press.

Hu-DeHart, Evelyn. 1989. "Coolies, Shopkeepers, Pioneers: The Chinese of Mexico and Peru (1849–1930)." *Ameriasia* 15 (2): 91–116.

Hu-DeHart, Evelyn. 1994. "Chinese Coolie Labor in Cuba in the Nineteenth Century: Free Labor of Neoslavery." *Contributions to Black Studies* 12 (5): 38–54. https://scholarworks.umass.edu/cibs/vol12/iss1/5/.

Hu-DeHart, Evelyn. 1995. "The Chinese of Peru, Cuba, and Mexico." In *Cambridge Survey of World Migration*, edited by Robin Cohen, 220–22. Cambridge: Cambridge University Press.

Hu-DeHart, Evelyn. 1998. "Latin America in Asia-Pacific Perspective." In *What Is in a Rim? Critical Perspectives on the Pacific Region Idea*, 2nd ed., edited by Arif Dirlik, 251–78. New York: Rowman and Littlefield.

Hu-DeHart, Evelyn. 2010. "Indispensable Enemy or Convenient Scapegoat? A Critical Examination of Sinophobia in Latin America and the Caribbean, 1870s to 1930s." In *The Chinese in Latin America and the Caribbean*, edited by Walton Look Lai and Tan Chee-Beng, 65–102. Leiden: Brill.

Huesmann, James. 1991. "The Chinese in Costa Rica, 1855–1897." *Historian* 53 (4): 711–20.

Human Rights Watch. 2019. "Nicaragua Events of 2018." https://www.hrw.org/world-report/2019/country-chapters/nicaragua.

Hunter, Alan. 2009. "Soft Power: China on the Global Stage." *Chinese Journal of International* Politics 2: 373–98.

Huntington, Samuel. 1996. *The Clash of Civilizations and the Remaking of the World Order*. New York: Touchstone Books.

IADB (Inter-American Development Bank). 2012. "Resolution DE-150/12 Costa Rica: Loan and Guarantee 2804/OC-CR—Reventazón Hydropower Project." Adopted October 19, 2012. http://idbdocs.iadb.org/wsdocs/getdocument.aspx?docnum=37022625.

ICDF (International Cooperation and Development Fund). 2019. *2019 Annual Report*. https://www.icdf.org.tw/public/MMO/icdf/2019AnnualReport.pdf.

Instituto Nacional de Estadística y Censos, Costa Rica. 2011. 2011 Census Statistics. http://www.inec.go.cr/censos/censos 2011.

Inter-American Commission on Human Rights. 2019. "Nicaragua: Special Monitoring Mechanism for Nicaragua; Situation of Human Rights in Nicaragua." May 2019. https://www.oas.org/es/cidh/actividades/visitas/2018Nicaragua/Newsletter-MESENI-May2019.pdf.

Inter-American Dialogue. 2018. "China's Transport Infrastructure Investment in LAC: Five Things to Know." November 13, 2018. https://www.thedialogue.org/blogs/2018/11/chinas-transport-infrastructure-investment-in-lac-five-things-to-know/.

Ivanov, Kalin S. 2007. "The Limits of a Global Campaign against Corruption." In *Corruption and Development: The Anti-corruption Campaigns*, edited by Sarah Bracking, 28–45. Basingstoke, UK: Palgrave Macmillan.

Jacques, Martin. 2009. *When China Rules the World: The End of the Western World and the Birth of a New Global Order*. New York: Penguin.

Jenkins, Mauricio, Gerardo Esquivel, and Felipe Larraín B. 1998. "Export Processing Zones in Central America." Harvard Institute for International Development Working Paper No. 646. https://papers.ssrn.com/sol3/papers.cfm?abstract_id=168174.

Jenkins, Rhys. 2019. *How China Is Reshaping the Global Economy: Development Impacts in Africa and Latin America*. Oxford: Oxford University Press.

Joseph, Gilbert, Catherine LeGrand, and Ricardo Salvatore, eds. 1998. *Close Encounters of Empire: Writing the Cultural History of US-Latin American Relations*. Durham, NC: Duke University Press.

Keliher, Macabe, and Hsinchao Wu. 2015. "How to Discipline 90 Million People." *The Atlantic*, April 7, 2015. http://www.theatlantic.com/international/ archive/2015/04/xi-jinping-china-corruption-political-culture/389787/.

Kinloch, Frances. 2015. *El imaginario del canal y la nacion cosmopolita: Nicaragua siglo XIX*. Managua: Instituto de Historia de Nicaragua y Centroamérica de la Universidad Centroamericana.

Kinosian, Sara, and Carlos Pérez Osorio. 2018. "How Nicaragua Uses Anti-terror Laws against Protesters to Suppress Dissent." The Intercept, November 11, 2018. https://theintercept.com/2018/11/11/nicaragua-protests-terrorism-daniel-ortega/.

Koop, Fermin. 2019. "Belt and Road: The New Face of China in Latin America." Dialogo Chino, April 25, 2019. https://dialogochino.net/26121-belt-and-road-the-new-face-of-china-in-latin-america/.

Kurlantzick, Joshua. 2007. *Charm Offensive: How China's Soft Power Is Transforming the World*. New Haven, CT: Yale University Press.

La nación. 2010. "Empresa China quiere trasladar obreros del estadio a condominios." July 26, 2010. https://www.nacion.com/el-pais/servicios/empresa-china-quiere-trasladar-obreros-del-estadio-a-condominios/YILSI3463FF6HDNMFVY W5R3BKE/story/.

La nación. 2011. *Revista estadio nacional*. Magazine supplement, March 2011.

La prenda libre. 2017. "China envía 20 chinos para terminar La Platina en una semana." January 12, 2017. https://laprendalibre.com/2017/01/12/ china-envia-20-chinos-para-terminar-la-platina-en-una-semana/.

LaFeber, Walter. 1984. *Inevitable Revolutions: The United States in Central America*. Exp. ed. New York: W. W. Norton.

Latour, Bruno. 1993. *We Have Never Been Modern*. Translated by Catherine Porter. Cambridge, MA: Harvard University Press.

Lau Sandino, J. Fabio. 2007. *Un trazo de su historia*. Asociación China de Guatemala. Managua: Nicaragua.

Lau Sandino., J. Fabio. 2016. *La inmigración China y sus Asociaciones en Panamá, Centroamérica y Belice*. Managua, Nicaragua: Asociación China de Nicaragua.

Lausent-Herrera, Isabelle. 2011. "The Chinatown in Peru and the Changing Peruvian Chinese Community(ies)." *Journal of Chinese Overseas* 7: 69–113.

Lee, Ana Paulina. 2018. *Mandarin Brazil: Race, Representation, and Memory*. Stanford, CA: Stanford University Press.

Lee, Erica. 2005. "Orientalisms in the Americas: A Hemispheric Approach to Asian American History." *Journal of Asian American Studies* 8 (3): 235–56.

Lee, Hsin-fang, and William Hetherington. 2018. "Tsai Discusses Taiwan's Workforce with SICA Head." *Taipei Times*, May 31, 2018. http://www.taipeitimes.com/ News/taiwan/archives/2018/05/31/2003694045.

Leon Azofeifa, Moises. 1988. "Chinese Immigrants on the Atlantic Coast of Costa Rica: The Economic Adaptation of an Asian Minority in a Pluralistic Society." PhD diss., Tulane University.

Levitt, Matt. 2012. "Shaky Start for Mayor's Chinatown." Tico Times, March 2, 2012. https://ticotimes.net/2012/03/01/shaky-start-for-mayor-s-chinatown.

Li, Jie. 2006. "Soft Power Building and China's Peaceful Development." *China International Studies*, Winter 2006, 164–79.

Li, Ling. 2016. "The Rise of the Discipline and Inspection Commission, 1927–2012: Anticorruption Investigation and Decision-Making in the Chinese Communist Party." *Modern China* 42 (5): 447–82.

Li, Wei. 1997. "Ethnoburb versus Chinatown: Two Types of Urban Ethnic Communities in Los Angeles." *Cybergeo European Journal of Geography*, Dossiers, doc. 70, December 10, 1998. https://doi.org/10.4000/cybergeo.1018.

Lin, Jan. 1998. *Reconstructing Chinatown: Ethnic Enclave, Global Change*. Minneapolis: University of Minnesota Press.

Lin, Weiqiang, and Brenda Yeoh. 2014. "Transpacific Studies: A View from Asia." In *Transpacific Studies: Framing an Emerging Field*, edited by Janet Hoskins and Viet Thanh Nguyen, 41–63. Honolulu: University of Hawai'i Press.

Ling, Huping. 2012. *Chinese Chicago: Race, Transnational Migration, and Community since 1870*. Stanford, CA: Stanford University Press.

Londono, Ernesto. 2018. "From a Space Station in Argentina, China Expands Its Reach in Latin America." *New York Times*, July 28, 2018. https://www.nytimes.com/2018/07/28/world/americas/china-latin-america.html.

Look Lai, Walton, and Tan Chee-Beng, eds. 2010. *The Chinese in Latin America and the Caribbean*. Leiden: Brill.

López, Ismael, and Yimou Lee. 2019. "Loan of $100 million from Taiwan Gives Lifeline to Nicaragua's Ortega." Reuters, February 19, 2019. https://www.reuters.com/article/us-nicaragua-protests-taiwan/loan-of-100-million-from-taiwan-gives-lifeline-to-nicaraguas-ortega-idUSKCN1Q903T.

López, Kathleen. 2013. *Chinese Cubans: A Transnational History*. Chapel Hill: University of North Carolina Press.

López Baltodano, Mónica. 2017. *La Entrega de un país: Expediente jurídica de la concesión canalera de Nicaragua, 2013–17*. Managua, Nicaragua: Creative Commons International.

Loría Chaves, Marlene, and Alonso Rodríguez Chaves. 2000. "Los inmigrantes chinos dentro de la comunidad costarricense (1870–1910)." PhD thesis, University of Costa Rica.

Loría Chaves, Marlene, and Alonso Rodríguez Chaves. 2001. "Los inmigrantes chinos a Costa Rica. Entre la explotación y la exclusión (1870–1910)." *Revista de historia* 44 (2): 159–92.

Ma, Laurence J.C., and Carolyn Cartier. 2003. *The Chinese Diaspora: Space, Place, Mobility, and Identity*. Boulder, CO: Rowman and Littlefield.

Manion, Melanie. 2009. *Corruption by Design: Building Clean Government in Mainland China and Hong Kong*. Cambridge, MA: Harvard University Press.

Marro, Nick. 2014. "The Unintended Consequences of China's Anti-corruption Drive." US-China Business Council. https://www.uschina.org/unintended-consequences-china%E2%80%99s-anti-corruption-drive.

Marroquín, Oscar Clemente. 2015. "Los socios de la corrupción." Diario la hora, July 10, 2015. https://web.archive.org/web/20150710192225/http:/lahora.gt/los-socios-de-la-corrupcion/.

Mars, Neville, and Adrian Hornsby. 2008. *The Chinese Dream: A Society under Construction*. Rotterdam: 010 Publishers.

Massey, Doreen. 1994. *Space, Place and Gender*. Cambridge: Blackwell.

Mata, Estéban. 2013. "Expertos alegan que gobierno los quitó tras criticar refinería china." *La nación*, June 20, 2013.

Matsuda, Matt. 2012. *Pacific Worlds: A History of Seas, Peoples and Cultures*. Cambridge: Cambridge University Press.

Mazza, Jaqueline. 2016. *Chinese Migration to Latin America and the Caribbean*. Washington, DC: Inter-American Dialogue. https://www.thedialogue.org/wp-content/uploads/2016/10/Chinese_Migration_to_LAC_Mazza-1.pdf.

McCall, Sarah, and Matthew Taylor. 2018. "Nicaragua's Grand Canal: Cuento Chino? Rhetoric and Field-Based Evidence on the Chinese Presence in Nicaragua." *Journal of Latin American Geography* 17 (2): 191–208.

McCord, William. 1993. *The Dawn of the Pacific Century: Implications for Three Worlds of Development*. New Brunswick, NJ: Transaction.

McFarlane, Colin. 2011. *Learning the City: Knowledge and Translocal Assemblage*. Malden, MA: Wiley Blackwell.

McFarlane, Colin, and Ben Anderson. 2011. "Thinking with Assemblage." *Area* 43 (2): 124–27.

McKeown, Adam. 2008. *Melancholy Order: Asian Migration and the Globalization of Borders*. New York: Columbia University Press.

Mearsheimer, John. 2006. "China's Unpeaceful Rise." *Current History* 105 (690): 160–62.

Mearsheimer, John. 2014. "Can China Rise Peacefully?" *National Interest*, October 25, 2014. http://nationalinterest.org/commentary/can-china-rise-peacefully-10204?page=show.

Mearsheimer, John. 2019. "Realism and Restraint." *Horizons Journal of International Relations* 14 (Summer): 12–29.

Meyer, Peter. 2016. *U.S. Foreign Assistance to Latin America and the Caribbean: Recent Trends and FY 2016 Appropriations*. Congressional Research Service report prepared for members of Congress. https://fas.org/sgp/crs/row/R44113.pdf.

MOFA (Ministry of Foreign Affairs, Taiwan). 2007. "Act of Relations between Costa Rica and China." *La nación*, September 10, 2007. http://www.nacion.com/opin ion/foros/Acta-relaciones-Costa-Rica-China_0_1000100039.html.

MOFA (Ministry of Foreign Affairs, Taiwan). 2009. "Partnerships for Progress and Sustainable Development: White Paper on Foreign Aid Policy." May 2009. https://www.mofa.gov.tw/Upload/RelFile/1120/588/f26446b6-b904-44c1-aa2d-1ec5f0d7d8dd.pdf.

Molenaers, Nadia, Sebastian Dellepiane, and Jorg Faust. 2015. "Political Conditionality and Foreign Aid." *World Development* 75 (November): 2–12.

Mon, Ramon. 2013. "The Chinese of Panama Also Have a Story to Tell . . ." *Revista* 12 (3): 46–48.

Muir, Sarah, and Akhil Gupta. 2018. "Rethinking the Anthropology of Corruption." *Current Anthropology* 28 (S18): S4–15.

Murillo, Álvaro.
    2013. "Ni tan barrio ni tan chino." *La nación*, June 1, 2013.

Myers, Margaret, and Kevin Gallagher. 2019. *Cautious Capital: Chinese Development Finance in LAC, 2018*. Washington, DC: Inter-American Dialogue. https://www.thedialogue.org/wp-content/uploads/2019/02/Chinese-Finance-in-LAC-2018.pdf.

Myers, Margaret, and Carol Wise, eds. 2017. *The Political Economy of China–Latin America Relations in the New Millennium: Brave New World*. New York: Routledge.

Narins, Thomas, and John Agnew. 2019. "Missing from the Map: Chinese Exceptionalism, Sovereignty Regimes and the Belt Road Initiative." *Geopolitics* 25 (4): 809–37. https://doi.org/10.1080/14650045.2019.1601082.

Nicolaci da Costa, Ana. 2018. "How the World Is Grappling with China's Rising Power." BBC News, October 26, 2018. https://www.bbc.com/news/business-45948692.

Nye, Joseph. 2004. *Soft Power: The Means to Success in World Politics*. New York: Public Affairs.

Nye, Joseph. 2005. "The Rise of China's Soft Power." *Asian Wall Street Journal*, December 29, 2005.

OAS (Organization of American States). 1996. Inter-American Convention against Corruption. Adopted March 29, 1996. http://www.oas.org/en/sla/dil/inter_american_treaties_B-58_against_Corruption.asp.

Obregón Valverde, Enrique. 2012. "Barrio chino sin chinos." *La nación*, March 14, 2012. http://www.nacion.com/archivo/Barrio-chino-chinos_0_1256274633.html.

Ong, Aihwa. 1999. *Flexible Citizenship: The Cultural Logics of Transnationality.* Durham, NC: Duke University Press.

Ong, Aihwa, and Stephen Collier, eds. 2004. *Global Assemblages: Technology, Politics, and Ethics as Anthropological Problems.* Malden, MA: Blackwell.

Ong, Aihwa, and Donald Nonini. 1997. *Ungrounded Empires: The Cultural Politics of Modern Chinese Transnationalism.* New York: Routledge.

Palacios, Claudia. 2015. "Acuerdo de Energuate y Jaguar Energy antecedió el escandalo de corrupción." Diario la hora, July 10, 2015. https://web.archive.org/web/20150710231754/http:/lahora.gt/acuerdo-de-energuate-y-jaguar-energy-antecedio-el-escandalo-de-corrupcion/.

People's Daily. 2008. "China, Latin America Join Hands in Creating Model for South-South Cooperation." November 22, 2008. http://english.peopledaily.com.cn/90001/90776/90883/6538421.html.

People's Republic of China. 2008. "Policy Paper on Latin America and the Caribbean." June 11, 2008. http://www.gov.cn/english/official/2008-11/05/content_1140347.htm.

People's Republic of China. 2016. "Policy Paper on Latin America and the Caribbean." November 24, 2016. http://english.www.gov.cn/archive/white_paper/2016/11/24/content_281475499069158.htm.

Petersen, Kurt. 1992. "Maquiladora Revolution in Guatemala." In *Global Production: The Apparel Industry in the Pacific Rim*, edited by Edna Bonacich, Lucie Cheng, Norma Chinchilla, Nora Hamilton, and Paul Ong, 268–86. Philadelphia: Temple University Press.

Pinheiro-Machado, Rosana. 2018. "The Power of Chineseness: Flexible Taiwanese Identities amidst Times of Change in Asia and Latin America." *Journal of Latin American and Caribbean Anthropology* 23 (1): 56–73.

Pisu, Mauro, and Federico Villalobos. 2016. "A Bird-Eye View of Costa Rica's Transport Infrastructure." OECD Economics Department Working Papers, No. 1323. http://dx.doi.org/10.1787/5jlswbwvwqjf-en.

Prensa libre. 2015. "Así operó la red de tráfico de influencias." July 9, 2015. https://www.prensalibre.com/guatemala/justicia/asi-opero-la-red-de-trafico-de-influencias/.

Putnam, Lara. 2002. *The Company They Kept: Migrants and the Politics of Gender in Caribbean Costa Rica, 1870–1960.* Chapel Hill: University of North Carolina Press.

Putnam, Lara. 2013. *Radical Moves: Caribbean Migrants and the Politics of Race in the Jazz Age.* Chapel Hill: University of North Carolina Press.

Radio Free Europe/Radio Liberty. 2018. "US Secretary of State Says Washington Focused on Ties with Latin America." December 1, 2018. https://www.rferl.org/a/u-s-secretary-of-states-pompeo-ties-with-latin-america/29632239.html.

Rahnema, Majid, and Victoria Bawtree, eds. 1997. *The Post-Development Reader.* London: Zed Books.

Ramo, Joshua Cooper. 2004. *The Beijing Consensus.* London: Foreign Policy Centre.

Ray, Rebecca, Kevin Gallagher, Andrés López, and Cynthia Sanborn. 2017. *China and Sustainable Development in Latin America: The Social and Environmental Dimension*. New York: Anthem.

RECOPE (Costa Rican Petroleum Refinery). 2012. *Modernización de refinería: Un proyecto de vital importancia*. https://www.recope.go.cr/wp-content/uploads/2012/11/Proyecto_descriptivo_Modernizacion_Refineria.pdf.

Rico. 2015. "Costa Rican Ambassador to China Has Only a High School Diploma." Q News, March 7, 2015. https://qcostarica.com/costa-rican-ambassador-to-china-has-only-a-high-school-diploma/.

Rivas, Zelideth María, and Debbie Lee-DiStefano, eds. 2016. *Imagining Asia in the Americas*. New Brunswick, NJ: Rutgers University Press.

Robinson, St. John. 2010. "The Chinese of Central America: Diverse Beginnings, Common Achievements." In *The Chinese in Latin America and the Caribbean*, edited by Walton Look Lai and Tan Chee-Beng, 103–28. Leiden: Brill.

Rose-Ackerman, Susan. 2012. "International Actors and the Promises and Pitfalls of Anti-corruption Reform." *University of Pennsylvania Journal of International Law* 34 (3): 447–89.

Rosenberg, Mark, and Luis Solis. 2007. *The United States and Central America: Geopolitical Realities and Regional Fragility*. New York: Routledge.

Rothwell, Daniel. 2010. "The Chinese Revolution and Latin America: The Impact of Global Communist Networks on Latin American Guerrilla Groups." *World History Connected* 7 (3). https://worldhistoryconnected.press.uillinois.edu/7.3/rothwell.html.

Rothwell, Daniel. 2013. *Transpacific Revolutionaries: The Chinese Revolution in Latin America*. Routledge Studies in Modern History. New York: Routledge.

Ruales, Vanessa. 2018. "Cleaning Up: The Brazilian Judiciary Roots Out Corruption." *Harvard Political Review*, March 24, 2018. https://harvardpolitics.com/world/cleaning-up-the-brazilian-judiciary-roots-out-corruption/.

Ruíz, Gerardo. 2015. "CHEC confirma a diputados inminente aumente en costo para ampliar Ruta 32." *El financiero*, May 6, 2015. http://www.elfinancierocr.com/economia-y-politica/CHEC-inminente-ampliacion-carretera-Limon_0_732526747.html.

Ruíz, Horacio. 1992. "Reabren la zona franca." *La prensa*, April 7, 1992.

Russell, Benjamin. 2019. "Costa Rica's 'Before and After' Corruption Scandal Casts a Long Shadow." *Americas Quarterly*, August 5, 2019. https://www.americasquarterly.org/content/costa-ricas-and-after-corruption-scandal-casts-long-shadow.

Sakai, Naori. 2019. "The Regime of Separation and Performativity of Area." *Positions* 27 (1): 241–76.

Scheper-Hughes, Nancy. 2002. "Min(d)ing the Body: On the Trail of Organ-Stealing Rumors." In *Exotic No More: Anthropology for the Contemporary World*, edited by Jeremy MacClancy, 33–63. Chicago: University of Chicago Press.

Schlesinger, Stephen, and Stephen Kinzer. 1983. *Bitter Fruit: The Story of the American Coup in Guatemala*. New York: Anchor Books, Doubleday.

SETENA (National Environmental Technical Secretary). 2016. "Resolución Nº 1892-2016-SETENA." October 11, 2016. http://www.centralamericadata.com/docs/RES18922016ampliacionruta32CR.pdf.

Shah, Nayan. 2001. *Contagious Divides: Epidemics and Race in San Francisco's Chinatown*. Berkeley: University of California Press.

Shambaugh, David. 2013. *China Goes Global: The Partial Power*. Oxford: Oxford University Press.

Shen, Simon. 2012. "Online Perceptions of Latin America." *China Quarterly* 209 (March): 157–77.

Silva, Manuel. 2017. "Taiwán gano negociación para tramo de la CA-9." *El periódico*, August 3, 2017. https://elperiodico.com.gt/noticias/economia/2017/08/03/taiwan-gano-negociacion-para-tramo-de-la-ca-9/.

Siu, Lok. 2005. *Memories of a Future Home: Diasporic Citizenship of Chinese in Panama*. Stanford, CA: Stanford University Press.

Slack, Edward. 2010. "Sinifying New Spain: Cathay's Influence on Colonial Mexico via the Nao de China." In *The Chinese in Latin America and the Caribbean*, edited by Walton Look Lai and Tan Chee-Beng, 7–31. Leiden: Brill.

Smart, Alan, and Carolyn L. Hsu. 2013. "Corruption or Social Capital? Tact and the Performance of Guanxi in Market Socialist China." In *Corruption and the Secret of Law: A Legal Anthropological Perspective*, edited by Gerhard Anders and Monique Nuijten, 167–89. London: Routledge.

Smart, Alan, and Jinn Yuh Hsu. 2004. "The Chinese Diaspora, Foreign Investment and Economic Development in Latin America." *Review of International Affairs* 3 (4): 544–66.

Smith, Timothy, and Abigail Adams. 2011. *After the Coup: An Ethnographic Reframing of Guatemala 1954*. Champaign: University of Illinois Press.

Solano, Ricardo Javier. 2017. "Embajador tico en China cesado por falta de resultados." Crhoy.com, April 5, 2017. https://www.crhoy.com/nacionales/embajador-tico-en-china-cesado-por-falta-de-resultados/.

Solinger, Dorothy. 2002. "Labor Market Reform and the Plight of the Laid-Off Proletariat." *China Quarterly* 170 (June): 304–26.

Solís, Ottón. 2013. "China: Cobre que Costa Rica paga." *La nación*, June 14, 2013.

Song, Yanbin. 2013. "Saludos del señor embajador." *La nación*, February 8, 2013.

Soto Quirós, Ronald. 2005. "Discursos y políticas de inmigración en Costa Rica: 1862–1943." *Iberoamericana* 5 (19): 119–33.

Soto Quirós, Ronald. 2009. "Percepciones y actitudes políticas con respeto a la minoria china en Costa Rica, 1879–1911." *Historia y espacio* 5 (32): 165–23.

Talley, Ian, and Robbie Whelan. 2018. "US Ramps Up Nicaragua Sanctions, Citing Corruption, Abuses." *Washington Street Journal*, November 27, 2018. https://www.wsj.com/articles/u-s-ramps-up-nicaragua-sanctions-citing-corruption-abuses-1543348857.

Tarnoff, Curt, and Marion Leonardo Lawson. 2009. *Foreign Aid: An Introduction to U.S. Programs and Policy*. Congressional Research Service, February 10, 2011. https://digital.library.unt.edu/ark:/67531/metadc103053/.

Thunø, Mette. 2002. "Reaching Out and Incorporating Chinese Overseas: The Trans-territorial Scope of the PRC by the end of the 20th Century." *China Quarterly* 168 (December): 910–29.

Tico Times. 2011. "Do You Speak Mandarin?" July 7, 2011. http://www.ticotimes.net/2011/07/07/do-you-speak-mandarin.

Torres Rivas, Edelberto. 1993. *History and Society in Central America*. Translated by Douglas Sullivan-González. Austin: University of Texas Press.

Transparency International. 2020. "Nicaragua Country Profile." https://www.transparency.org/country/NIC.

Tsing, Anna Lowenhaupt. 2005. *Friction: An Ethnography of Global Connection*. Princeton, NJ: Princeton University Press.

UNICEF. 2016. "Migration Profile: Nicaragua, 2010–15." https://esa.un.org/miggmg profiles/indicators/files/Nicaragua.pdf.

United Nations, Political and Peacebuilding Affairs. 2019. "CICIG: International Commission against Impunity in Guatemala." https://dppa.un.org/en/mission/cicig.

UNODC (United Nations Office on Drugs and Crime). 2004. *United Nations Convention against Corruption*. https://www.unodc.org/documents/treaties/UNCAC/ Publications/Convention/08-50026_E.pdf.

US Department of State and US & Foreign Commercial Service. 2016. "Country Commercial Guide Summary: Costa Rica." Last updated August 22, 2016. http://2016.export.gov/costarica/doingbusinessincostarica/index.asp.

Van Wunnik, Lucas. 2011. "The Multinational Firm in the Maquiladora Industry of Nicaragua (2007 v. 1998): More of the Same." *Annales de geographie* 3 (679): 266–97.

Villalobos Clare, Jorge. 2013. "Las verdades del proyecto Ampliacion y Modernizacion de la Refineria." RECOPE, June 2013. https://www.recope.go.cr/wp-content/ uploads/2013/06/AMR_Las_verdades_del_proyecto.pdf.

Von Feigenblatt, Otto. 2009. "Costa Rica and the Two Chinas." *Journal of Alternative Perspectives in the Social Sciences* 1 (2): 400–434.

Walker, Gavin. 2019. "The Accumulation of Difference and the Logic of Area." *Positions* 27 (1): 67–98.

Walker, Gavin, and Naori Sakai. 2019. "The End of Area Studies." *Positions* 27 (1): 1–31.

Wang, Helen. 2010. *The Chinese Dream: The Rise of the World's Largest Middle Class and What It Means to You*. Scotts Valley, CA: CreateSpace.

Watkins, Derek, K. K. Rebecca Lai, and Keith Bradsher. 2018. "The World, Built by China." *New York Times*, November 18, 2018. https://www.nytimes.com/interac tive/2018/11/18/world/asia/world-built-by-china.html.

Weber, Max. 1968. *The Religion of China*. Edited by Hans Gerth. New York: Free Press.

Wedel, Janine, Chris Shore, Gregory Feldman, and Stacy Lathrop. 2005. "Towards an Anthropology of Policy." *Annual Review of Anthropology* 600: 30–51.

Wedeman, Andrew. 2004. "The Intensification of Corruption in China." *China Quarterly* 180 (December): 895–921.

Weinland, Don. 2019. "China Banks in Foreign Infrastructure Retreat." *Financial Times*, April 5, 2019.

Wilson, Bruce. 2014a. "Background Paper on Costa Rica." Work Product 3, Corruption and Governance Improvement in Global and Continental Perspectives, Anti-Corruption Policies Revisted Project. German Institute of Global and Area Studies, European Union.

Wilson, Bruce. 2014b. "Costa Rica's Anti-corruption Trajectory: Strengths and Limitations." Chr. Michelsen Institute, Anti-corruption Policies Revisited Project. https://www.cmi.no/publications/5228-costa-ricas-anti-corruption-trajectory.

Wise, Carol. 2020. *Dragonomics: How Latin America Is Maximizing (or Missing Out on) China's International Development Strategy*. New Haven, CT: Yale University Press.

World Bank. 2011. "World Bank Applies 2009 Debarment to China Communications Construction Company Limited for Fraud in Philippines Roads Project." Press release. July 29, 2011. http://www.worldbank.org/en/news/press-release/ 2011/07/29/world-bank-applies-2009-debarment-to-china-communications-construction-company-limited-for-fraud-in-philippines-roads-project.

World Bank. 2018. "Belt and Road Initiative." March 29, 2018. https://www.worldbank. org/en/topic/regional-integration/brief/belt-and-road-initiative.

World Bank. 2021. "GDP per Capita (Current US$): Latin America & Caribbean." Accessed February 28, 2021. https://data.worldbank.org/indicator/NY.GDP. PCAP.CD?locations=ZJ.

Wuthnow, Joel. 2008. "The Concept of Soft Power in China's Strategic Discourse." *Issues and Studies* 44 (2): 1–28.

Xiang, Biao. 2014. "The Pacific Paradox: The Chinese State in Transpacific Interactions." In *Transpacific Studies: Framing an Emerging Field*, edited by Janet Hoskins and Viet Thanh Nguyen, 85–108. Honolulu: University of Hawai'i Press.

Xinhuanet English News. 2012. "Costa Rica Opens World's Newest Chinatown." December 6, 2012. http://news.xinhuanet.com/english/culture/2012-12/06/c_132023731.htm.

Xinhuanet English News. 2018. "China Becomes Second Largest Trading Partner of Latin America." November 29, 2018. http://www.xinhuanet.com/english/2018-11/29/c_137640261.htm.

Xinhuanet English News. 2019. "Belt and Road Helps Latin America to Achieve UN 2030 Agenda, Says ECLAC Official." April 26, 2019. http://www.xinhuanet.com/english/2019-04/26/c_138011601.htm.

Young, Elliott. 2014. *Alien Nations: Chinese Migration in the Americas from the Coolie Era through World War II*. Chapel Hill: University of North Carolina Press.

Yu, Henry. 2018. "Unbound Space: Migration, Aspiration, and the Making of Time in the Cantonese Pacific." In *Pacific Futures: Past and Present*, edited by Warwick Anderson, Miranda Johnson, and Barbara Brookes, 178–206. Honolulu: University of Hawai'i Press.

Yuen, S. 2014. "Disciplining the Party." *China Perspectives* 3: 41–47.

Yun, Lisa. 2008. *The Coolie Speaks: Chinese Indentured Laborers and African Slaves of Cuba*. Philadelphia: Temple University Press.

Zhan, Mei. 2009. *Other-Worldly: Making Chinese Medicine through Transnational Frames*. Durham, NC: Duke University Press.

Zhang, Li. 2002. "Spatiality and Urban Citizenship in Late Socialist China." *Public Culture* 14 (2): 311–34.

Index

Page numbers in italics refer to figures.

CPSIA information can be obtained
at www.ICGtesting.com
Printed in the USA
LVHW030449050921
696997LV00009B/1175